Praise for the tools in *Writing at Work*
From participants in Plain English Foundation writing workshops

Applying these tools in our office has helped us all think much more clearly as well as write more effectively. It also takes us half the time to write a report.

Neil's approach makes what could be a dry subject very engaging. I especially enjoyed the grammar! He has reignited my love of the English language.

It makes excellent use of live samples, which turns writing theory into reality. It is highly relevant to real-world writing tasks.

A practical and well-structured program. I didn't realise you could approach writing in such a systematic way. While the concepts behind the tools are sophisticated, they are surprisingly easy to use.

I was initially sceptical that I would learn anything new about writing, but this was well worth the time invested. This was the best workplace training I have done in over 20 years.

Since using these tools, our documents are one third shorter without compromising content. Think of all the toner we'll be saving!

I always knew that our writing wasn't working well, but now I understand why. More importantly, I know what to do about it.

I now see my readers as real people instead of faceless recipients of documents.

Every professional should learn these tools—especially managers. It helped me cut my editing work in half.

I've been to several writing courses, but this one was the best by far. A real eye-opener!

Neil James has been writing at work for nearly 20 years in government, the media and corporate communications. He is currently Executive Director of the Plain English Foundation in Australia, which combines plain English training, editing and evaluation with a public campaign for clearer public language.

In recent years, Neil has presented writing workshops to thousands of professionals across Australia in government, law, business, engineering, education, finance and the environment. He has written style manuals and reports, drafted plain language standards and developed document templates—all the while refining the methods for *Writing at Work*.

Neil has a doctorate in English from the University of Sydney and has worked as a policy officer in the NSW Cabinet Office, as a program manager in the Ministry for the Arts, as a producer at SBS television and as associate publisher with Halstead Press Publishers. He is the author of two books—*Writers on Writing* (2000) and *The Complete Sentimental Bloke* (2002)—and has published over 50 articles and essays in publications as diverse as the *Times Literary Supplement* and the *Daily Telegraph*.

Neil is increasingly sought after as a speaker on plain language at international and national conferences and in the media, where he features regularly on ABC Radio.

Neil James
Executive Director of the
Plain English Foundation

Writing at Work

How to write clearly, effectively and professionally

ALLEN&UNWIN

Plain English Foundation

First published in 2007

Allen & Unwin
83 Alexander Street
Crows Nest NSW 2065
Australia

Phone: (61 2) 8425 0100
Fax: (61 2) 9906 2218
Email: info@allenandunwin.com
Web: www.allenandunwin.com

National Library of Australia
Cataloguing-in-Publication entry:

James, Neil, 1966- .
Writing at work : how to write clearly, effectively and professionally.

Bibliography.
Includes index.
ISBN 978 1 74175 218 2 (pbk.).

1. English language - Written English. 2. Report writing.
3. Technical writing. I. Title.

808.066

Index by Garry Cousins
Internal design by Bookhouse
Illustrations/maps by Ian Faulkner
Set in 12/14 pt Adobe Jenson Pro by Bookhouse
Printed by South Wind Productions, Singapore

10 9 8 7 6 5 4 3 2

Contents

Introduction 1

Planning

1 Readers 13
2 Content 30
3 Structure 50

Structure

4 Focus 79
5 Persuasion 97
6 Coherence 116
7 Design 134

Expression

8 Tone 153
9 Grammar 169
10 Words 188
11 Clutter 205
12 Verbs 222
13 Sentences 241

Review

14 Punctuation 261
15 Style 280
16 Editing 297
17 Proofing 313

Further reading 330
Chapter notes 343
Acknowledgements 361
Index 363

Dedicated to
the 4000 professionals
who took up the challenge
of reviewing the way that they write,
and in doing so road-tested
the methods in this book.

Introduction

Writing at work

This book is for busy professionals who write at work. Whether you are in finance, engineering or the public sector, in a law firm, a university or a corporation, your most regular product is probably a document. If writing-related tasks take up at least a quarter of your day—or will do so in the future—then this book is for you.

The problem this book seeks to address is that our education often did not prepare us adequately for workplace writing. It focused on making us technically proficient in our fields, not on how to write effective letters, memos or proposals when we actually got there. Yet after mastering your specialty, few skills are as important to your career as the ability to write well.

In 2004, the American National Commission on Writing surveyed 120 major American corporations that collectively employed eight million people. It found that writing is a threshold skill, offering the ticket into a professional career. Up to two-thirds of salaried staff have to write at work. As many as eight out of 10 companies in some sectors assess writing during hiring, and one-half assess it during promotion. Follow-up research in 2005 found that writing was even more important to American state government agencies, which together employed some three million people.

Despite the importance of writing, the Commission also found that one-third of professionals do not write effectively in their jobs. American companies are spending US$3.1 billion a year on training to bridge the gap. The state-level public sector spends another US$250 million.

The professionals turning up to all this training paint a confusing picture of workplace communication. Some feel that there is little wrong with their writing, and that it is rightly shaped by technical needs that can't be compromised. Others are anxious that they are getting their grammar wrong, and are looking for some guidance. Some are just fed up with their documents being rewritten all the time. Most agree that their writing is at times hard to read and is not always suitable for its intended audience. Yet they are sceptical about whether these problems can be fixed.

This scepticism is understandable. As a graduate professional, you often start your career thinking that the essay structure reigns supreme and that the academic style you aped to pass exams would serve equally well at work. It comes as a shock when these don't do the job.

Early in your career, you start using document structures you don't fully fathom, and work hard at mastering a mix of technical language, officialese and corporate-speak. Yet everything you write is endlessly rewritten by managers offering explanations like 'it sounds better this way', or 'that's just how you have to do it'. This means writing several drafts of every document.

When you eventually do write longer reports, you find that agreeing with colleagues about the placement of a comma can become a bit of a brawl. The most senior people impose their personal preferences, leaving others wishing for more objective writing standards.

As your career progresses, you do more editing than writing, but the time spent on the task increases exponentially. You rewrite everything that comes your way, shaking your head about the standards of graduates and burying yourself in a mountain of text. You work late to clear the backlog so you can get on with your 'real' work.

If you progress to executive level, your focus switches to efficiency. You have so little time to read the text coming at you from all angles that you just want to cut to the chase. Most documents are too long, not very clear, and far too hard to read. You notice how long it takes your organisation to send out even simple letters, and that they don't really strike the right tone. You wonder whether you can reform communications just as you would any other workplace system.

If any of these problems sound familiar to you, *Writing at Work* offers an objective and systematic method to help you solve them. All of the tools in this book have been road-tested with some 4000 professionals working with real workplace documents in government, law, engineering, finance, insurance, business, utilities, health, community services and the environment. Whatever your level of skill or seniority, you can benefit from their experience.

Criteria for effective writing

The first challenge in improving your writing is to move on from the rigid and limited approach we all learned at school. This may help you judge whether your grammar is correct, but not whether a passage is effectively written. For example, would you prefer to read this:

> At this point in time, it will be necessary for you to provide further documentary evidence with regard to the gaps identified in the correspondence in order to progress your application to the formal assessment process.

Or this:

> Before we can formally assess your application, you will need to send us more evidence about the gaps we identified in our letter.

Both versions are grammatically correct, but one of them is more effective for its readers. Workplace writing demands far more than correct grammar to succeed, and that calls for more sophisticated criteria of effectiveness.

Precision

Each sentence in your writing should have one and only one meaning, expressing exactly what you intend. Professionals use a formal and technical language in an effort to maximise precision, so it surprises them when someone takes a different meaning from their text. If this has ever happened to you, it is because your language was ambiguous. You will need some tools to evaluate your draft more objectively.

Clarity

Not only should your meaning be precise, but it should be crystal clear. Some professionals set up a false dichotomy between these two qualities. Lawyers argue that to be exact they have to sacrifice clarity, and readers must simply put up with it. Others prefer technical jargon because it captures their content in an easy shorthand. Yet what point is there in being 'exact' if your reader does not understand you? The second challenge of effective writing is to strive equally for clarity and precision.

Readability

The third challenge is just as difficult: making your message as easy to read as possible. You can gauge your document's readability by asking whether readers will comprehend everything they need after just one reading. If they have to reread several passages more than once, then your text scores poorly. They will start to skim the document, and that puts your purpose at risk. Fortunately, there are some simple language techniques you can learn to make your text readable as well as technically accurate.

Efficiency

Failing these challenges will inevitably lead to inefficiency. You will use too many words to express your intended meaning—just like the sample did above. Most organisations can reduce their documents on average by 25 per cent, and commonly by one-third, without losing content. This saves time and effort for writers as well as readers—and reduces editorial tussles between writers and reviewers.

Usability

If there is one thing that separates workplace writing from creative writing, it is that writing at work has a practical purpose. Readers will often use a document to help them accomplish a specific task, such as filling out a form or using a piece of equipment. In such cases, you can measure your effectiveness by how well your readers succeed in that task. Too often, professionals gather little information about the actual use of their work, concentrating on the content rather than the task it serves.

Persuasiveness

If your writing is not intended to instruct, it will probably seek to persuade your reader to a point of view. To succeed here, you must craft a careful argument that defines an issue, develops some analysis and secures support for a recommendation. Professionals generally attempt to persuade through an impressive vocabulary or through sheer volume of material. There are far more effective techniques you can use to make your case.

Let's face it: achieving all of these things is challenging. That's why the National Commission on Writing found that one-third of workplace writers are failing to meet their employer's standards. It's also why I wrote this book.

The methods for writing at work

When professionals see a gap in their writing skills, they often head off to a bookshop to see what is available on the subject. That's when confusion really sets in.

In front of them is a wall of writing books, bandying about terms like technical writing, information design, discourse analysis, business communications, usability testing, psycholinguistics, transformational grammar, civic rhetoric, plain English, readability, style and usage. Many are written by academics in each field, extolling the virtues of their specific approach. Which one do you pick?

The truth is, there is something to be gained from all of them, and they share many of the same foundations. But buying them all would mean setting up a small library when a single volume is all you have time for. *Writing at Work* has prepared that volume for you by drawing from each discipline the tools that are most relevant to the modern workplace. The fields you will most often encounter are:

- Traditional grammar
- Rhetoric
- Plain English
- Technical writing
- Information design
- Editing

Traditional grammar and rhetoric were among the earliest disciplines developed by Greek philosophers. Grammar will help you understand the mechanics of writing by explaining the different types of words and how they function in a sentence. Without grammar, you cannot tease out why a particular sentence 'sounds wrong', let alone explain it to a colleague whose work you are reviewing.

Classical rhetoric was arguably the first complete account of effective communication. The Greek and Roman rhetorical manuals were 'how to' books on giving an effective speech—then the leading form of public communication. While some no doubt peddled the cheap debating tricks that gave rhetoric its sense of empty or misleading language, philosophers and orators such as Aristotle and Cicero turned it into a rigorous craft.

By the time of the Roman Republic, Cicero identified five 'canons' of rhetoric: invention (developing content), arrangement (structuring content), style (expressing content), delivery (speaking effectively) and memory (remembering your text). As writing replaced speech as the main form of public exchange, we gradually whittled rhetoric down to the study of style, but in doing so we neglected the powerful tools of invention and arrangement. *Writing at Work* revisits the best of the classical texts and finds much that is still of practical use.

Many of the original concepts of rhetoric have re-emerged over the last 50 years within disciplines like technical writing, communications, plain English and information design. These all restore the reader as a major focus for effective communication, and set handy principles for structuring documents, expressing ideas effectively, and making the most of technology so that the design can support the message. Along the way, they have evolved more complex methods for analysing outcomes and testing drafts with readers. More importantly, they refined their methods through actual use in the working world. *Writing at Work* will draw on some of the most recent and relevant research from these disciplines about writing in a professional context.

Over the last century, the rise of mass media has greatly accelerated communication. As publishing and broadcasting evolved, quality control by the editor evolved with it. Editing practice applies proven techniques to make communication more effective for its intended audience. In particular, *Writing at Work* will show you some tricks of the trade that book and newspaper editors use, and how you can apply them in your workplace.

The stages of the writing process

To apply all these tools effectively, you also need to understand the writing process itself. We often think of writing as a one-dimensional act, but in fact it has several stages:

The writing process

Research

↓

Planning

↓

Drafting

↓

Structure review

↓

Expression review

↓

Proofing

Different writers work through these stages in different ways. Some like to do a lot of planning, outlining the overall structure—and even what each paragraph is going to say—well before they start drafting. Most tend to dive into the task without much structure to guide them, and use the writing process itself to work out what they want to write.

The best balance is somewhere in between, spreading your time evenly between stages. If you neglect some, you will have to apply more effort in others. For example, if you spend a lot of time planning, you will probably need to do less reviewing, but you risk leaving too little time for drafting. If you tend to dive in, you will invariably write a longer draft than necessary and will need to review your text more systematically at the end of the writing process.

How to use this book

Writing at Work is structured both horizontally and vertically, and you can access the tools it offers in a number of ways. First, it mimics the writing process itself. The book starts with chapters on planning and content development, moves through structure and design, and ends with expression and review. If you're weak in one area you can go directly to a specific topic to find tools of immediate use. If you want to upgrade your writing skills across the board, you can also read the book from start to finish.

When you reach each chapter, you can access its material in order of priority in three recurring sections: **the toolbox, the living language** and **power tools**. The toolbox gives you some quick and easy tools to work with straight away. This will be the area you turn to while writing a document, particularly when you are between drafts. You could also skip through the book, stopping only at toolbox sections, to get a practical overview of each area.

When you are ready to explore each chapter in more detail, you can delve into the living language section. This charts the intellectual and historical contexts of the toolbox, explaining how these tools developed, where they have evolved and why they remain useful. It will explain what disciplines such as classical rhetoric and cognitive psychology actually do, and how they are relevant to you. The living language sections cover some interesting history while at the same time reinforcing the concepts in the toolbox.

The final section, power tools, has the most advanced material in each chapter. You won't need it to get started on improving your writing, but will return to it as you master the earlier tools. This section will also be useful as your career develops and your writing roles become more complex and challenging.

As an example of this structure, Chapter 13 on sentences begins the toolbox by looking at three principles: having one idea per sentence, keeping a low average sentence length, and varying your sentence length. The living language section then looks at the structures that Greek and Roman orators first identified as giving sentences rhythm and bite. The power tools section covers the grammar, including common sentence patterns, to help you diagnose problems and edit your text.

The challenge ahead

Be prepared: some of what you encounter will challenge ideas you didn't even know you had about writing in a professional environment. This is a book not just about workplace writing, but about how to reform workplace writing. The experience of doing just that with more than 30 organisations and 4000 people has taught me that this is not easy. It calls for new skills, but equally for changes in attitudes to templates, style guides and systems.

Writing at Work is part of the broader reform of our public language that has been gaining momentum over the last 20 to 30 years. It attempts to forecast how effective workplace writing will read in the future. Applying these tools will not only improve your writing but also promote your career.

Planning

1 Readers 13
2 Content 30
3 Structure 50

Tools covered in this section

The reader checklist	16
The scale of document testing	23
The content checklist	31
The topic checklist	32
The stasis system	39
Conclusion testing	40
Free-writing	43
Brainstorming	44
Mind-mapping	45
The six thinking hats	45
Force-field analysis	47
Fishbone diagrams	48
Analytical document models	52
Informational document models	56
Structural outlining	58
The structure checklist	60
The structure mapping checklist	65

1 Readers

At a glance

The toolbox

- Work cooperatively with your readers 14
- Understand the communication process 15
- Apply the reader checklist 16

The living language

- Why audience was the focus of classical rhetoric 19
- How we lost sight of the reader 21
- Restore the reader to your writing 22

Power tools

- Test how well your documents work 23
- Record your readers' responses 24
- Review your readers' needs 24
- Assess your text against standards 25
- Run reader surveys and focus groups 26
- Conduct usability testing 27
- Run some field tests 28

The toolbox

Work cooperatively with your readers

One evening in the British town of Barnard Castle, the Teesdale District Parish Council sat down for its regular meeting. On the agenda was a document describing itself as a 'Local Development Framework Core Strategy Sustainability Appraisal Scoping Report'. The text of the report was no clearer than its title, using jargon like this to describe an unemployment rate of nearly 6 per cent:

> The Indices of Multiple Deprivation (IMD) Rank of Employment Deprivation shows the areas with a high level of involuntary exclusion from the world of work. Approximately 5.9% of the population are classified as Employment Deprived.

Councillor Alan Wilkinson objected that the 'report was incomprehensible to any normal person. Nobody talks like this,' he said. 'Nobody reads books written like this. Frankly, it's a turn-off, and it's not surprising that we are having trouble attracting new members.'

Wilkinson's response is familiar to workplace readers throughout the world. How often have you read a document that was equally hard to follow? Unfortunately, the council's response to this criticism is also far too common. Council member Newton Wood said this is 'just the way council reports are written, and if you want to be a councillor you need to understand that. If you go to France, they speak French. Here in the council, we speak like this.'

This attitude lies at the heart of what is wrong with workplace writing. Rather than seeing writing as a collaborative process, with writers and readers achieving outcomes of common interest, professionals too often see it as a one-sided transaction, with the writers dictating content and style, and the readers having to accept it. To read a district council report, you need to learn the language. If anything goes wrong in your communication, it is the reader's fault because it is the reader's obligation to know that language.

But a district council is not a foreign country, and there is no reason why it should write reports as if using a foreign tongue. It is unlikely that all of Newton Wood's fellow councillors shared his benign view of Teesdale prose. In the contemporary workplace, readers no longer have the time to wade through such dense jargon. Like Councillor Wilkinson, they will increasingly protest when a document does not meet their needs, and that means the document will fail. It doesn't matter how good your content is or how much effort you put into it—alienate your readers and your document will fail.

KEY TIP Write for your reader rather than yourself.

Understand the communication process

Picture the transaction that happens when you write. At its simplest, workplace writing translates a purpose into an outcome through the exchange of a document:

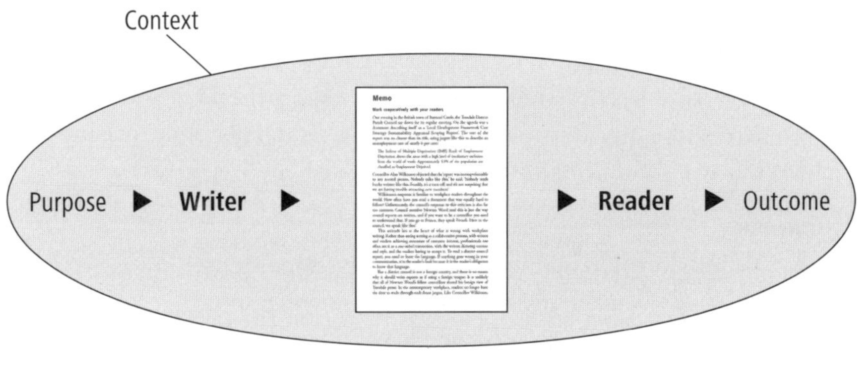

The two key participants are the writer and the reader. The writer will start with a purpose, develop the content and choose how to express it. These activities will be the main focus: how to be technically correct and complete, and perhaps also reflect the effort involved. The writer may also be thinking about professional status, and use elevated language to impress the reader.

Although this is understandable, it ignores the one critical barrier between your document and your intended outcomes: your readers. Effective workplace writers understand this and learn how to adapt their content to their readers' needs. This means you must master a range of structures and styles. In one document, you might include a great amount of detail, written with specialist terms to save time for a technical reader. In the next document—perhaps on the very same topic—you may cull some content and simplify the style to reach a public reader.

One is no better or worse than the other. Each is simply being effective for its readers. Either document could fail if given to the reader it was not intended for.

Apply the reader checklist

To help you judge how to adapt your content, ask yourself 10 questions:

The reader checklist

1 Who are my readers?

Background

2 How educated are my readers?
3 What knowledge do they bring to the document?
4 What attitudes will they have about my document?

Differences

5 Are some readers more important than others?
6 Are there any tensions between my readers?
7 Do my intentions differ from those of my readers?

Outcomes

8 What do my readers need from my document?
9 What do I want my readers to do in response?
10 What do I want to achieve by writing this document?

Using these checkpoints during drafting will help you make more informed choices about what content to include, how to structure it, and the best way to express it.

Let's take the case of Sara, a customer service officer in an insurance company. Sara is preparing a report about the recent denial of a customer's claim. The customer has written contesting the denial, and Sara must review the decision, recommend whether to overturn it, and draft a final letter. The context is fairly complex, and she needs to protect the company's interests at the same time as preserving its relationship with the customer.

Sara uses a reader checklist to identify her two main readers: her manager, who has to approve the final letter; and the customer, who will need to be persuaded that the company's decision was fair. But she realises that there is a third, unseen reader: a future reader of the file. Her documents will need to record the review process in enough detail for someone to understand it fully—especially if that person is in a court of law. Using the 10 checkpoints, Sara's map looks like this:

	Reader 1	Reader 2	Reader 3
1	Manager	Customer	Future reader of file
2	High education	Unknown education	High education
3	High knowledge	Low knowledge	Unknown, likely medium to high knowledge
4	Looking to be comprehensive and reduce risks to company.	Potentially hostile about decision, will need to be persuaded if claim is denied.	Will be looking for evidence of a thorough review.
5	High importance, because without approval, document won't go.	Highest importance, ultimately the document needs to persuade the customer.	Low priority initially, but will become higher if customer continues with claim.
6	Will want detail to cover the company's back.	Will be intolerant of detail and want to get straight to the point.	Will want the most detail to assess the process we went through.
7	Will want to minimise risks to the company.	Will be hostile if decision goes against him.	May not agree with our decision.
8	Details to check content.	Key message quickly.	Enough details to follow entire process.
9	Approve and sign letter.	Agree with our position and end claim.	Understand and reinforce our decision.
10	Complaint ends with minimal cost to company.	Complaint ends with customer understanding why claim was denied.	Will support and uphold the decision.

After just five minutes of sketching her readers, Sara identifies her main challenge. Her first reader is her manager, and the success of the document will come in gaining his support. He tends to put the company's interests first, and likes a lot of detail. Sara also knows that this is the opposite of what her final reader is looking for, because her research has established that the original decision was valid. She will need to explain clearly that the claim simply does not fall within the scope of the policy.

Sara decides that she can strike the best balance by covering the detail of the case in a memo while reducing the text for the customer. To keep the customer reading beyond the opening, she also decides to acknowledge his point of view before explaining why the policy doesn't cover the claim.

Here is Sara's letter:

> Dear Mr Gold,
>
> Thank you for your recent letter disputing the claims assessment we sent you on 10 January 2004.
>
> We have considered your reasons carefully, but unfortunately we have decided to deny your claim.
>
> While this claim is commonly covered in insurance policies of this type, your particular policy does not cover the event you describe. Had it done so, the premiums for the policy would have been substantially more than what you paid for your insurance.
>
> I have attached for your information the policy document with the relevant sections highlighted. You will see that the part of the document relating to your claim—section 5—does not include the circumstances you outline.
>
> We regret that your existing policy did not cover you in this case. I would welcome the opportunity to help you review your current insurance to ensure that your future cover is adequate. You can contact me on my direct line, 278 1451.
>
> Yours sincerely,
>
> Claims Review

Sara's manager is happy with the memo but nervous about the letter. It doesn't seem long enough, he says, and could expose the company to further action. He is particularly worried about the opening, which gets straight to the point and sets a sympathetic tone. We don't want to thank the guy, he says, and the decision is not unfortunate, it's simply reality.

Sara explains to the manager why she feels her letter will succeed. From the insurer's point of view, this is a clear-cut case of a policy not covering a particular event, but the customer clearly thinks otherwise. While the company should not pay a claim it is not obliged to, it can still be sympathetic to the customer and acknowledge his point of view. Her manager agrees to try this approach, but warns that it will likely present further opportunity for the customer to appeal the decision. Much to his surprise, the customer rings back having accepted the decision and wanting to discuss options for strengthening his future cover. Sara has turned a potential conflict into an opportunity to secure further business.

The reader checklist helped Sara to prepare a more effective document by walking in the shoes of her readers and understanding the tensions between them. In similar circumstances, too many workplace writers tend to write for their manager or from their own perspective. This may satisfy you, but it may not achieve your outcomes. This does not mean pandering to everything your readers want, but understanding their background and point of view, and communicating with them cooperatively. It's what they will look for every time they read a page of your writing.

The living language

Why audience was the focus of classical rhetoric

The vital role of the audience was at the heart of the earliest theories about effective communication. Over 2000 years ago, classical rhetoricians focused on audience because the main form of public exchange was the oration. In early Athenian democracy, any citizen could stand up and argue for a particular action, and being a gifted communicator gave you power and influence. But when you deliver a speech, the audience gives immediate clues to how your words are being received. Speakers who face a bored silence or a hostile howl can fail in a very public way. Athenian citizens needed techniques to anticipate an audience's response and avoid a public defeat. The first teachers of public speaking emerged and became quite the fashion in the fifth century BC. They named their craft rhetoric, from the Greek word 'rhetor', meaning orator.

Many of the early manuals on rhetoric earned it a bad name. They were accused of offering cheap debating tricks and methods for dishonest manipulation. This sense of rhetoric as empty or misleading language survives to this day, but Plato was its instigator. He became a staunch opponent of the craft, particularly after the mob was persuaded to condemn Socrates to death. Ironically, it was a student at Plato's Academy who countered this criticism and established rhetoric as the most influential theory of communication for the next 15 centuries. This was a clever bloke called Aristotle.

With all the logic of a natural philosopher, Aristotle developed the craft of rhetoric as a rational and systematic method of communication. He wrote about how to develop arguments to support your case, how to structure them for maximum impact, and how to deliver them in the style most appropriate to a given audience. He devoted entire sections of his *Ars Rhetorica* to understanding character and emotion, arguing that only by knowing your audience and what motivates them can you persuade them to your point of view.

By the time of the Roman Empire, democracy was far more contained than in Plato's day, but oratory had not lost its importance. One of the empire's greatest lawyers became the most successful proponent of rhetoric. Cicero's surviving works divided the craft into five areas for study:

1 Inventio—the discovery of arguments.
2 Dispositio—the structure of a speech.
3 Elocutio—the style used to express your case.
4 Pronuntiatio—the delivery of the speech.
5 Memoria—methods for memorising your speech.

Here was a complete tool kit for the orator, offering practical methods to develop content, structure it, express it and deliver it word-perfect. It did not mandate one particular form of speech but laid down the skills for adapting each speech to its audience. What began as a practical method for public speaking had evolved into a fully fledged theory of communication.

As writing gradually replaced speaking as the main form of public exchange, the principles of rhetoric were carried with it. When European scholars began rediscovering classical texts in the Middle Ages, they applied the same principles to the art of letter writing, which they called the 'ars dictamanus'.

Rhetoric was considered so important that it was one of the three core subjects in a four-year Bachelor of Arts degree. Rhetoric was also at the core of grammar school education in Britain and retained its influence through the Reformation and into the Renaissance. Throughout these centuries, works on rhetoric preserved the core notion that writers needed to adjust their arguments, structure and style to suit a particular reader.

How we lost sight of the reader

So what happened? If the dominant theory about communication placed such primacy on the reader, how did we arrive at such a blatantly indifferent title as 'Local Development Framework Core Strategy Sustainability Appraisal Scoping Report' and the take-it-or-leave-it attitude of Councillor Wood? The answer lies in part with a shift proposed by the scholars Agricola and Peter Ramus in the 15th and 16th centuries.

Ramus reduced the traditional five canons of rhetoric to just two: the style and delivery. From then on, he argued, the invention and arrangement of arguments were to become the separate province of logic or dialectic. Rhetoric's remaining role was simply to give the argument an ornamental dress. This shift in perspective found increasingly fertile ground during the Age of Reason in the 17th century, and was reinforced by Francis Bacon's division between reason and imagination. Science and logic were to be the preserve of reason, and rhetoric, in its narrower sense of style, should survive as the preserve of the imagination alone.

This had profound consequences for the way we communicate. Content was to be governed solely by logic, which was universal, objective and unconcerned by its audience. The only element that you might adjust for your reader was your style, because the reader no longer governed content.

Here lies the genesis of Councillor Wood's attitude. As the Western world entered the industrial age, the primacy of content was secured. As the professions emerged and workplaces became increasingly complex, the distance between writers and readers widened. Writers no longer had the pressure of a yawning audience shifting in its seats and glancing out the window to tell them whether their message was getting through. Many writers started to forget that it mattered. They focused on making documents complex and impressive rather than rhetorically effective. Like the authors of the Teesdale report, they lost sight of their readers.

Restore the reader to your writing

Only in the last 50 years have we seriously begun to rediscover our readers. A 'new rhetoric' movement has emerged, returning to some of the oldest notions about effective communication. New disciplines such as technical writing use rhetorical principles to adapt technical content to its intended audience. While an engineer or designer knows what makes a complex piece of machinery work, the technical writer has the task of helping the ordinary user to operate it. These trends have come together in fields such as user-centred design and usability testing. Companies have discovered that the best way to develop a product or document is to start by considering its users and design the product accordingly.

Emerging fields such as linguistics have also deepened our understanding of the relationship between writers and readers. In 1967, H.P. Grice published an influential account of the 'contract' that exists between the two, and the conventions that each tacitly accepts when they communicate. Key to this is the 'cooperative principle', which states that readers begin a text assuming it will communicate effectively. For a writer to maintain that cooperation, their document needs to have four general qualities:

1. Quantity—it should contain no more nor less information than the reader needs.
2. Quality—it should have enough evidence to support what it puts forward.
3. Relation—it should be relevant to the reader.
4. Manner—it should be clear, well focused, unambiguous and easy to read.

The good news is that most of your readers at the outset will assume these qualities are there, and may go to considerable lengths to read them into your document. The bad news is that, if you fail to achieve or maintain these qualities, you will lose your reader's cooperation. The Teesdale District Council report violated the conventions of quantity and manner to such a degree that it drew public condemnation.

This book will reintroduce many of the traditional techniques of classical rhetoric combined with some of the most recently developed methods for effective communication. It will restore the reader as the central focus for workplace writing. To help you meet your readers' needs, we will start with one of the newest disciplines: document testing.

Power tools

Test how well your documents work

It is one thing to understand the importance of your readers but quite another to know how to meet their needs. Your readers may be remote from you, giving you scant or no feedback. This is why it is easy to neglect them altogether. Yet there are a number of ways to test whether your documents will work for your readers. Here is a scale of 10 common testing methods, ranked in order of complexity.

The scale of document testing

	Method	Description
1	Reader feedback	Learning from responses received about completed documents.
2	Document outcomes	More formal monitoring of the track record of your documents.
3	Self-review	Formally assessing your document from a reader's perspective.
4	Peer review	A third party review of how your document meets readers' needs.
5	Review against standards	Systematic analysis of a document using some formal criteria.
6	Expert evaluation	Formal evaluation by an external expert using industry standards.
7	Surveys	More systematic feedback from readers about your writing.
8	Focus groups	Formal discussion with a sample of representative readers about their views.
9	Usability testing	Formal testing of how a document actually works in a simulated environment using representative readers.
10	Field testing	Assessment of how a document works in a real environment.

Record your readers' responses—levels one and two

At the lowest end of the testing scale is a reader's actual response. This may be as simple as a signature approving a proposal or the return of the document for further work. For many, this is the only test of their writing, but it is a blunt way of promoting your work and your career. You will eventually develop a notion of your readers and how to meet their needs, but you will score a lot of failures along the way. Don't make this your only form of testing.

The next, more systematic test sets some measurable document outcomes in advance. When writing a sales letter, for example, you could set a target for the percentage response to your offer, or the revenue it generates. If you are writing for an internal audience, your benchmark might be the take-up rate of your recommendations. For an informational document such as an operations manual, the outcome might be falling error rates or fewer calls for technical support.

Review your readers' needs—levels three and four

If low-level testing finds that your documents are falling short, the first form of intervention is a more rigorous self-review. Here, the focus shifts to analysing the likely success of your document before you finish it. You can incorporate audience analysis into every stage of writing and editing. During planning, for example, the reader checklist will help you decide on the best structure, the appropriate level of detail, how to design the text, and what tone to strike. While you review how coherent your document structure is, the map can be a guide on how likely you are to get your readers' cooperation. Lastly, in reviewing written expression, assess whether vocabulary, sentence length and tone are appropriate to your readers.

You can also ask a third party to assess your draft. Give it to some colleagues—preferably in an unrelated area—and ask them how the target audience might respond. If you are writing about a technical subject for a non-technical audience, give it to someone with no technical background. Of course, this kind of test is partly hypothetical because you have to put yourself in the shoes of your readers. If your reader map is thorough or you have a strong sense of your reader, this may be all that you need. If not, then the leap will be more difficult. That's when you move to the next level of testing.

Assess your text against standards—levels five and six

When you reach level five on the testing scale, you will use more structured methods to review your work against predetermined standards. This may be how consistently you have used a set template, or whether you are following your organisation's style guide. You could also use a readability formula to test how difficult your writing is for your audience to follow. Every chapter of this book offers tests and benchmarks to help you evaluate your work. Here are 12 tests you can apply during drafting and editing, which the following chapters will illustrate in more detail.

A selection of document tests

	Test	Assessment purpose
1	Reader checklist	How well your text meets the readers' identified needs. (Chapter 1)
2	Conclusion checking	The reasoning and evidence supporting your content. (Chapter 2)
3	Structure mapping	The structure design, headings, navigation, complexity and balance. (Chapter 3)
4	Core message test	The level of focus and balance between the key points and the details. (Chapter 4)
5	Proof analysis	The quality of analysis and its likely persuasiveness. (Chapter 5)
6	Design checklist	How well the visual elements reinforce the content. (Chapter 7)
7	Tone scale	How your text will sound to the reader and what voice it establishes. (Chapter 8)
8	Readability	How easily readers will work through the text and absorb the content. (Chapter 10)
9	Key words	The efficiency of expression. (Chapter 11)
10	Active voice	The precision, directness and clarity of the verbs. (Chapter 12)
11	Style checklist	How your text complies with standards for language, punctuation, numbers, grammar and sourcing. (Chapter 15)
12	Proofing checklist	The final quality control to find and eliminate errors. (Chapter 17)

When selecting which of these measures to use, consider their relevance, scope and cost. When time is short, it is unlikely that you'll be able to apply them all, so choose those that will tell you the most about your document. If, for example, you are writing for a readership with low levels of education, then a readability check will probably be highly relevant. If your readers are more technically oriented, then conclusion testing will help you check the completeness of your facts and the evidence supporting your conclusions. When writing for a hostile readership, you may find a proof analysis of most benefit. Structural mapping will come into its own for a longer report.

If time is of the essence, use the reader checklist and the most relevant second test. But beware of the limits of a narrow testing regime. A document can be highly readable yet still fail if its content is muddled or its structure is a mess. You might carefully test your content but not the basics of spelling, grammar and punctuation, and your reader may still dismiss your conclusions. The more tests you can apply, the better your document will be.

Of course, evaluating your text against particular standards is fine if you can judge what level is appropriate for your reader. Where you do not have this expertise, you can call in an external expert. Over the past 20 years, communications consultants have developed some effective methods for estimating how well a text will work with its intended readership. Some offer formal accreditation or a quality mark to attest that a document meets a standard. Others are even willing to defend a client's writing if it comes before a court.

Run reader surveys and focus groups—levels seven and eight

While expert evaluation offers some assurance that your document will succeed, all standards share one important limitation: they are estimates based on general experience of how readers respond to documents. While it is likely this can be adapted to your context, there is no guarantee that it will work for your unique reader. There is ultimately only one way to tell what your readers think about your documents: ask them.

You can survey readers at two levels: by asking them to assess a specific document, or by asking them about their general experience of reading your documents. The first form of survey is a more formal version of the reader response at level one on the testing scale. Instead of recording a signature alone, for example, you could add a couple of questions about your writing, such as how long it took to read a document or how clear the reader found the text. Some companies add these to a cover sheet for all internal documents. Government agencies often ask readers to estimate the time it takes to complete a form. These mini-surveys are usually limited to one or two questions and to documents that will return to the writer. But even one or two questions can give you vital feedback, so look for any opportunity to build these into your documents.

More commonly, when a workplace has identified problems with its communication, it will commission a formal survey of readers. This offers a snapshot of more general trends and problems. Try not to make a survey too long or complicated, or you may find that very few readers participate. Use multiple-choice options or ask readers to circle numbers on a scale, and include space for further comments. Even short surveys will quickly pinpoint problem areas.

Some organisations extend their surveying by setting up more formal interviews or focus groups. These are particularly useful in drawing out more qualitative responses, and mapping them in greater detail than the surveys alone. But while the depth and quality of information will increase, so too will the expense. You will need dedicated staff or a consultant to design the research, chair the groups, and pay your participants something for their efforts. This makes focus groups an expensive exercise for individual documents, but there will be times that expense is justified.

Conduct usability testing—level nine

The next form of testing is more time-intensive again, but also more reliable. Usability testing combines the oldest rhetorical principle of audience focus with the contemporary skills of technical writing, industrial design, human factors engineering and cognitive psychology. It is particularly useful when your document has practical, functional outcomes that many readers will achieve by using it. The classic example is a user manual for computer hardware or software.

At its core, a usability test takes a product and asks a representative sample of readers to use it under controlled circumstances. The results are then evaluated and used to refine that product. Successful testing can give you great return for your investment. For example, when the Digital Equipment Corporation first released its RALLY software, sales were slow. Rather than scrap the product, the company analysed its users and the tasks the users wanted the software to perform. The company used this information to revise its interface, and tested it continuously with representative users. Sales of the revised product lifted by 80 per cent.

The features of usability testing include:

- testing a document continuously through the cycle of drafting
- testing iteratively, with each test informing the next stage of development
- using empirical measures and rigorous protocols
- making writing a more collaborative process, involving writers, engineers, marketers and other specialists
- testing a document using real people doing real tasks
- shifting the culture towards a user-centred approach
- applying usability to any kind of product or interface.

As powerful as testing is, it does have some limits. It can be expensive and impractical for some kinds of documents or readers. If you are writing a report for a government minister, for example, you are hardly likely to persuade her to participate in a test. A routine memo to a colleague is never going to justify the costs. In these cases, you should turn to forms of testing lower down the scale. Secondly, a usability test can never perfectly reproduce a real-world environment, no matter how hard you try. While the results are highly likely to reveal how the product will fare, they are never a guarantee.

Run some field tests—level 10

You can overcome some of these limits by conducting a field test instead of a simulated usability test. This means going to where your reader will use your document and observing how well it works there. Where this is feasible, a field test will give you the greatest degree of assurance that your document is effective. The disadvantage is that by the time you release a document it is in such an advanced stage that it will be more costly to correct. It is best not to leave your testing so late. Test your texts from your readers' perspectives as early and as often as you can.

The document testing scale shows that there is no longer any excuse for keeping your readers at a distance. Many workplaces see testing as a complex and time-consuming exercise that they can ill afford. At the higher end of the scale, usability or field tests are costly, and are best reserved for documents that warrant the effort and expense. This might be, for example, the operating instructions for a product that will be used by thousands or even millions of customers. Comprehensive and regular testing throughout the development of the product then becomes essential. It is less essential if your reader is a single colleague with whom you can easily discuss your document. For every level in between, there are several testing methods you can select. If the Teesdale District Council had applied even one test, it could have avoided public condemnation of its scoping report.

2 Content

At a glance

The toolbox

- Overcome writer's block 31
- Apply the content checklist 31
- Define your topic clearly 32
- Clarify your purpose 34
- Scope your research 35
- Draw some findings and conclusions 36
- Set targets for results 37

The living language

- Know the three types of content 38
- Use the stasis system to judge a past action 39
- Test the conclusions for a future action 40

Power tools

- Explore contemporary content techniques 43
- Develop content creatively 43
- Try some structured content techniques 45

The toolbox

Overcome writer's block

If there is a single experience that every writer shares, it is the terror of the blank page. Whether you are a prize-winning novelist or a website author, you have probably experienced writer's block. In the workplace, this is mainly a problem with content—not knowing enough about your topic or what you want to say about it. You may have parts of the puzzle in your mind, but if you start writing at random it can take you in haphazard directions. You come to a standstill. It's time to step back and develop your thinking in a more structured way.

There are four steps to developing the content of any document:

1. Defining your topic.
2. Gathering information about it.
3. Evaluating that information.
4. Developing your ideas in response.

Of course, these steps are not always as linear as this. You will evaluate as you gather information, and you will research partly with some idea of what you want to say. But if you take shortcuts with one or more steps, chances are you will find yourself staring at a blank screen.

A content checklist can guide you through the steps, keep your focus on ideas and help you let go of anxieties about your draft.

Apply the content checklist

The content checklist

Topic and purpose

1. What is the topic or problem you are writing about?
2. What kind of document are you writing?
3. What do you want to achieve by writing it?

Research

4. What prompted you to write this document?
5. What information do you need to gather about your topic?
6. What sources will you need to consult?

Findings and conclusions

7 What findings emerge from your research?
8 What conclusions can you draw about your topic?
9 What reasons and evidence support these conclusions?

Results

10 What actions should follow the reading of your document?
11 What outcomes do you want to achieve as a result of those actions?
12 How can you measure the success of your document?

Define your topic clearly

Defining a topic poorly will result in a poor document. Be as specific as you can, and revisit your definition as you research. Often you will start out with a general subject, but find that the key issue is a smaller subset, or even something else altogether. Many professionals use the writing process itself to refine their topic. This is entirely valid, but it is also inefficient. Changing your topic midstream will waste much drafting effort, so think before you write.

Let's illustrate the first steps in the checklist with the experience of Jack, a policy officer in a government planning department. Jack is preparing a ministerial briefing note on whether to exempt a property developer from an infrastructure levy that helps to fund roads, sewers and public transport. His minister has previously granted exemptions in similar circumstances. The topic appears straightforward, but Jack teases it out with a simple topic checklist.

The topic checklist

1 **What** is the topic?
2 **Who** is involved?
3 **When** does it take place?
4 **Where** does it take place?
5 **How** does it happen?
6 **Why** is this of interest or concern?

Jack starts answering these questions easily enough:

1 What—whether to grant an exemption to an infrastructure levy.
2 Who—Premium Properties.

3 When—now and for the life of the project.
4 Where—the Punt Road development.
5 How—the minister has discretionary power under the Act.

So far, the topic presents no surprises, but the final question causes Jack to shift his thinking:

6 Why
—developer argues that his case is similar to other exemptions.
—granting the exemption may create a more general precedent.
—requests for exemptions seem to be growing.
—too many exemptions may reduce the money available for infrastructure.
—this could leave an area without adequate access to transport.
—one-off exemptions may make the system unclear and complex.

Asking why an issue is important will usually clarify your topic. If you can't explain to yourself why something is significant, you probably can't convince your reader either. After doing so, Jack re-works his entire topic checklist:

1 What—the need to review the infrastructure levy exemption system.
2 Who—specific request from Premium Properties, but potentially all developers.
3 When—now and for future development projects.
4 Where—at Punt Road and all future developments.
5 How—use of discretionary powers under the Act.
6 Why
—current system may be inconsistent.
—income from levy may limit the infrastructure that communities need.
—current situation is creating uncertainty among developers.
—current system is becoming complex to administer.

Always try to think through your topic before leaping into writing. Jack's new approach had greater value for his agency because it identified and sought to resolve the underlying problem. It also saved him a lot of rewriting.

KEY TIP | Think before you draft.

Clarify your purpose

Once you have a clear topic, decide on what kind of document you are writing. Most documents tend to emphasise one of three aims: persuasion, information and entertainment.

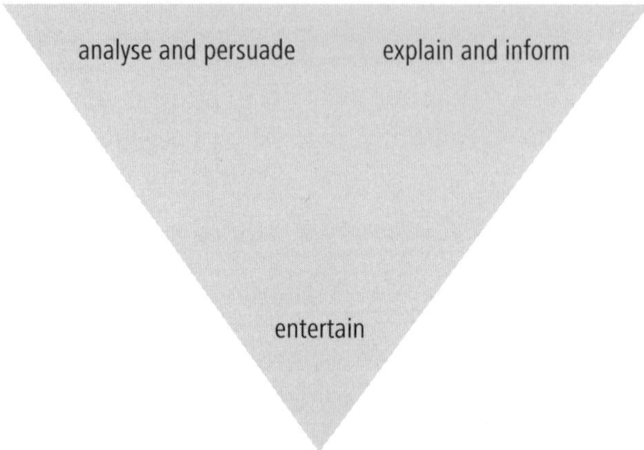

Because workplace writing is utilitarian, it generally doesn't need to be entertaining, so most documents at work will fall in a spectrum between persuasion and information. At one end, documents such as reports or submissions gather information about a problem, subject that to some kind of analysis, draw conclusions and recommend an appropriate action. They will explain a problem, but their ultimate goal is to persuade a reader to act on their recommendation.

At other times, your document will simply need to inform rather than make a case for a particular action. This might be an information brochure, a legal contract, a warranty for a product, the instructions for assembling it, or a letter outlining changes to a service. The purpose here is not to analyse the instructions, nor to comment on the contract conditions or the service, but simply to inform the reader about them.

Of course, many documents will combine both elements. When responding to customer complaints, you need to inform them of the company's policy and persuade them that it is valid. If you are changing a service, you will need to persuade the customer that your product remains good value. Jack was writing an analytical document that would need to persuade his minister. That means gathering careful evidence during his research.

Scope your research

A mistake typical of workplace writers is spending too much time on research. It is always much easier to gather facts than to start writing, but suddenly you find you have only one day left to meet your deadline. To avoid this trap, scope your research at the start.

Start by asking what has prompted the need for your document. Always double-check that a problem really exists by reviewing the original source. Jack begins with the correspondence from Premium Properties and finds a slight ambiguity in the original letter. This makes him ask: is the company asking for an exemption for a particular development or for all its future developments?

Checking the source helps Jack list all the information he will need: details of all levy payments; some history about Premium Properties; the background of the infrastructure levy itself; the way that exemptions have been granted in the past; and possible alternatives to the system. Before rushing off to the nearest source, however, he scopes his research tasks. Even when time is short, always plan your research.

There are three kinds of sources you can go to:

1 Primary—written or oral.
2 Secondary—written documents.
3 Tertiary—synthesised accounts of more general subjects.

To lay a strong foundation for your document, follow these three principles:

1 Turn first to primary sources, then secondary, then tertiary.
2 Assess the credibility of all your sources.
3 Keep clear records of your sources.

Jack's primary sources are both written and oral. He jots down the places he can go and estimates the time it will take:

Primary sources	
Department files	1 day
Department staff	0.5 day
Stakeholder organisations	1.5 days
Other agency staff	1 hour
Minister's staff	1 hour

Secondary sources

Media coverage	2 hours
Discussion in professional journals	1 day

Jack has less than five days to submit his document. There is too much work here for the available time, so he prioritises. The key information is in the department's own files or held by planning staff. There is value in touching base with the minister's office and looking at media articles. Although stakeholder organisations would be relevant, their position would be predictable. Likewise, professional journals would be too time-consuming. Jack gave himself two days for research and thinking, and two-and-a-half days for writing.

Draw some findings and conclusions

When the research is done, it is time to draw out the most relevant findings. Sift your material to develop your analysis—the bridge between descriptive fact-gathering and the analytical interpretation of those facts.

Jack finds a wealth of material on file and interviews three planning staff who have some experience of the levy exemptions. His main findings are:

- The levy was introduced in 1992 to defray the costs of infrastructure in growth areas.
- It has raised $780 million.
- In 2001, the previous minister first used a little-known provision to exempt a developer from a levy if 'the circumstances warrant it'.
- Since then, 12 developers have been granted exemptions.
- The circumstances of Punt Road are identical to those of similar previous exemptions.
- Cases for which exemptions have been granted are widening.
- The number of approaches for exemptions is increasing.
- The cost to the State in lost revenue is estimated at $68 million and is growing.
- The situation is starting to attract negative media coverage.

You now enter the more interesting part of the content development process: drawing conclusions. The greatest value that workplace writers bring to their organisations is judging how best to respond to a problem.

Lacking confidence about your conclusions is the surest way to suffer writer's block. Many writers respond by starting to write up their fact finding with the hope that the conclusions will emerge. The content checklist can help you develop conclusions in a more structured way.

Jack uses the content checklist to list some tentative conclusions:

- It would be hard not to grant an exemption to Premium Properties.
- Growing use of exemptions is threatening the original purpose of the levy.
- The exemptions are creating uncertainty and becoming complex to administer.
- While granting this exemption, we should also develop a new policy for the future.

You can then test the reasons and evidence that support your conclusions by listing them. Jack's research notes gave him what he needed:

- The precedents of three previous cases similar to that of Premium Properties.
- The year-by-year numbers showing growing exemptions.
- Quotations from developers and media about uncertainty.
- Details of administration time spent by the department.
- Projected loss of revenue if the situation continues.

The living language section below has a further tool on testing your conclusions.

Set targets for results

The final part of the content checklist helps you to map out your recommendations about an issue or a problem. What exactly needs to happen? What should your readers do in response? This will often be to approve your decision and sign the document, but think beyond the initial step and about the final outcomes. Jack summarises his outcomes as:

- Approval by minister.
- Letter to Premium Properties.
- More revenue available for infrastructure development.
- Fall in number of requests for exemption.

- Increase in revenue raised by levy for infrastructure.
- Increase in proportion of developers paying full levy.

Using a content checklist as his guide, Jack had researched and developed the content of his document in two days. When he sat down to write, the draft flowed smoothly. He also used his checklist to negotiate some content verbally with his manager, which meant it was readily approved.

Many of the questions in the checklist may seem obvious, but approaching your task in a structured way will save you time, improve your content and avoid the horrors of the blank page.

The living language

Know the three types of content

Coming up with content is one of the oldest problems in public and professional communication. It was the primary focus of classical rhetoricians such as Cicero and Quintilian, who developed detailed systems for identifying an issue and exploring the arguments that will address it. Some of these techniques have been preserved down the centuries, while others are only recently being rediscovered in the workplace. To supplement the content checklist, we are going to look at two simple tools that work as well today as they did during the Roman Republic.

Classical rhetoric started by defining the three types of contexts you need to develop content for:

1. Judicial—making a judgement about a past action.
2. Deliberative—finding solutions for a future action.
3. Ceremonial—commemorating a person or topic.

Ceremonial speeches were far more common in classical times than they are today, when the closest thing most people do is give a farewell speech for a colleague. But judicial and deliberative contexts are just as relevant today as they were 2000 years ago, so these will be our focus.

Use the stasis system to judge a past action

The judicial context was particularly attractive to the Romans, and much of their rhetorical theory related to how to make a case in the law courts. Lawyers still use many of these techniques, but so can workplace managers when they must judge, for example, the effectiveness of a previous decision or the performance of their staff.

Cicero taught what he called the 'stasis' system for developing a judicial case. This examines a situation through four key 'stopping points':

1 Issues of fact
2 Issues of definition
3 Issues of quality
4 Issues of process

These stopping points can help you judge a past action. Robyn uses the stasis system when she is asked to prepare a report about the alleged misconduct of Joel, one of her junior team members. She starts by gathering facts about the conduct itself, concentrating solely on what can be established objectively. She verifies several points of poor performance, including late arrival at work, mistakes in completed work and the late delivery of projects. These are the issues of fact.

Robyn then considers these facts against definitions of misconduct and poor performance. Fortunately, these are clearly defined in the human resources policies. She judges that the facts fit the definition of poor performance, but probably not that of misconduct. These are the issues of definition.

The third issue under Cicero's system is the issue of quality. Were there any extenuating circumstances? How severe was the behaviour? What was Joel's attitude? His response to Robyn is indifference about his behaviour and hostility towards her review—and that can only count against him. These are the issues of quality.

The final issue is that of process. Have the established and relevant procedures or laws been followed? In this case, the problems had been raised continually with Joel in writing, following a clear pattern of escalation. The process has been conducted properly, and Joel had every opportunity to correct his behaviour. There were no issues of process.

Cicero proposed these four stopping points as the likely areas of dispute in any judicial process, whether a major court case or a minor incident. Use these to go to the heart of a case and gather what you need for an effective judgement. Robyn decides that there was no misconduct, but there was certainly poor performance. Joel's refusal to respond to reasonable attempts to correct his behaviour leads to the company dismissing him. Using the stasis system, Robyn brought this about without exposing her employer to claims of unfair dismissal.

Test the conclusions for a future action

The second context that classical rhetoricians discussed involved a deliberative decision about a future action. Here, you are not judging the past, but assessing how to solve a problem or choose between different future options. Writing of this kind does not turn so much on issues of definition or quality. Instead, the success of your solution will flow from how rigorously you have tested your conclusions.

We can adapt some core concepts of rhetoric into a simple four-point system:

1 Question—the topic or problem.
2 Conclusion—your response or solution.
3 Proof—the arguments that support your conclusion.
4 Refutation—the arguments that oppose your conclusion.

This checklist is useful when you are part-way through your research and struggling to develop strong conclusions. You can test out potential conclusions by subjecting them to these steps. Even doing so mentally will help you to reject weaker options and focus on those that you can back with strong arguments. More importantly, this structure forces you to move from the monologue of your research to a dialogue with your readers. What arguments will convince your readers to support your conclusions?

The crucial step is to evaluate your proof—the reasoning behind your conclusions. Just as a simple checklist can help you refine your topic, five steps will quickly identify any weaknesses in your supporting arguments:

1 Claim
2 Reason
3 Evidence
4 Concessions
5 Warrants

If your question is a simple one, you can put your conclusion into the claim slot and then evaluate it. If, on the other hand, your conclusion needs to be backed up with a range of supporting arguments, then it is worth testing each one in turn.

The first step is to ask your reasons for the claim. This usually follows a 'because…' statement. In the Premium Property example, Jack's first conclusion was that the minister should grant the exemption because exemptions had been granted in similar circumstances, and not doing so would expose the state to legal challenges. His second conclusion was that the whole system should be reformed because it was becoming hard to administer, attracting criticism and failing to meet its purpose. If you can't explain your reasons as succinctly as this, you may need to revisit your claim.

The next step is to identify the evidence that supports your reasoning. Assess your evidence using five simple tests:

1 Sufficiency
2 Representativeness
3 Accuracy
4 Relevance
5 Authoritativeness

Jack decided he would need to include most of his evidence to build a sufficient case, including the amount raised by the levy, the growing number of exemptions and the media coverage—all accurate, relevant and genuine information. Coming mostly from the department's records and published sources, it was also authoritative. Because his estimate of lost revenue came from a less reliable oral source, he double-checked it and found that it did indeed call for qualification. If he hadn't checked it, his recommendation might have been rejected or the decision based on misleading evidence.

The qualification related to unconnected policy changes that may have independently influenced the trend of lower revenue for the infrastructure levy. While Jack's revised estimate of economic impact was lower, it was still enough to support his conclusion. But by acknowledging the qualification in his document, Jack was making a concession that anticipated a reader's question. Too often, we leave concessions out of our content for fear that they will damage our argument. This is understandable, but it carries its own risk. The chances are that your reader will light on the same question, and that will undercut your case much more than acknowledging the limit yourself. You will also gain credibility from being open with your reader. Of course, if a concession is so significant that it threatens a claim altogether, it is time to revise your thinking.

If you are dealing with a fairly complex argument, you may also need to add some 'warrants'. In *The Craft of Research*, the American academics Booth, Colomb and Williams describe warrants as short explanations of why a reason supports a claim, or why some evidence is relevant to a reason. Too often, we tend to leave these out because the connections seem obvious. But if they are not clear to your reader, even the most powerful reasons and evidence will not win your case.

Jack included several warrants in his documents to support his claims, carefully selecting those that he felt the Minister would question. He explained clearly, for example, why the State would be exposed to legal action if it didn't grant an exemption, and exactly how the levy was failing to meet its intended purpose. These were warrants connecting his reasons to his claims. While most of his evidence was clearly linked to his reasons, he also felt he should explain why the critical media sources he used were worth heeding. He didn't spell out every connection in the chain of argument, but strengthened the potentially weak links.

The final step in testing your ideas comes from swapping seats with your readers completely. Ask yourself what other reasons might refute your claims. Test out all possible reasons, evidence and warrants using the same steps. This is an essential part of the dialogue with your reader. Anticipating and answering alternatives is one of the most powerful things you can do to win support.

Of course, you will not want to do this so much that it destroys your own case. If a powerful argument stands validly against your conclusion, mention it but reason that the overall benefits outweigh the costs. Ignoring a strong opposing point will almost certainly leave you open to attack. If you find that the counterclaims seem to be stronger than your own case, then return to the drawing board and rethink your conclusions. This is the value of evaluating your content critically.

Power tools

Explore contemporary content techniques

While some of the most effective techniques for developing content are the oldest, we have hardly been standing still for 2000 years. In recent decades, several new tools have emerged specifically for workplace documents. Six of the most useful are:

1 Free-writing
2 Brainstorming
3 Mind-mapping
4 Six thinking hats
5 Force-field analysis
6 Fishbone diagrams

Some of these techniques tap into the creative side of your brain. Others work best in group situations when you are writing as a team. The final two are of most help when you have a more specific problem to solve.

Develop content creatively

Free-writing is the least structured of the techniques. You simply sit down with a pen or at the keyboard, then, thinking about your topic, write whatever comes into your head regardless of its relevance or worth. The idea is that free-writing jump-starts the creative process. Here's an example of free-writing that Leigh used to write a sales report. Leigh is a sales representative for a distributor of quality coffee. She is paid partly by her salary and partly by commission worked out from averaging sales on the past two quarters and the predicted sales for the next. Her report must be accurate while retaining the confidence of her manager. After free-writing for less than five minutes, Leigh went over the text and bolded key themes and words.

> **Sales generally flat this quarter**, with most outlets reporting falls in patronage, lucky my **client base is varied** because while the **cafes lost customers particularly the Saturday morning crowd** who tend to drop in for a coffee and a focaccia and read the Saturday papers, although personally getting out of bed and immersing yourself in another throng

> voluntarily seems a waste of energy but they do drink a lot of coffee. But while these tend to get very antsy about **rises in interest rates** like the two that we had the month before last, the **corporate world is less affected** by this don't know why but they seem to be doing all right and that is **keeping up the weekday patronage.** This also helps out the **cafes which provide take-away service near office buildings** as well, really builds up their **morning customer base,** at least according to Grant from Café Crowd who reckons it's now about 40 per cent of his business and he deserves to do well what with his wife and the cancer but he reckons that this **diversity is going to be the saving grace** in the months ahead and cafes that can adapt will do well. It makes me glad I've got the broad mix of outlets that I have because it makes me less susceptible to swings of fortune so things should **stay flat or be slightly better but no worse in the quarter ahead.**

Within minutes, Leigh had the essence of her report:

> Sales were flat this quarter.
> This was caused by fall in trade due to interest rate rises and consumer sentiment.
> However, in the next quarter my results should be stable or slightly ahead.
> This is because my client base is diverse:
>
> - cafes losing Saturday morning crowd
> - some compensating with weekday take-away sales
> - restaurants catering to corporate customers are increasing patronage.
>
> Suggest that we market to sectors doing well, but maintain a diverse client base.

Brainstorming is similar to free-writing in that it is initially unstructured, focusing purely on getting words down onto the page or onto a whiteboard. Instead of writing in a stream of consciousness, however, you note ideas in point form. While doing so, put any critical attitude on hold, as this will help you escape well-established attitudes to a particular problem. Concentrate first on generating ideas, no matter how off the wall they may seem. Only after the ideas peter out do you then return to what you have produced and evaluate what will be workable. The next chapter on structure will illustrate brainstorming and how you can convert it to a draft document outline.

Brainstorming is a useful way of harnessing the ideas of a team, but this needs a strong facilitator. Often, you can give it a bit more structure by using the mind-mapping technique. This starts by placing a question or problem in the centre of a whiteboard or a large piece of paper. You then think of ideas related to the central topic, and sub-branches of those ideas. Use different colours for different sections to reinforce the concepts you are developing. You will quickly develop the content for your document.

This technique is also useful when you are facing an impossible deadline. Ian is a corporate services manager in an insurance company. He has two hours to prepare a presentation to his executive about his ideas for a new mail handling system. He knows the subject well as he just trialled a new system, but he has not yet written up the results. Now he has virtually no time to come up with some coherent and persuasive content. He turns to mind-mapping on a large whiteboard. His diagram is shown on the next page.

The mind map took 20 minutes to prepare. Ian then outlined the structure for his presentation and mentally walked himself through it. He typed up a one-page summary using the same categories and handed this out at the meeting. The presentation was logical and focused, and the executive approved his recommendation.

Try some structured content techniques

Edward de Bono's 'six thinking hats' technique is a useful way of evaluating a problem from several different angles. The idea behind it is that most people tend to bring one dominant perspective to a problem. A manager advocating a particular course of action will tend to write about its positive features without always assessing its faults. Technical staff may look at a problem purely through available data without considering the emotional responses people might have. To make sure you have considered a proposal from every angle, think about it through six perspectives in turn:

- White hat—analytical thinking, working with available data.
- Red hat—emotional response and gut feeling.
- Black hat—the pessimist, considering the worst case scenario.
- Yellow hat—the optimist, looking for all the positives.

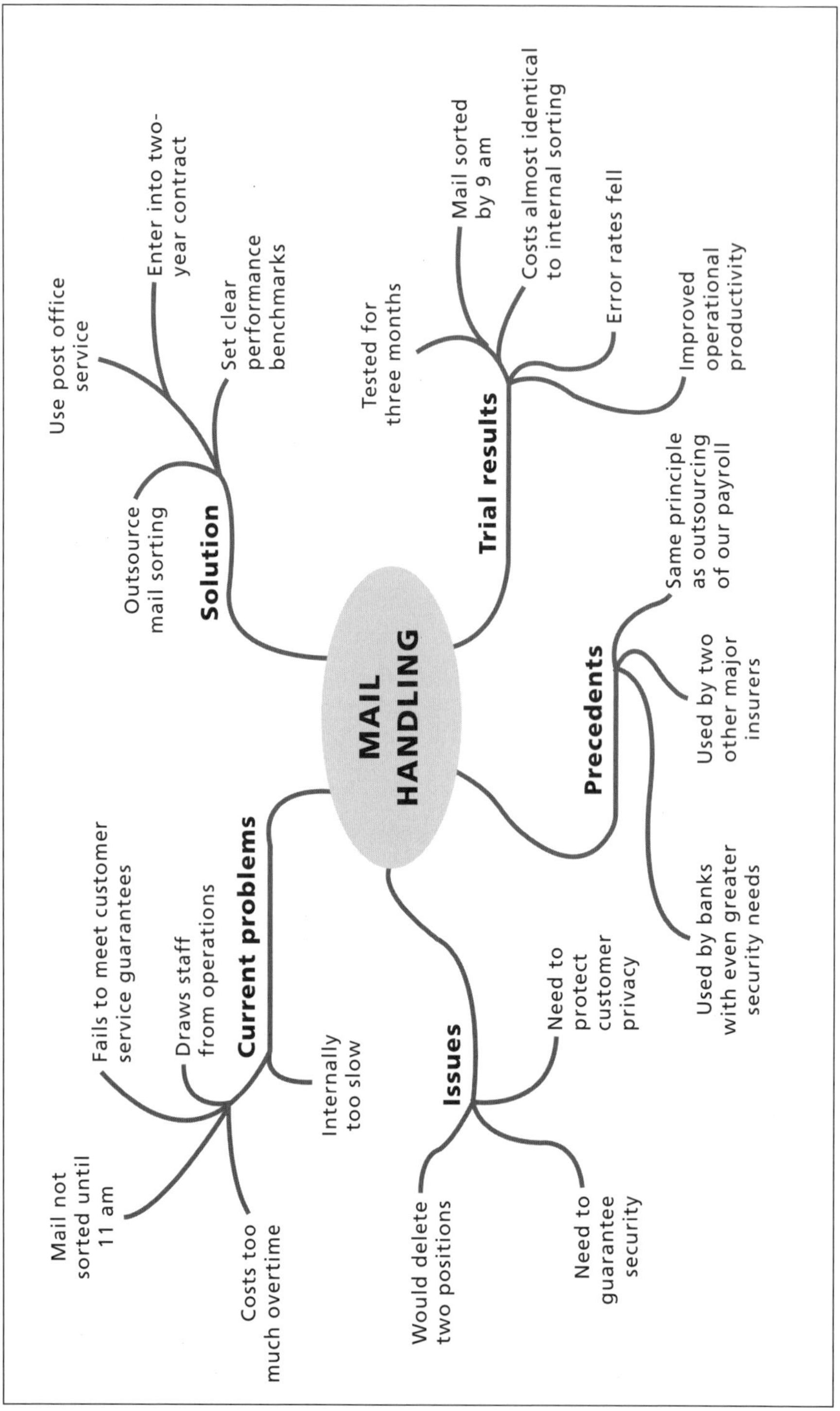
MAIL HANDLING
Solution
Outsource mail sorting
Use post office service
Enter into two-year contract
Set clear performance benchmarks
Trial results
Tested for three months
Mail sorted by 9 am
Costs almost identical to internal sorting
Error rates fell
Improved operational productivity
Precedents
Same principle as outsourcing of our payroll
Used by two other major insurers
Used by banks with even greater security needs
Issues
Need to protect customer privacy
Need to guarantee security
Would delete two positions
Current problems
Fails to meet customer service guarantees
Draws staff from operations
Internally too slow
Mail not sorted until 11 am
Costs too much overtime

- Green hat—your creative thinking, open-minded and unfettered by criticism.
- Blue hat—the traffic cop, considering and directing the thinking between hats.

This technique is highly effective in group situations, particularly where you need to harness the strengths of some strong personalities who tend towards one hat or another. Asking people to limit their perspective to one view at a time can open everybody up to alternative ways of looking at a problem. When you have explored the idea from every angle, you can reach a consensus more easily about the most balanced decision.

Hedda has been asked to reduce the costs of her company's current car packages for its mobile sales staff. Her main options are to provide smaller, cheaper cars, combined with staff increasing their contribution from salary sacrifice. Past experience tells her that nothing causes discontent quite like changes to car packages, so she decides to bring together a working group. This includes representatives of the sales force, the finance and the human resources departments. She deliberately asks people to put on the hat they are not used to wearing. The value of getting participants to see the situation from another perspective is immediately apparent, and the group quickly reaches a consensus that supports her case.

The final two techniques are particularly strong when you are assessing a specific problem. Force-field analysis will help you to assess whether to proceed with an action by rating the forces working for and against it. Take a piece of paper and write down the proposal or idea in the centre. List all of the forces supporting it on one side and those opposing it on the other, scoring each force from 1 (weak) to 10 (strong).

This will let you more easily visualise the environment the plan will have to contend with, and where you may have to adjust your intentions. After exhausting all the possible pros and cons, add up the scores on each side. This will help you judge whether the decision is likely to succeed.

Fishbone diagrams look like the skeleton of a fish. Also known as cause-and-effect diagrams, these were developed by Kaoru Ishikawa in the 1960s to analyse the causes of a particular situation. They can help to evaluate a particular problem, or to assess the factors that will make a successful product. Here is an example of a fishbone diagram assessing the causes of falling sales for a retail chain:

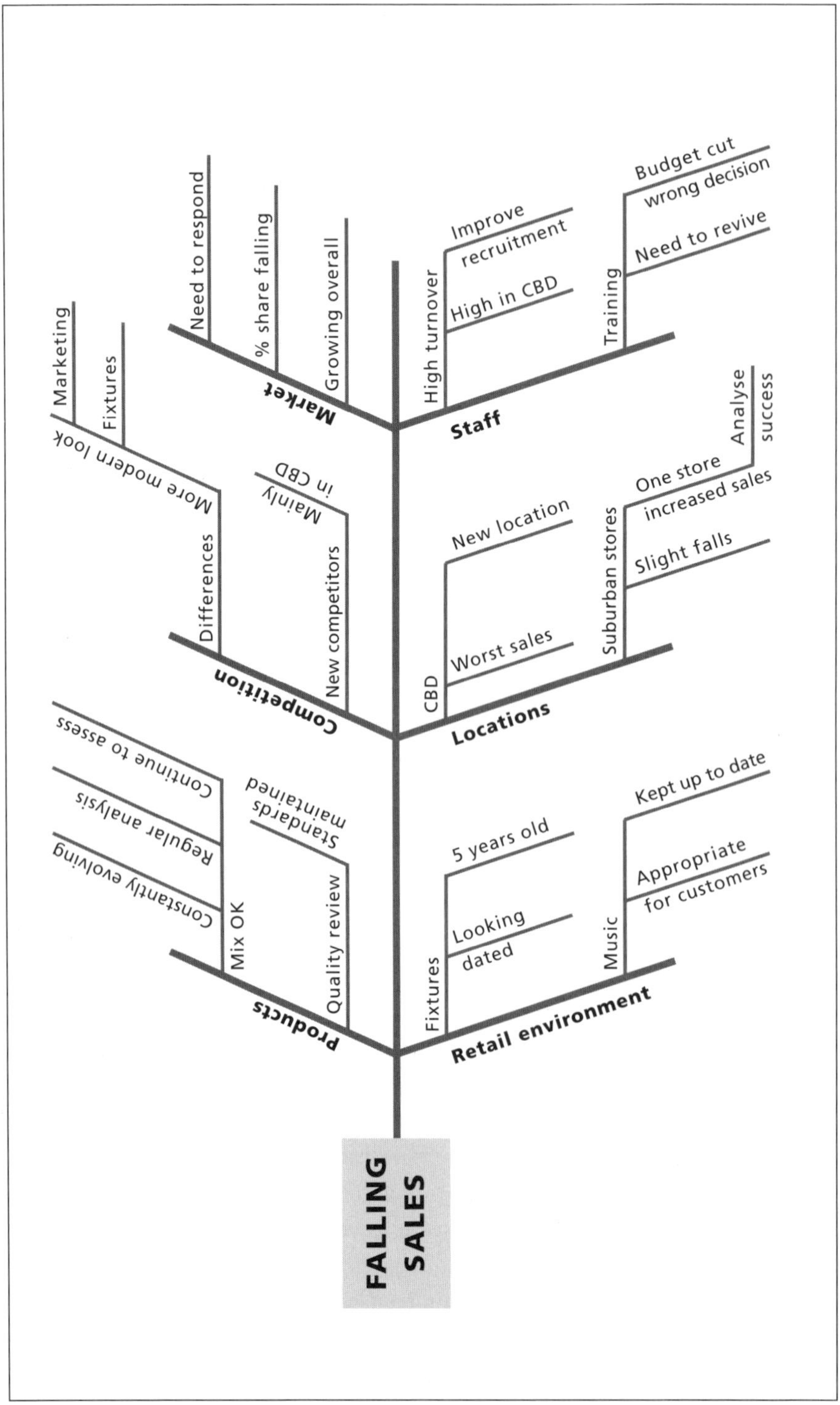
FALLING SALES
Market
Need to respond
% share falling
Growing overall
Staff
High turnover
Improve recruitment
High in CBD
Training
Budget cut wrong decision
Need to revive
Competition
Differences
More modern look
Marketing
Fixtures
New competitors
Mainly in CBD
Locations
CBD
New location
Worst sales
Suburban stores
One store increased sales
Analyse success
Slight falls
Products
Mix OK
Continue to assess
Regular analysis
Constantly evolving
Quality review
Standards maintained
Retail environment
Fixtures
5 years old
Looking dated
Music
Kept up to date
Appropriate for customers

Following a format such as this gives you an immediate structure for your thinking. Like all the content techniques in this chapter, this offers a practical way to wrestle with your topic and develop your content. The best-written documents in the world will still fail if the thinking behind them is sloppy. Experiment with these techniques and you will find that your ideas will become sharper and you will seldom face the terrors of the blank screen.

3 Structure

At a glance

The toolbox

- Put some order in the house 51
- Use issue–discussion–action for simple documents 52
- Avoid narrative where you can 52
- Telescope your documents wherever possible 53
- Use exposition in longer documents 54
- Use instruction for procedures 56
- Try question and answer for disconnected text 57
- Experiment with mosaic structures 57

The living language

- Use structural outlining to move from planning to drafting 58
- Apply the structure checklist 60

Power tools

- Apply structure mapping to longer reports 65
- Review the structural design 65
- Avoid unnecessary complexity 66
- Assess the structural balance 66
- Use headings consistently 66
- Use numbering to aid navigation 67

The toolbox

Put some order in the house

Structuring a document is a lot like building a house. With the best content in the world, all you have are the raw materials. To turn these into something usable, you need some architecture to guide your readers from one room to the next. But how do you create that structure? What contents are needed? What environment will your document be read in? How long will your readers have to visit and for what purpose?

Many workplace writers start building walls before they have a complete plan. They end up wasting resources on a mansion when a simpler structure would do. They put the most important elements in the wrong part of the house. How often have you unearthed what you needed most from a letter right at the end, then had to reread the thing from the top?

Fortunately, document architecture is not as complex as housing. There are seven common models you can work with:

1. Issue—discussion—action
2. Narrative
3. Telescoping
4. Exposition
5. Instruction
6. Question and answer
7. Mosaic

The first four structural models are better employed for analytical documents such as reports and submissions, where you analyse a problem and develop a solution. The last three are more suitable for descriptive documents where your purpose is to inform rather than persuade, such as a web page, a policy or some instructions.

Use issue—discussion—action (IDA) for simple documents

The first structure is probably the easiest, dividing a document into three simple parts. You start by defining a topic, then move into discussing it before recommending a response.

Issue
The problem or situation

Discussion
Its implications and your conclusions

Action
What should be done to address the issue

This works well in short documents such as emails or memos under one page, particularly if the topic is straightforward. Also turn to IDA if you have to respond to something immediately.

Avoid narrative where you can

When you are writing a more comprehensive submission or report, the three-part IDA structure will not give you enough room to work with. The most common structure professionals turn to next is the narrative. This uses the information-gathering process itself to structure a document, tracing the writer's journey from setting the scene, deciding on methods for investigation, conducting research, summarising findings, drawing conclusions and (finally) framing recommendations.

This is a logical architecture that mirrors the scientific method, so it is hardly surprising that it is prevalent in technical professions such as engineering and science, as well as in the academy. It is particularly useful when your readers' primary aim is to assess the research itself as much as the conclusions that result from it.

Yet the narrative structure has one major drawback: it is not reader-friendly for non-technical readers or for busy people. For readers who do not need to assess the research, the chief interest lies in the last rooms of your house. To get there, they will skim your document, or start reading it from the back. This causes frustration and inefficiency. Avoid narrative structures for most workplace documents.

Background
Scene setting and history

↓

Methods
The research design

↓

Research
The actual investigation

↓

Findings
Results of what you found

↓

Conclusion
What it all means

↓

Recommendation
What should happen now

Telescope your documents wherever possible

Increasingly, organisations are turning to the telescoping structure as a more reader-friendly approach than narrative. Instead of structuring according to the research process, telescoping sequences your information in descending order of value, with the key material first, followed by the details. Readers can absorb the most important content, then decide how much subsidiary information they need. Each section of the document expands in the way that a telescope does from a viewing lens to a magnifying lens.

Telescoping structures have been adapted from the techniques used in newspapers, which need to balance the interests of a diverse readership. A standard news report has a lead paragraph that summarises the entire story, followed by the key facts of the story and their significance, and finally the supporting detail, including the background history, the quotes and the less significant facts. Newspapers know that few readers work through story after story from beginning to end. Telescoping lets them draw the information they need with maximum efficiency and interest.

Key information
Summary
Conclusions
Recommendations

Evaluation
Primary analysis and evidence,
along with most important context

Detailed information
Outlining the topic's full history,
processes, research or findings
Mainly descriptive detail, but also some analysis.

Time-pressured workplaces are now applying this principle to great effect. Telescoping empowers readers to choose for themselves how much they read. Some professionals are uncomfortable with it for that very reason, but you have to be realistic about how people will read your work. A study by James Souther found that decision-makers read different parts of a report to very different extents. All read the summary if there was one, and 60 per cent went on to read the introduction. Only 15 per cent read the main body, while 50 per cent skipped straight to the conclusion. Telescoping puts what they most need at the start, then sequences the information in descending order of value.

Telescoping does have one main drawback. It generally divides a piece of writing into three sections, and this is less sustainable for longer documents. In more complex reports, you will want to combine it with other models. The best one to use is exposition.

Use exposition in longer documents

Exposition is the standard approach to structuring an essay. It builds an argument by identifying an issue, analysing one aspect at a time, then forming a conclusion. It is similar to narrative, except that the main body of the document is built on a series of topics or themes instead of the steps of the research itself.

Introduction
Outline of the overall topic

↓

Theme 1
Detailed discussion of one aspect of the topic

↓

Theme 2
Detailed discussion of next aspect of the topic

↓

Theme 3
Detailed discussion of next aspect of the topic

↓

Conclusion
Findings and recommendations

Graduates often come into the workforce believing that this structure —which they learned at school—works in the real world as well. Exposition certainly works well in an educational environment because the context is somewhat artificial. You write an essay for teachers who already know what you are about to tell them. They are reading your work to assess your understanding of the topic and your ability to construct a coherent argument. It doesn't matter so much that the conclusions come at the end, because the journey is as important as the destination. This carries right through academic writing.

In the workplace, by contrast, you are often writing to someone who knows nothing of your subject matter. A public reader is not paid to wade through your prose and can easily toss it aside. A colleague who is paid to read it will want to do so as quickly and efficiently as possible, and that doesn't always mean reading it from start to finish.

Exposition comes into its own in the workplace in longer reports, where the simpler structure of telescoping is usually not complex enough to contain the scope of material. But see if you can combine it with some telescoping by adding an executive summary at the start, and perhaps some chapter summaries at the beginning of each section. You can also use simpler structures such as IDA to order the subsections within each chapter.

KEY TIP | In longer documents, consider using different structures at different levels.

Analytical documents have the advantage of built-in variety. By presenting some facts, then drawing conclusions about them, you automatically give your document some light and shade. Even the narrative structure can carry a reader along from one part of the story to the next. Sometimes, however, you will need to write an informational document that has very little variation in content and will not fit into an analytical structure. All you can do is pile fact after fact after fact after fact after fact. That's when you turn to some different structural models.

Use instruction for procedures

The most common informational document is a set of instructions. This might present the directions for operating machinery or for assembling and using a particular product. It might set out guidelines for calculating leave entitlements, setting a secure password or processing accounts payable. Here, a chronologically based structure comes into its own. There might be six steps in setting up the spam filter on a computer, of which the most important are steps two and four, but there is little point telescoping the text by bringing them up to the front. Unless the sequence is followed in order, the process will fail.

Introduction
Purpose of instructions

↓

Context
What your reader will need

↓

Step 1
The first actions

↓

Step 2
The next phase

↓

Step 3
The final phase

↓

Completion
What the end result should be

Try question and answer for disconnected text

Other kinds of informational documents do not have the advantage of a clear sequence. A policy document about leave entitlements, for example, will need to cover several different circumstances that relate to different staff, but there is no time or process connection between them. Here, the question-and-answer structure can work well. It identifies a series of likely questions that your readers will have, providing short answers to each one.

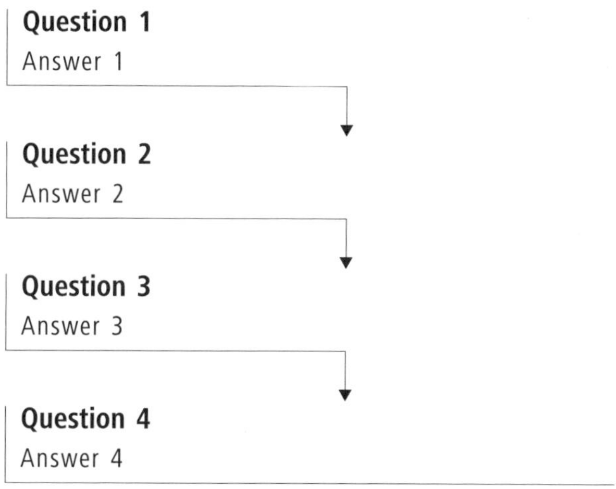

The question-and-answer structure is effective for websites and intranet sites where a diverse readership needs to access small but different parcels of information. You can often identify the 'frequently asked questions' that you have actually received. But beware of the limits of this structure. It works well if you have half-a-dozen questions, each of which is answered by a few paragraphs only. Any larger than this, and it will become unwieldy.

Experiment with mosaic structures

Sometimes you will have more than a dozen information groups, or they will be too long to work well in a question-and-answer format. Yet your document still does not have a linear flow from one section to the next. You might have some primary text, but then some secondary bits and pieces that don't flow from it. An increasingly common example is the web page, but information brochures and short promotional publications also fall into this category. In these cases you are dealing with a mosaic structure.

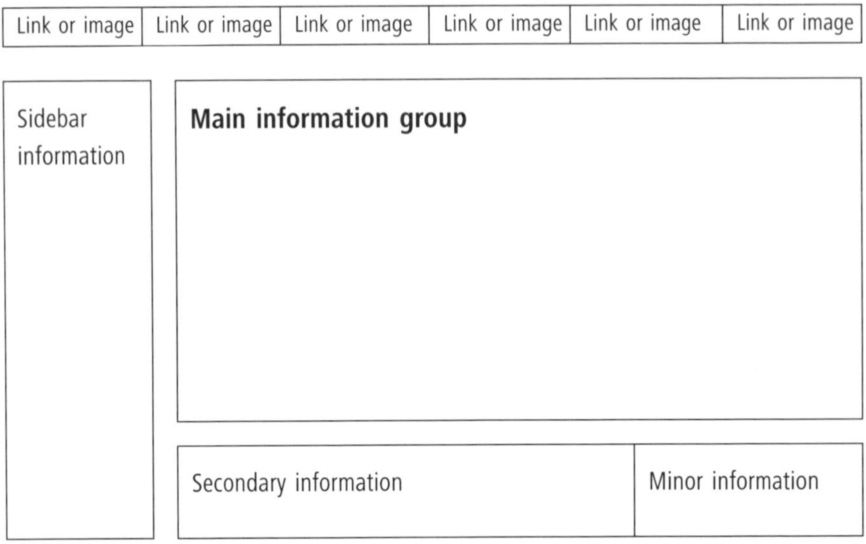

The mosaic structure in some ways returns to the non-linear text of old illuminated manuscripts. These carried a main body of text, but often commentary in the margins, glosses above the text, and elaborate illustrations that contained their own messages and narratives. The reader was used to moving around between information groups. In the online age, we are again becoming used to jumping around a document rather than reading it from start to finish. Use this trend to your advantage.

The living language

Use structural outlining to move from planning to drafting

Adding the seven structure models to your writing toolbox will accelerate the planning of any document. You can test which model will work for a document by completing some quick structural outlines. Let's illustrate how this works though a case study from the retail sector. Carmen is a retail manager preparing a report to the general manager of a retail chain. The company's stores are experiencing increasing stock losses through theft, but also a rise in customer complaints about the heavy-handedness of in-store security staff. The company outsourced its security to an external contractor 18 months ago.

Carmen has been asked to investigate the problem and recommend solutions. After interviewing staff, talking to the contractor, reviewing customer complaints and assessing financial information, she used the brainstorming technique in the previous chapter to set down the content for her report, and it now needs a structure. Here is the content she developed:

Security problems in Clothing Depot stores

Initial problems	Customer complaints Stock losses	
Staff views	Sales staff interviews Sales staff attitudes to security	
Security contractor	The outsourcing of security Restructuring of contractor Security staff turnover Recruitment practices	
Option 1	Replace contractor	2 years remain on contract Termination provisions weak Payout costs high
Contractor views	Interviews with security staff Meeting with contractor	
Option 2	Training	Contractor responsibility Costs and benefits Extending induction
Review of files	Review of sales and stock Review of complaints	
Flow-on impacts of problem	Staff time Impact on profits Threat to market share	
Option 3	Systems improvements	Upgrade security devices Promote procedure manual Raise sales staff awareness
Recommendations	Training and systems upgrades Replace contractor when due Strengthen termination clause Improve complaint handling	

Apply the structure checklist

To move from an unstructured list of content to a draft architecture, ask yourself six questions:

The structure checklist

1. Can you group some content together?
2. Would you merge some areas within these groups?
3. What are the main messages in each group?
4. Which groups are most important?
5. What is the logic or connection between groups?
6. What structure models could you use to link the groups?

Working through the structure checklist, Carmen starts by grouping and merging some areas:

Problems	Customer complaints Stock losses Staff time Impact on profits Threat to market share	
Options	1. Replace contractor	2 years remain on contract Termination provisions weak Payout costs high
	2. Training	Contractor responsibility Costs and benefits Extending induction
	3. Systems improvements	Upgrade security devices Promote procedure manual Raise sales staff awareness
Recommendations	Training and systems upgrades Replace contractor when due Strengthen termination clause Improve complaint handling	
Investigation	Staff views	Sales staff interviews
	Contractor views	Interviews with security staff Meeting with contractor
	Review of files	Review of sales and stock Review of complaints

Causes	The outsourcing of security Restructuring of contractor Security staff turnover Recruitment practices Sales staff attitudes to security	

Her next step is to consider the sequence to connect all the areas. Looking at the main headings down the left side of the page, Carmen realises there is a simple connection between them: her research process. She has started with the problems, investigated the causes, developed some options and drafted some recommendations. The easiest structure to pick would be narrative:

Outline using narrative model

A	Problems	Customer complaints Stock losses Staff time Profits and market share
B	Investigation	Sales staff interviews Security staff interviews and meeting with contractor Review of customer complaints Review of sales and stock info
C	Findings	Outsourcing security major cause Security staff turnover worsened Sales staff attitudes Contractor restructuring and poor recruitment
D	Options	1. Replace contractor 2. Training for all staff 3. Systems improvements
E	Recommendations	Replace contractor when due Training and system upgrades Strengthen termination provisions Improve complaint handling

Carmen now has a draft architecture, but is it the best structure she could use? She has answered five of the six questions on the checklist to her satisfaction, but one question worries her: where is the most important information? There is no doubt that sections D and E have the key material, although there is some important information in the first three sections as well. But this report is likely to be at least a thousand words long, and she knows that the general manager does not like reading long reports.

Carmen uses the draft outline to discuss the structure with her manager. He agrees that their boss hates reading through long accounts of research, and suggests making the options themselves the focus of the report. Looking again at the structural models, Carmen decides that an exposition structure might work better. Here is the outline she comes up with:

Outline using exposition model

Introduction	Problems: Stock losses Staff time Profits and market share Causes: Security contractor Sales staff attitudes Options: 1. Replace contractor 2. Training 3. System improvements
Option 1— Replace contractor	Arguments for: Outsourcing of security is major cause Contractor restructuring led to high turnover and poor recruitment Arguments against: 2 years remain on contract Termination provisions weak Payout costs high Evidence: Security staff interviews and meeting with contractor

Option 2— Invest in training sales staff and/or contractor staff	Arguments for: Sales staff attitudes contribute to problem Need to improve internal complaint handling Extending induction of contractor staff would contain training costs Arguments against: Training of security staff is a contractor responsibility The costs of training security staff may outweigh the benefits Evidence: Sales staff interviews Review of customer complaints
Option 3— Systems improvements	Physical security: Upgrade in-store security devices Staff systems: Promote procedure manual Raise awareness of complaint handling
Conclusions	1. Replace contractor only when due and strengthen termination provisions in new contract 2. Invest in training internal staff to improve complaint handling 3. Bring forward upgrade of physical security system

Carmen finds as she works on the new outline that her thinking evolves, so some of the topic areas change as she goes. The exposition structure brings her more important analytical content to the front. She also finds herself letting go of much of the process detail that was prominent in her narrative structure. But before going back to her manager, Carmen decides to test out the new structure against a telescoping outline. She is still concerned by the key conclusions coming right at the end, and can imagine the general manager skipping straight from the introduction to the conclusion. She wants him to read more of the body of the report as well. Here is her final outline:

Outline using telescoping model

1. Overview	Problems: Stock losses Staff time Profits and market share Causes: 1. Security contractor outsourcing, recruitment and turnover 2. Sales staff attitudes and internal complaint handling contribute Recommendations: 1. Replace contractor when contract expires 2. Invest in some staff training and improve complaint handling 3. Strengthen security systems
2. Options available	Option 1—Replace contractor: 2 years remain on contract Termination provisions weak Payout costs high Option 2—Invest in some training: Internal staff training needed with extension of induction for security staff Full training of security staff contractor responsibility Option 3—System improvements: Upgrade in-store security devices Promote procedure manual
3. Details of investigation	Security staff interviews and meeting with contractor Sales staff interviews Review of customer complaints

Carmen is surprised by how well the telescoping structure works. Although the logical flow of both the narrative and exposition appeals to her, she recognises that the general manager will actually read more of her content in this final version. He will likely only read the overview, but now the key part of her analysis is in this section rather than being spread throughout the report. Her immediate manager will want to look more carefully at the discussion of options, but both readers will likely only skim the details of the research itself. Yet this final section remains an important part of the report for the record. As it turns out, her manager approves the telescoping structure and signs it straight through. The general manager approves the recommendations within a day and praises the report. Structural outlining had helped Carmen to test several structures before drafting to make sure she used the most effective architecture for her purpose.

Power tools

Apply structure mapping to longer reports

If you are writing a short document, it is likely that the draft text will be close to the blueprint in your structure outline. If you need to, you can usually refine the structure as you draft or edit. In longer documents, however, you will inevitably have to redraw parts of your blueprint. You will probably add new sections that are not in your outline. You will certainly need to add subsections as you write. You may draft too much text in one section, only to let other sections drain away. If you are writing a report as part of a team, different writers will take the text in different directions. It takes discipline to stand back and look at your overall outline.

You can evaluate the architecture of a longer document by drawing up a structure map. This sets out the hierarchy of information in more detail than your initial outline. Drawing the map is very easy: simply list all the headings, the subheadings and the sub-subheadings, formatted as a table. If there is already draft text, include in the map the number of paragraphs in each section, as well as any tables or figures.

With the map complete, apply a five-point checklist to assess your architecture:

The structure mapping checklist

1. Structural design
2. Complexity
3. Balance
4. Headings
5. Numbering and navigation

Review the structural design

Structural design concerns the models discussed earlier in this chapter. Are you using telescoping, exposition or narrative, or an informational structure such as questions and answers? Which model is most effective in conveying your content to your readers? What structures are you using in subsections? Does the structure foreground the most important material for your reader?

Avoid unnecessary complexity

Complexity is the feature that the structure map will pick up most clearly. What is the sheer volume of headings and subheadings, and how many levels does the report have, both horizontally and vertically? It is a good idea to print out your map and tape it together in one long document. The result may shock you. Ask yourself whether the framework looks complex or easy to follow. Could readers hold most of the map in their heads?

It is generally best to avoid more than six to eight main chapters, even in a long report, and try not to go down to more than three levels of subheading in each chapter. See if you can move chapter material into an appendix instead. Calculate the average number of paragraphs per heading. If your score is two or less, then you have probably over-structured your document.

Assess the structural balance

Balance is a more difficult concept. It stems from reader expectations that a long text will be divided into reasonably equal sections. This helps readers because they form a mental map of where the next break will come and what will follow. If the reading terrain varies too much, the readers will stop to refocus. They may backtrack, which draws attention to the architecture itself and away from your content.

Spot lack of balance by looking for white space in your map, such as between major chapters, or between subsections. A structure is out of balance, for example, if some chapters jump from a second level to a fourth level heading while others do not. The content may have called for this as you drafted, or it may be that different writers invested more energy in particular sections. The map will help you to re-balance the architecture.

Use headings consistently

Headings are crucial in longer documents. They act as the corridors and doorways that divide your house into rooms and arrange the walkways within them. There are three types of headings you can use:

1. Descriptive—Demand pressures.
2. Question—Has demand fallen?
3. Analytical—Demand has fallen.

Descriptive headings help your reader navigate the text through its main topics. These are the most common in workplace writing, to the point of being over-used. Question headings are becoming more common, and engage a reader by generating curiosity: what is the answer to the question? But too many questions can be annoying, so don't overdo them. Analytical headings are the hardest to write and the least common. They summarise the conclusions in each section. They are harder to write in a succinct form, but extremely powerful. Even readers skimming the text will still get your main messages from analytical headings. Carefully placed, analytical headings can summarise an entire report.

The key with headings is to use more than one type, but be consistent at each level. If your second level headings are partly questions and partly descriptions, your readers will have to think twice about where they are in the house. Descriptive headings often work well at the higher end of the heading hierarchy, followed by question headings, then analytical headings. Each chapter has a main topic, divided by the questions each discusses, with answers at the third level—where they are most likely to occur.

Also make your document headings as precise as possible. You may have used general headings when drafting your document, so adjust them to convey as much meaning as possible. If your readers had only your headings to go on, would they still get the gist of your document?

Use numbering to aid navigation

Closely related to headings is the use of numbering. It is generally best to use numbers at the highest level of the hierarchy of headings. This gives your readers a quick snapshot of how many main sections there are. They are also often useful at the next level, using a decimal system such as 1.1, 1.2, 1.3, 1.4 and so on. Numbering below this level tends to be counterproductive and unnecessarily complex. Unless you are writing a contract or an act of parliament that will need precise cross-referencing, avoid numbering paragraphs.

Finally, ask yourself how easy it would be for a reader to navigate around your document:

- Does your executive summary mirror the structure of the main text, helping readers move between them?
- Are there cross-references if they would be useful?
- If your readers opened the report at any page, would they be able to tell quickly where they were in the structure?

Adjust your navigation if you need to.

To illustrate structure mapping, we will take a single chapter from a government report on a fisheries licensing buy-back scheme. This scheme attempted to increase the sustainability of the sawtooth fish and manage the social and economic consequences for the communities involved. Read the original map at the end of the chapter and apply the checklist.

Working through the sawtooth report reveals some clear shortcomings. The chapter structure uses exposition, but without a summary it buries the more important conclusions. There is unnecessary complexity in that the chapter goes down to a fourth level of heading in some sections, and there are too few paragraphs per heading. The chapter is also out of balance, with some significantly blank real estate between sections. The headings mix up different types at the same level, but the report does use more than one heading type and the headings are reasonably precise. The numbering, however, is at the wrong end of the scale. The paragraph numbers do little to aid navigation. We can improve the report's impact by adjusting each of these elements. Suddenly, the edited map comes down to a much more balanced outline.

Compared with the original structure, the edited structure:

- telescopes by placing the key conclusions and recommendations up front
- uses exposition for the rest of the chapter, but reduces it from three sections to two
- reduces complexity by eliminating the E level subheadings
- reduces the overall number of headings by a third
- balances the structure more evenly between B, C and D levels
- uses numbering at a higher level of the hierarchy to aid navigation
- makes the heading styles more consistent at each level.

The content of the chapter was fine and it hasn't changed. All we have done through structure mapping is evaluate and amend the architecture to convey that content more effectively. Of course, this was only one chapter in a longer report. Even so the map ran to four pages. When you map an entire report, it can run to 10 or 20 pages. While each part of the architecture seems justified when you are drafting an individual section, the map helps you to view the structure from above and adjust it to make the report much more effective.

Original structure—sawtooth report

A head	B head	C head	D head	E head	Para #
Part 3 Report Findings	REDUCING SAWTOOTH FISHING TO SUSTAINABLE LEVELS	How much licensed sawtooth volume did DOF need to buy back?	*How much licensed sawtooth volume did DOF buy back?*		3.1 3.2 Fig 3A 3.3 3.4 Fig 3B
			Central Coast and Pearly Bay FMAs		3.5
			Jamestown and Spear Shelf FMAs		3.6 3.7
	DOF'S MANAGEMENT OF THE VOLUNTARY LICENCE REDUCTION PROGRAM	Did DOF secure the reduction in licensed sawtooth volumes within budget?		*Initial targets* *Reduction*	3.8 3.9 3.10 3.11 3.12 3.13 Fig 3C
		Did DOF deliver the reduction in licensed sawtooth volume over time?			3.14
		Did DOF and the Fisheries Finance Corporation administer the Voluntary Licence Reduction Program according to the guidelines?			3.15 3.16

A head	B head	C head	D head	E head	Para #
	CONCLUSION				3.17 3.18 3.19 3.20
	MANAGING THE SOCIAL CONSEQUENCES OF REDUCED FISHING	Assisting fishing industry workers			3.21
			What are the objectives of the Worker Assistance Program?		3.22
			Who is eligible for assistance?		3.23 3.24 3.25
			What assistance is to be provided?		3.26 3.27
			Is the Department for Communities meeting the Program objectives?		3.28
				Assistance provided	3.29 3.30 Fig 3D
				Employment outcomes	3.31 3.32 3.33 Fig 3E

A head	B head	C head	D head	E head	Para #
			How much will it cost to assist workers?		3.34 3.35 Fig 3F 3.36
		Assisting processing and transport contractors			3.37
			What are the objectives of the Contractor Assistance Program and who is eligible for assistance?		3.38 3.39 3.40 3.41
			What assistance is to be provided?		3.42 3.43 3.44 3.45 3.46
			Has this assistance been provided?	*Business elements*	3.47 3.48 Fig 3G 3.49 Fig 3H 3.50 Fig 3I 3.51

A head	B head	C head	D head	E head	Para #
			Applications on hold		3.52 3.53 3.54
			How much will the Contractor Assistance Program cost?		3.55 3.56 3.57 Fig 3J 3.58
	CONCLUSION	Worker Assistance Program			3.59
		Contractor Assistance Program			3.60
	RECOMMENDATIONS				3.61 3.62 3.63
			RESPONSE		

Edited structure

A head	B head	C head	D head	Figs
Part 3 Report Findings	SUMMARY AND CONCLUSIONS	1. Sustainable fishery management		
		2. Managing social consequences		
	RECOMMENDATIONS			
	1. SUSTAINABLE FISHERY MANAGEMENT	Did DOF reduce sawtooth volumes within budget?	Government target achieved	Fig 3A Fig 3B
			Program under budget	Fig 3C
		Is the Voluntary Licence Reduction Program on schedule?	Program ahead of schedule	
		Did DOF reduce licences according to guidelines?	Program administered within guidelines	
	2. MANAGING SOCIAL CONSEQUENCES	Was the Worker Assistance Program effective?	Program objectives are clear	
			Program is meeting objectives	Fig 3D Fig 3E
			Program costs are growing	Fig 3F
		Was the Contractor Assistance Program effective?	Program objectives are clear	Fig 3G

A head	B head	C head	D head	Figs
			Assistance is well directed	Fig 3H Fig 3I
			Some delays are creating uncertainty	
			Program costs are growing fast	Fig 3J
		How is DOF responding?	DOF accepts our recommendations	

Structure

4 Focus 79
5 Persuasion 97
6 Coherence 116
7 Design 134

Tools covered in this section

The core message statement	80
The core message test	81
Value analysis	98
The three modes of persuasion	105
The proof analysis checklist	108
The three elements of coherence	117
Paraphrasing	118
The paraphrasing checklist	118
The checklist of paragraph structures	126
The 'old before new' principle	127
The subsection checklist	131
The table of transitional words	132
The type checklist	135
The page design checklist	143
The graphics checklist	148

4 Focus

At a glance

The toolbox

- Sharpen your focus 80
- Write a core message statement 80
- Apply the core message test 81

The living language

- Know the difference between thinking and communicating 88
- Structure your documents rhetorically 90

Power tools

- Communicate key information at the start 91
- Generally deliver bad news early 95
- Make your core message transparent 96

The toolbox

Sharpen your focus

Anyone who has looked down the lens of a camera knows that it takes some time to get the focus right. Where you first cast your eye is not always what you end up wanting to see, so you must refocus the lens to sharpen the image. The same process applies to your documents, except that instead of bringing a physical object into view, you are foregrounding facts and ideas.

To highlight the most important elements in a document, look at the balance between the essential information and the background details. What is your core message, and where is it in the document? Does it come at the beginning, right at the end, or is it spread throughout? Is it surrounded by so much subsidiary information that your reader risks losing the focus altogether?

Write a core message statement

While we don't have a handy knob to turn as we might on a camera, there is a simple tool you can apply: the core message test. Summarise the entire text in just three sentences. Even complex documents can be brought into sharp relief this way. Here are two examples summarising the core message of longer documents:

> Recent press coverage and complaints have highlighted the need for better communication with our rural clients. Other utilities have introduced the model of a rural communication network with some success, and our rural offices support the idea. We should fund a consultancy to assess the feasibility of this model.

> The IT Help Desk has been overwhelmed with support requests relating to the new database software. The new procedure document outlines a clearer step-by-step process that staff can use to record customer details. It should reduce processing time and errors, and cause less frustration for staff and customers contacting the call centre.

If you have trouble writing such a succinct summary, break your core message statement into three parts:

1 Topic—what is the subject or problem?
2 Analysis—what are your conclusions and why?
3 Action—what should happen in response?

To complete your core message, write one sentence on each part.

Apply the core message test

With your core message at hand, read every paragraph to assess which content is essential, and which content is blurring the main message. Mark this up in your paragraph margins by placing:

- ✗ next to a paragraph the reader doesn't need
- ✓ next to a paragraph that is essential
- ↓ next to a paragraph you can reduce, and underline content you will keep
- ↑ next to a paragraph that needs more information
- ? against a paragraph if you are not sure the reader needs it.

This will give you a focus map to follow to sharpen the text. Drafting inevitably includes more words than your reader needs. The trick is to decide which elements are most relevant, and keep the focus on them.

KEY TIP | If in doubt, cut it out.

To illustrate how this tool works, let's look at a ministerial submission that Monique drafted. Monique works in a government agency and has been closely involved with her topic. Her submission is over 1000 words long, which she feels is as short as it can be without compromising her content. Her director, on the other hand, knows that it is far too long for its intended reader, the Minister for Heritage. The minister receives about two dozen submissions every day, and she simply doesn't have time to read 24,000 words a day.

Monique's director has already asked her to shorten the document, and she has come back with this text, arguing that it is as short as she can make it. She feels the detail needs to be there so that anyone coming to the file in future will understand the reasoning behind the new policy. To test the focus, the director summarises its core message using the topic/analysis/action structure, and comes up with this:

	Core message statement
Topic What is the subject or problem?	Whether to establish a Heritage Repairs Management Agency to reduce the maintenance costs for government-owned heritage buildings.
Analysis What are your conclusions and why?	The proposal will improve heritage outcomes and reduce the net costs of repair by up to $20 million over the next five years.
Action What should happen in response?	The minister should approve the proposal in principle and sign the attached letter.

Monique agrees that this is a fair summary of the submission. Her director then asks her to apply the core message to focus the document using the ticks, crosses and arrows. Monique finds that as she marks up the text, her perspective shifts:

SUBMISSION

To: Minister for Heritage and Environment
From: Monique Seine
Re: **REDUCING COSTS TO THE STATE OF REPAIRING HERITAGE PROPERTY**

PURPOSE

To advise the Minister on the feasibility and timing of the adoption of recommendations of the Public Works Management Committee and seek approval in principle for implementation. ✗

BACKGROUND

<u>The Public Works Management Committee (PWMC) produced a report in November 2005</u> titled 'Reducing Repair Costs of State Heritage Properties'. Briefly, the purpose of the report was to suggest ways and means for agencies to manage repairs of government-owned heritage properties, in an efficient and cost-effective manner. ↓

The report concluded that individual agencies often do not have the expertise to take heritage considerations fully into account when maintaining their properties. This leads to costly follow-up work and threatens heritage values. The PWMC strongly recommended the establishment of a Central Heritage Repairs Management Agency (CHRMA) within the Department of Heritage and Environment. ✓

The report has now been reviewed by a working party chaired by the Heritage Office and consisting of representatives from the Department of Works, the Department of Planning and Housing, the Treasury, the Premier's Department, the Department of Education, the Department of Transport, and the Department of Heritage and Environment. The committee's report on the review is attached. ↓

In reviewing the PWMC report valuable input was provided by a number of other State agencies that have heritage properties within their respective portfolios. The working party also initiated consultation with industry and community stakeholder organisations such as the Australian Institute of Architects, the Heritage Community Council, the Railway Historical Society, the Friends of Forsythe House and the Heritage Builders Association. These groups also provided submissions to the PWMC during their enquiries. ↓

ISSUES

During our review government agencies and other stakeholders interviewed generally supported the principle of the establishment of a CHRMA. The only likely contentious point was whether it would be compulsory for all agencies to refer repair needs to the CHRMA. ✓

It is the view of the working party that it should not be a compulsory process, as many agencies were found to be managing heritage repair work quite well with effective systems ✓

and processes in place. Other agencies, however, advised that they viewed managing and undertaking heritage property repairs as a distraction from their core business that impacted on their productivity and business objectives.

If approved, it is intended that the CHRMA should manage repairs only on behalf of those agencies seeking assistance. All repair requests referred to the CHRMA would be assessed, with repair works then being outsourced to private heritage builders on a tender basis in consultation with the agency involved. CHRMA would then oversee and assess the works against set milestones. The costs of the repairs would be paid through the usual budget allocations of the individual agency concerned. To promote early take up, the CHRMA would not charge for its services, although it may consider a management fee in the future. ✓

The only compulsory referral of repair responsibilities to the CHRMA would be where an agency is disposing of a heritage property in need of repair. Disposal details would then be referred to the CHRMA and where appropriate (depending on the repair needs) the repairs would be outsourced to an approved private repair provider before disposal. The CHRMA would case manage and monitor the repairs with the provider as it would with other repair works referred to the agency. It would also assess whether heritage conditions should be placed on the contract for sale. ↓

It was estimated by the PWMC that in the five-year period to the 2000–2001 financial year, there was approximately $22M of additional costs to the State because of poorly managed repairs to heritage buildings that necessitated further works. This experience has made agencies cautious in proceeding with repairs to heritage buildings, leading in some cases to further deterioration which it is estimated will escalate the costs of eventual repairs. ✓

The working group, based on its consultations, is of the view that the backlog of heritage repairs is in the order of $220M, and that continuing additional costs of between $15–20M over the next five-year period due to inexpert management and further delays would not be considered unreasonable. While it is difficult to ascertain how much of this amount will be saved through more effective coordination of heritage repairs, it is confidently expected that the establishment of a CHRMA will cost less than the revenue saved from a whole-of-government perspective. ↓

As the works to heritage buildings will be paid for through regular budget allocations in each agency, the cost to government in resourcing the CHRMA would be minimal. The salary package cost would include three full-time staff, totalling $290,000 (including on-costs) and once-off expenses in office systems at a cost of approximately $70,000. A proposal will be prepared to Treasury to cover these costs through the annual budget supplementation process. Treasury representatives on the Working Group indicated informally that favourable consideration would be given to such a proposal. ✓

Costs associated with the repair works would be borne by the relevant agencies and hence there would be no further cost to government for heritage building repairs. The establishment of a CHRMA would also help to regularise the costs of heritage works to the government across the board and provide a more consistent approach to managing these assets. ✗

Once established, the CHRMA would initiate recruitment of a pool of preferred repair providers from which it can draw. The tender documents would be prepared and approved by the State Contracts Control Board and major stakeholders would contribute and be part of the selection process. ↓

The Department of Heritage and Environment will prepare a report on the CHRMA in 12 months subsequent to its establishment to measure the CHRMA performance in managing State heritage repair needs and the effectiveness of centralising heritage property repairs on behalf of other agencies. ↓

RECOMMENDATION
It is recommended that the Minister:

1. Approve in principle the Public Works Management Committee recommendation for the establishment of a Central Heritage Repairs Management Agency as part of the Department of Heritage and Environment. ↓

2. Sign the attached letter to the Premier and Treasurer outlining the proposal and requesting that it be included in the forthcoming budget supplementation. ↓

What was your experience of reading the submission? Did your concentration wander? How hard did you have to work at sifting out the key information? Monique classified only six of the 17 paragraphs with ticks. More than half could be shortened. The underlining also showed that the important information was spread out. A busy minister would skim the text. Monique agreed that she needed to keep focused on the core message. Her final document was just 40 per cent of the original length.

SUBMISSION

To: Minister for Heritage and Environment
From: Monique Seine
Re: **IMPROVING STATE HERITAGE PROPERTY REPAIRS**

PURPOSE

To gain approval for a Central Heritage Repairs Management Agency (CHRMA) within the Department of Heritage and Environment.

BACKGROUND

A 2005 report by the Public Works Management Committee (PWMC) concluded that agencies often do not have enough heritage expertise when maintaining some properties. This leads to costly follow-up work and threatens heritage values. The PWMC strongly recommended the establishment of a central repair agency in the Department of Heritage and Environment.

Since this recommendation, an interdepartmental working party chaired by the Heritage Office has reviewed the proposal, in consultation with a range of other agencies and industry and community stakeholders (see attachment A).

ISSUES

The PWMC estimated that over five years to July 2001, the State paid about $22 million in extra costs because of poor heritage repairs that required further work. Agencies are now cautious with heritage repairs, leading to extra delays and costs. The working group estimates that extra costs of $15–20 million are likely over the next five years as well.

All agencies and stakeholders support the establishment of a CHRMA. The only contentious point is whether to make it compulsory. Many agencies are managing heritage repair work well, while others view it as a distraction from their core business.

> The current proposal is therefore to manage repairs only for agencies seeking help. The CHRMA will provide expertise and coordination, and prepare tenders for a pool of private heritage builders to do the work. It will then oversee the works against set milestones, in line with State Contracts Board requirements. The only compulsory referral would be where an agency is disposing of a heritage property, in which case the CHRMA would also assess heritage conditions.
>
> The works themselves will be paid from regular budget allocations in each agency. The only costs for the CHRMA are set-up costs of $70,000, and recurrent costs of $290,000 for three full-time staff. Treasury has indicated that favourable consideration would be given to funding this through budget supplementation. We will review the CHRMA in 12 months.
>
> **RECOMMENDATION**
> That the Minister approve in principle the establishment of a Central Heritage Repairs Management Agency as part of the Department of Heritage and Environment and sign the attached letter to the Premier and Treasurer.

Using a core message statement in this way will help you to gain some objective distance on your work and make the necessary cuts to improve its focus. It is all too easy to convince yourself that your readers need the detail. The core message statement will help you to test whether this is actually the case.

The living language

Know the difference between thinking and communicating

Ideally, you would not need a handy focus knob to adjust your documents because they would come out sharp and clear first time around. Unfortunately, the way we investigate a problem and develop a solution inevitably leads us into distracting detail. When thinking about a topic, you will gather some facts, interpret those facts and then draw some conclusions. You have to work through the research to make an effective judgement.

This thinking structure is fundamental to the scientific method, which we could summarise in the following steps:

- Hypothesis
- Method
- Results
- Discussion
- Conclusion

Because this approach is so important to problem solving, professionals assume that documents should automatically follow the same pattern. The report template that many public sector organisations use echoes this sequence:

- Issue
- Background
- Current position
- Advice
- Comment
- Recommendation

You can also find it in this structure, which is common in contemporary audit reports:

- Audit issue
- Background
- Methods
- Findings
- Conclusions
- Recommendations

While these are valid thinking structures, they turn the focus of a document towards the research process itself. This is appropriate where the reader's purpose is primarily to assess the research, as it is in scientific and academic papers. For the workplace, however, it tends to reduce the focus on what is of more importance: the conclusions and the recommendations. Your workplace readers are more likely to be interested in the results than the journey.

If your organisation uses a thinking structure such as the narrative model for its documents, always apply the core message test to bring your most important material into sharp relief. Be ruthless with the details of the journey you took, and reduce the text to the essential context, the analysis and the conclusions. Where you have more freedom, see if you can use a communication structure that will be more effective for your readers.

To clarify the difference, imagine you are walking in the local park. You notice that a particular area is rather deserted. As you walk into that area, you see someone running with a newspaper above his head. You hear a familiar bird call, and you look up and see movement in the trees. Suddenly, a magpie swoops on you, so you hot-foot it away from his territory.

The next week, you are walking in the same park with a friend, and you notice that a different area seems deserted. You hear the same bird calls and see movement overhead. You recognise the sequence of events and conclude that you are about to be attacked. How do you communicate that to your friend? Do you take the narrative approach, starting with the background of last week, then relating each observation in turn, concluding that you are about to be attacked, and making a recommendation that you run? Or do you start by saying that you are about to be attacked, and explain the details once you are safely away?

The content in both approaches is the same, but the focus is different. In the first version, you would stubbornly persist with using the thinking structure as your communication structure. The story becomes the focus. In the second, you focus on what is of immediate importance to your audience. The Roman orator Quintilian expressed the difference well when he wrote, 'The [part] to be spoken first is not the one to be thought out first.' Yet this is exactly what many workplaces do, and they condemn their readers to long, unfocused documents.

Structure your documents rhetorically

The early rhetoricians certainly understood the value of narrative as a thinking structure, but also the dangers of using it inflexibly as a communication structure. Cicero, for example, identified several sections in a speech:

- Exordium—introduction.
- Narration—statement of facts.
- Partition—separation of points agreed to and points in dispute.
- Confirmation—presentation of arguments.
- Refutation—response to opposing arguments.
- Peroration—conclusion and appeal to audience.

The outline here looks very similar to the document skeletons that use a narrative model. But Cicero also recognised that you should adapt this structure to your particular audience and circumstances. That might mean beginning with the statement of facts, or with a single strong argument. You might leap into the proof after a very short introduction. At other times, you could start by refuting the arguments of an opposing view and leave out the narrative altogether. By all means use the research process to develop your content, but don't be bound to communicate it in the same order. Let the focus change with the circumstances.

Quintilian likened the craft of structure to that of generalship in war. No successful general commands an army by deploying it in the same way regardless of the terrain, or the opposition forces, or the weather conditions, or the state of the troops. An effective commander will deploy them as needs reveal themselves, and change that deployment as those needs change.

So think about your focus strategically. If you have to use a narrative structure, apply the core message test to sharpen the focus. But where you can, try to structure your document to bring what is most important into the foreground. This is the second practical application of the core message test.

Power tools

Communicate key information at the start

When you have applied the core message test and marked up your text, the ticks will reveal what is most important in your text. You can then consider how to structure the document to focus your reader's attention on it. If the ticks are spread throughout the document, then you are probably using a thinking structure as your communication structure.

See if you can consolidate what is important and bring it to the front using a telescoping model.

Read the following memo from an industry organisation representing pharmacists, which is telling members about recent changes to legislation and their potential impact on pharmacy practice. The text is marked up using the core message test.

Issuing sick certificates

Pharmacists may be aware of the recent Work Choices amendments to the *Workplace Relations Act 1996*. The amended legislation states that 'registered health practitioners' may issue medical certificates for sick leave if in the registered health practitioner's opinion the person is unfit for work. ✓ The definition of 'health practitioner' has been broadened and now includes pharmacists. It appears that while health practitioners are allowed to issue medical or sick certificates under the Act and Regulations this can only be done in relation to their area of practice, and where the terms of the professional registration permit them to do so. This right of pharmacists to issue sick certificates is still not clear under the new legislation.

PSA has sought and received legal advice on whether the Work Choices amendments to the *Workplace Relations Act 1996* permit pharmacists to issue sick certificates. PSA has been advised that:

- Under the Act and Regulations health practitioners can only issue sick certificates where this is within their area of practice and expertise, and where permitted to do so by the conditions of their registration.
- Under the terms of registration for pharmacists, there is no express power to issue medical certificates and issuing sick certificates would fall outside a pharmacist's area of practice and expertise because this is not covered by the *Competency Standards* and *Professional Practice Standards* that apply to pharmacists.

- Accordingly, notwithstanding the broader definition of 'health practitioner' within the Act to include pharmacists, the right of health practitioners to issue sick certificates does not extend to pharmacists. ✓

PSA's advice is that if pharmacists did issue sick certificates, they would be acting in a manner inconsistent with the provisions of the *Workplace Relations Act 1996* and accompanying Regulations and placing themselves at legal risk by acting outside their area of practice and professional competence. As such, they may not be protected by their professional indemnity insurance.

On the basis of this advice, PSA recommends that if pharmacists are asked for a medical certificate by a customer this request be refused on the basis of advice they have been provided. ✓ Pharmacists who ignore this advice and issue a medical or sick certificate do so at their own risk. Pharmacists should consider whether they will be covered by their insurance arrangements if they choose to issue medical certificates and they may also be breaching their terms of registration if they choose to do so. ✓

The amendments to the *Workplace Relations Act 1996* are recent, and it is possible that the whole issue of who can or should be entitled to issue sick certificates will no doubt receive further attention within the health industry and within government. PSA will be monitoring the situation, and if there are any changes to legislation or the way it is applied which affect the advice set out above, PSA will advise pharmacists at that time.

PSA has sought an opinion from the insurer, Pharmaceutical Defence Limited, but this has not been received yet.

Notice how spread out the key message is, even in this short document. Unlike Monique's draft, the problem is not excessive detail. We need to reconsider the sequence itself to improve the focus. We can bring the core information together at the front, then follow with the details using a question-and-answer format.

Issuing sick certificates

> Recent changes to legislation broaden the definition of 'health practitioners' that are allowed to issue certificates for sick leave. Our legal advice is that the changes do not extend these rights to pharmacists, and that members signing certificates may compromise their insurance or breach the terms of their registration. We recommend that pharmacists not issue sick certificates until the law is clarified.

What is the current legal advice?
The PSA has received legal advice on whether the recent Work Choices amendments to the *Workplace Relations Act 1996* permit pharmacists to issue sick certificates. It states that:

- Health practitioners can only issue sick certificates where this is within their area of practice and expertise, and where permitted to do so by the conditions of their registration.
- Under the terms of registration for pharmacists, there is no express power to issue medical certificates. Issuing sick certificates would fall outside a pharmacist's area of practice and expertise because this is not covered by the *Competency Standards* and *Professional Practice Standards*.
- Although the Act broadens the definition of 'health practitioner' to include pharmacists, this does not extend the right to issue sick certificates.
- If pharmacists did issue sick certificates, they would place themselves at legal risk by acting outside their area of practice and professional competence. In such cases, they may not be protected by their professional indemnity insurance.

What does the PSA recommend?
On the basis of this advice, the PSA recommends that pharmacists explain to customers that they are not authorised

to issue medical certificates. Pharmacists who ignore this advice and issue a medical or sick certificate do so at their own risk.

Why is the situation uncertain?
The confusion has emerged because the recent Work Choices amendments to the *Workplace Relations Act* state that 'registered health practitioners' may issue medical certificates for sick leave if in their opinion the person is unfit for work. The definition of 'health practitioner' has also been broadened and now includes pharmacists. This suggests that pharmacists can issue certificates.

How might the situation change?
The amendments to the *Workplace Relations Act 1996* are recent and it is possible that the whole issue will receive further attention within the health industry and within government. We will monitor the situation and advise pharmacists if there are any changes that would alter our advice. We have also sought an opinion from the insurer, Pharmaceutical Defence Limited.

The reader has the entire issue in the first three sentences, and can scan the question-headings. We've improved the focus by adapting the structure to the context.

Generally deliver bad news early

Of course, in a memo to industry members, bringing the core message up front makes sense. But what if it delivers bad news? Do you hop straight into the message or beat around the bush for a while?

Some workplace writers prefer to detail all the reasons for a decision a reader might object to before telling them the result. But this is a rather naïve view of how your reader moves through the document. A bank customer who receives a letter about her loan application wants only one piece of information: yes or no. If that is on page two, she may be enraged by the time she reaches it. You can certainly write an introduction that acts as a softener or buffer before the bad news, but don't delay the main point longer than that.

Make your core message transparent

The core message test can also pinpoint how honest and transparent a document is, especially if there is a gap between what a reader takes as the core message and what the author intends. This happened to me a couple of years ago in a letter from my bank. 'Great news!' the letter trumpeted. 'We've simplified your accounts!' My accounts weren't overly complex, as I had only one at the time, but the letter went into great detail about how the bank was making my finances simpler. Then came the sting, and the real point of the letter. Buried towards the end of page two was the 'regrettable' detail about having to increase my fees—to improve products that I didn't need and hadn't asked for.

There were in fact two core messages competing for focus in the text. The bank's stated core message was:

Topic	We're writing about changes to your accounts.
Analysis	We've introduced a simpler structure.
Action	This will make it easier for you to manage your accounts.

The reader's core message was harder to glean:

Topic	We're writing about changes to your accounts.
Analysis	This will simplify the structure but affect the costs.
Action	We've increased the fees that you have to pay.

The bank chose a structure that deliberately shifted the focus of the document. Many readers would not have read as far as the second page. The bank had met its legal obligations while avoiding open and honest communication.

The core message test can help you to adjust your focus in several ways. It will reinforce the discipline of concise writing and guide you in structuring documents to highlight key information. If you are a reader, it can also help you to assess whether a writer is being open with you or trying to get you to focus elsewhere.

5 Persuasion

At a glance

The toolbox

- Understand the key parts of an argument 98
- Apply a value analysis to assess your argument 98
- Use the value analysis checklist 102

The living language

- Work with three modes of persuasion 105
- Remember deductive reasoning 106
- Use inductive reasoning if your reader has time to spare 107
- Use the proof analysis checklist for rhetorical arguments 108

Power tools

- Use proofs of consequence often 110
- Apply proofs of example carefully 111
- Use proofs of authority cautiously 112
- Select proofs of definition sparingly 113
- Avoid poor or false arguments 115

The toolbox

Understand the key parts of an argument

The most important task that workplace writers face is probably the hardest of all: persuasion. Whether you are dealing with a potential customer or a manager who needs to approve your report, the labour is the same. You need to convince them, and sometimes you need to change their mind.

Fortunately, you can approach this in a structured way. To be persuasive in your writing entails presenting an effective argument and engaging your readers in a constructive dialogue. By understanding their needs, presenting certain facts, drawing conclusions about those facts, and proving that your conclusions are valid, you are more likely to gain their support.

Understanding how to discover and present an argument is the core task of rhetoric. Aristotle called his craft 'the faculty of observing in any given case the available means of persuasion'. He believed that every argument had four key parts:

1. Introduction
2. Narration
3. Proof
4. Conclusion

For Aristotle, persuasion flows mainly from the narration and the proof. Narration presents the facts of a case, while the proof draws conclusions about those facts. And of these two, demonstrating proof is the most important by far. You can lay out all the facts you want, but until you interpret them and justify that interpretation, you will not change anyone's mind.

Apply a value analysis to assess your argument

The value analysis tool will help you to evaluate your argument by mapping the narrative and the proof. Of course, this will apply most to analytical documents. When you are writing a purely informational document, such as an instruction, your content will be mostly narration with very little interpretation. But you may still need some analysis to motivate your readers, so it is worth understanding the proofs you can use.

To apply the value analysis tool, mark up your document in the margin of each paragraph with an N or a P:

N Narration mainly describes or reports the facts of the situation. These paragraphs include the context of the document, a description of the problem you may be writing about, the methods you used, the views of those you consulted and the research findings.

P Proof identifies the analysis, which will be your argument, interpretation or opinion. It will cover the conclusions about the problem, any recommended action and the reasons that support them.

We often think of our information gathering as our 'analysis', and analytical skills are certainly involved in research. But you are distinguishing the structure of your argument by looking for the line between the facts of the case and your interpretation of those facts.

Having mapped the narration and proof, read the text again and add a further classification:

K Key material is added to the N and P paragraphs that contain the most important material. This might be your document's conclusion, main findings, or the key problem. Most of these will line up with your P paragraphs, although parts of the narration will also be key.

You now have a thumbnail map that shows where your background material is, where your analysis of it is, and where your key arguments are.

Angelo is the head of the IT division in a medium-sized corporation. He wrote a memo after three laptop computers and a scanner were stolen by someone who broke into the office. The general manager asked him to review the division's security. Angelo sees the theft as a one-off event and resents the intrusion into his area. He needs to persuade the general manager that everything is okay. How convinced are you by the argument in his memo?

MEMO

To: Suki Nakata, General Manager
From: Angelo Kostakidis, Director, IT Division
Re: **Security of IT Division**

Introduction

During the recent break-in to our BlueSky office, the IT Division lost three laptops and a scanner. The thieves also caused approximately $650 in damage to an external door. To prevent future theft, the General Manager requested a review of the current security practices in the IT Division. Secure Systems Pty Ltd was engaged to undertake a comprehensive review of the division's physical security as well as the underlying systems and processes for backups, bar coding and passwords.

Investigation

Secure Systems attended our premises last week and reviewed the following:

- current security policies and documentation on the intranet
- physical security of cabinets, doors and keys
- physical security of hardware such as computers and screens
- current bar coding of assets within the division
- passwords in the division and the backup of data
- staff security practices.

The security documentation reviewed included procedures for setting and changing passwords, locking cabinets and storage areas, backing up data onto the main server, locking all doors, and updating information on equipment with Asset Management. Secure Systems found that all procedures complied with company standards for security and were readily available to all staff.

Secure Systems then checked the locks and keys for 16 filing cabinets, two storage cupboards, six internal doors, four external doors and the file compactus. It located most of the 16 filing

cabinet keys in the cabinet locks or in a nearby desk drawer.
One storage cabinet was locked at the time of review and one N
was in use. Two of the internal doors were kept propped open
and none were locked overnight. All four external doors were
fitted with deadlocks to be locked overnight. The file compactus
was locked securely.

The consultant then reviewed the security anchors for all
computers, the storage of laptops and the current bar codes for
all office equipment. All relevant hardware had security cables N
and appropriate bar codes. Only the stolen laptops were stored
in a cabinet and were not attached to security cables. The
scanner was not attached to a cable at the time of the theft.

The investigation into password use found that most passwords
had not been updated regularly in accordance with the security
provisions, and some staff used the same password for access to
several different functions. Additionally, some passwords were
found not to be compliant with the company policy of using a N
mixture of characters and numbers and avoiding obvious names.
In some cases, the usernames and passwords were identical.
The system automatically makes backups once a week from
computers connected to the server and staff regularly transfer
working files from stand-alone computers and laptops.

Staff cited several reasons for the shortfall in compliance,
including time and work volume pressures, the continuation of N
past practice, lack of practicality of some of the requirements, K
and security efforts not being part of their individual job
descriptions. Secure Systems regarded these as an indication
of a 'cultural' gap that requires attention.

Discussion

Secure Systems' main recommendations concerned educating
staff about our security systems and reviewing the risks to N
the company's operations posed by any future theft. They also K
suggested consideration be given to reviewing the adequacy of
the current external doors and the possible introduction of an
alarm system.

> The review suggests that there is little at fault in our underlying security systems, and the theft of the laptops was simply an unfortunate event. However, we will remind staff of the importance of complying with company security policies for passwords. This will minimise future risks from theft. P K
>
> The installation of internal alarms as raised by the consultant would prove cost prohibitive given the current budgetary environment. P K

Use the value analysis checklist

After mapping your argument, ask six questions about your text.

The value analysis checklist

1. What structure does the document use?
2. What is the balance between narrative and proof?
3. How convincing is the proof?
4. What proportion of the document consists of the key material?
5. Where is the key material?
6. Can different readers easily find the information they need?

Angelo's memo is structured as a narrative. It sets out a problem, describes the investigation, reports the findings, then draws a conclusion. Logical, yes, but focused on the research, not on analysing that research. The N paragraphs make up more than 80 per cent of the memo. While some facts speak for themselves, without strong interpretation they will not be convincing. Only the last two paragraphs offer conclusions and they lack any reasoning to back them up. The core problem is a key element, as are parts of the findings, but overall, the proportion of key material is low, and comes at the end. This encourages a busy reader to skim the document, further reducing its persuasiveness.

This is exactly what happened to Angelo. The general manager did not agree with his conclusions and criticised the document for lacking analysis. 'Don't tell me endlessly about the research,' she said, 'explain how you drew your conclusions.' She also demanded that Angelo assess the potential risks to the company in more detail. A chastened Angelo looked at the document again. He used a value analysis to strengthen his argument by improving the balance between the narrative and the proof and placing more key material up front. This also shifted his thinking. He realised that he had previously made up his mind before starting to write. With a more rigorous look at his argument, he could no longer justify his conclusions.

KEY TIP Never rely on a long narrative to persuade your readers.

MEMO

To: Suki Nakata, General Manager
From: Angelo Kostakidis, Director, IT Division
Re: **Security of IT Division**

Summary

During the recent break-in to our BlueSky office, the IT Division lost three laptops and a scanner and suffered $650 in damage. A comprehensive review of the division's security revealed that our underlying systems are sound but that there is a 'cultural gap' in the awareness of IT staff about security. Because the theft of computers exposes the company to considerable risks, I recommend security training, coupled with stronger security through the installation of an alarm.

N
P
K

Discussion

Our previous risk analysis revealed a relatively low risk from this break-in, mainly related to the cost of replacing lost equipment. Given that most of what had been stolen was not expensive, the impact on the company was minimal. However, further analysis of the contents of the laptops stolen has revealed a much greater risk. One of the laptops contained a record of our IT protocols, as well as vital systems information that could be used to access our server. It also held an old but relatively complete customer database. This information is of great commercial value.

P
K

While it is likely that the break-in was conducted by petty P
thieves looking for computers to sell, there is still some chance
that sensitive files could end up with parties who might take
advantage of them. The impact on the company's business from K
system disruption or abuse of commercial information could be
significant.

To prevent further break-ins, we should reconsider the
installation of alarm systems. Although this will be difficult to P
fund in the current budget, the impact of further break-ins could
be far more costly. I will also allocate responsibility for securing K
the premises at the end of each day to specific staff members
who will sign off against a checklist.

We will also address the 'cultural gap' in staff attitudes by
holding a half-day seminar on information security. Secure P
Systems have a relevant training package, which they can
integrate with their security review. We will include information K
security as part of every performance review, and conduct rolling
security audits in the next three months.

Details of the investigation
[The same six paragraphs of the narrative followed.] N

Angelo's rewritten memo now has a much healthier ratio of proof to narration and considerably expands his discussion of the problem. He also uses a telescoping model rather than a research narrative. A one-paragraph summary is followed by the basic context, the analysis and the conclusions. All the key information is in the first half of the document—far more reader-friendly for a busy executive. He hasn't thrown away the details, but the reader can choose whether to read them. With this more persuasive document, Angelo got extra budget for his recommendations.

When you need to change someone's point of view, apply a value analysis to the text. Look at the balance of narration to proof and check where your key material is. This will quickly give you a sense of how successful your argument is likely to be.

The living language

It is easy to see the strength of an argument once it is on paper, but how do you come up with a proof in the first place? Rhetoricians call this the 'invention' of proofs.

Work with three modes of persuasion

Aristotle identified three means for persuading others to our cause:

1 The appeal of our character—ethos.
2 The appeal to emotion—pathos.
3 The appeal to reason—logos.

Perhaps the most under-recognised form of persuasion is that based on our 'ethos'—our professional and personal character. A reader will usually take into account a writer's skills, experience and track record. If the writer has credibility, the reader will trust the writer's judgement and be more open to persuasion. Aristotle wrote that 'character contains almost the strongest proof of all'. Never underestimate the importance of your ethos at work. It is your most valuable career asset.

Also remember that whenever humans interact, emotion is inevitably involved. We like to think that rationality is at the core of the workplace, but when it comes to persuading others, emotion is never far away. If you are in business to sell a product, you will appeal to the emotions of your customers as much as to their rational faculties. If you are a lawyer defending a client, you might appeal to jurors' emotions by pointing out the impact of prison on the defendant's family. When town planners are assessing future options for a community facility, they will need to take account of community feeling. You might want to exclude emotion as much as possible from your decision-making, but it is naïve to believe it will play no role when you are dealing with others.

Most professionals see the appeal to reason as the main way they persuade, through formal logic and carefully constructed evidence. We take pride in the objective nature of our work, particularly in technical professions such as engineering or science. But effective writing must draw from a wide range of rational argument. At one end there is the formal logic of mathematics. This is essential for quantitative questions such as the design specifications of a bridge that must bear a certain load. Here, you can derive your conclusions with a great deal of certainty.

But the real world also poses qualitative questions that cannot be answered with the same degree of exactness. Is the bridge worth building in the first place? Is the expense worthwhile? Will the bridge harm the surrounding environment? There are no formulas to answer these kinds of questions, but that doesn't mean you are any less rational when reasoning about them. The difference is that you cannot reach an answer with the same level of certainty as you do with mathematical questions—only a level of probability. And it is in the realm of probability that the techniques of argument come into their own.

To marshal the best possible arguments in your writing, it is worth remembering the two basic forms of logic that Greek philosophers identified 2000 years ago.

1 Deduction—which starts with a general premise to derive specific conclusions.
2 Induction—which uses specific examples to draw a general conclusion.

Remember deductive reasoning

Deductive reasoning starts with a generally accepted premise from which it draws a more specific conclusion. Aristotle called this process a syllogism. Its strength is that once readers agree with the premise, they cannot deny the conclusion deduced from it as long as your argument follows the rules of logic. Here is an example of a syllogism from the world of government:

> If a person owns a share in a residential property, they do not qualify for a first-home-owner grant.
>
> Jessie Smith already owns part of a residential property.
>
> Therefore Jessie Smith does not qualify for a first-home-owner grant.

Often, we use deductive reasoning with some of these elements implied rather than stated, but the same logic underpins our conclusions. The only ways you can counter a deductive argument are to question the premise or to challenge the chain of reasoning that leads to the conclusion.

Use inductive reasoning if your reader has time to spare

Inductive reasoning draws a conclusion, or inference, from a set of facts that serves as a basis for a prediction or generalisation. When you cannot prove something using deduction, you can argue for its probability by amassing evidence of its likelihood. You make a leap in judgement and generalise based on those facts. This is a staple of science, where repetition of an experiment increases the likelihood of its conclusions being true, but never precludes the possibility that one example might be discovered that will disprove it.

Until the 18th century, logic teachers illustrated inductive reasoning with the example 'all swans are white'. There was no way that this could be proved by deductive means, but no non-white swans had ever been recorded. Then Europeans arrived in Australia and discovered black swans. One example was enough to disprove the inductive argument. When the first specimens of black swans were sent back to Europe, it was thought that naturalists had faked them as a joke at the expense of their logic teachers. Shortly after, logic textbooks started to illustrate induction with the example 'all ravens are black'.

While deductive and inductive logic will take you far, they still fall short of the wide range of situations that workplace writers need to develop arguments for. Often you cannot reduce a situation to a premise and a conclusion. So writers use induction and collect large volumes of evidence to prove their case. But in a busy world, many readers will not tolerate so much material.

This is when you turn to rhetorical reasoning. This is a form of deductive proof that works like an abbreviated syllogism. It argues through a one-to-one correspondence that something is true because of something else. The major difference between the rhetorical proof and a syllogism is that it reaches a tentative conclusion from a probable premise, while a syllogism gives a definite conclusion from a true premise. Rhetoricians have identified hundreds of these, but the most common for workplace writing fall into four general areas.

Use the proof analysis checklist for rhetorical arguments

The proof analysis checklist

Proofs of consequence

1 Consequence
2 Cause and effect
3 Possibility

Proofs of example

4 Example
5 Comparison
6 Analogy

Proofs of authority

7 Authority
8 Precedent
9 Principle

Proofs of definition

10 Definition
11 Responsibility
12 Process

To illustrate how these proofs work, let's take a conclusion that our IT manager Angelo used in another (more successful) memo:

> Our version of Oracle database management software is no longer supported by Oracle. We should upgrade our software to the new version.

You could use straight deduction to argue for this conclusion:

> Organisations using unsupported software should upgrade their licences.
>
> We are using unsupported software from Oracle.
>
> We should upgrade our licence for Oracle software.

Logically watertight, but hardly convincing. Why should agencies upgrade their software? This may be clear to an IT manager, but not to others. Angelo could strengthen his case through inductive argument by quoting example after example of other organisations that have upgraded their licences, and what happens to those that do not. But there are two problems with using induction: where would he get this information, and who would want to read it in such volume?

So Angelo turns to rhetorical reasoning using the checklist, and quickly comes up with a dozen mini-arguments.

Rhetorical proofs	Conclusion
	We should upgrade our software licence to use a version of Oracle that is fully supported.
Proofs of consequence	
Consequence	Without support, error rates may increase, leading to failures in services.
Cause and effect	Our error rates in searches might be due to the out-of-date software.
Possibility	An upgrade is readily available for this software at minimal cost.
Proofs of example	
Example	In company x, not upgrading led to a system failure.
Comparison	Other companies have already upgraded their software.
Analogy	This would be like keeping a car when spare parts were not available.
Proofs of authority	
Authority	Using unsupported software does not comply with industry standards.
Precedent	We have already upgraded other comparable software.
Principle	Service failure would have unequal impact on our poorer customers.
Proofs of definition	
Definition	By definition, all database management systems need regular updating.
Responsibility	Under our customer service contracts, we are responsible for system upgrades.
Process	This need had been identified in our regular risk review.

Suddenly, you have 12 mini-proofs to strengthen your case. But that doesn't mean you use them all. Cicero wrote that it is good practice not to count your arguments but to weigh them. Use the most relevant and convincing arguments to persuade your readers. You may only use one or two. At other times, you may need half a dozen, backed with some inductive reasoning as well. To help you in your selection, we are going to look at the 12 rhetorical proofs in more detail.

Power tools

Use proofs of consequence often

Consequence is one of the most common and powerful rhetorical proofs. When you need to argue for or against a particular action, you can estimate its likely consequences. If these consequences matter to your reader, then they will be disposed towards your point of view. We use this kind of argument widely at work, often when we have specialist or technical information to impart:

> If agricultural systems fail to adapt to likely changes in water supply under climate change, they may have unrealistic water requirements, which could lead to an overall current system failure if water efficiency changes are not instilled.

Arguments using proofs of consequence are a form of cause-and-effect argument, with the effect being a future impact. Sometimes, however, you need to argue the cause of something that has already happened:

> To summarise, I think if we made our idea public like, say, 6 months prior to the release, SmartInspect could have been released earlier, with a different, slightly better feature set and would be more known. One thing's for sure, we won't make the same mistake again when creating our second product.

If you are using cause and effect, make sure you explain how the two are linked. In this case, I'm not so convinced that an earlier public announcement would have improved sales, so the writer would need to develop this argument to make it effective. It helps if the cause you are proposing is the most likely, and if you can rule out other causes, common causes or complex causes.

One proof that can clinch an argument is that of possibility. Arguing that your recommended action is readily achievable can help you win your case regardless of the strength of other proofs:

> The good news is that the solution is simple—buy some non-slip mats, or apply a high friction pool paint, or replace the tiles with a non-slip surface. These solutions do not need to cost much to install, actually fix the problem and lower the probability of injury.

Of course, you can also use this approach to argue against something, like an otherwise worthwhile proposal being impractical or costly.

Apply proofs of example carefully

The second set of proofs build support by using real or imagined examples. Government agencies do a lot of arguing by example when they respond to criticism of inaction:

> You raised the government's actions on water management. Yet major policy statements demonstrate our commitment to water, such as *Environment 2030, Our Rivers Our Future, A Plan for Growth Area Water Supply* and *Meeting Our Water Challenges.*

When you are arguing by example, make sure you give effective examples of what you are arguing for. This paragraph would need to explain how the documents mentioned translate into better water management.

You can also use one example as a mini-inductive argument to stand in for a raft of others. But it must be representative and not a random anecdote. If you use more than one example, offer different levels of detail in each to increase the inductive appeal.

One useful argument by example is a comparison between one situation and another. This can be positive or negative, depending on what you are arguing for:

> Our competitors have already announced expansion plans and the study to look at options will be vitally important to our ability to maintain market share in the longer term.

Back up any comparison you make with strong evidence. It helps if the two things being compared are measurable and you can offer facts and figures showing the link.

The third form of example argues for something by using a metaphor or analogy. This can be effective when the argument is directly relevant to the things you are comparing:

> In the future, disconnecting from the Internet will be as absurd as unplugging your phone after every call ...

Here, both examples relate to telecommunications, and the argument appears sound. The following analogy between wine and IT is less convincing:

> Wine is a fickle thing. To make a good vintage takes experience, an ability to perceive the specific local requirements, tremendous budgeting forethought, the diligence to follow mapped procedures with precision, detailed asset management of the inventory, and finally it must be proactively maintained at its optimum state to get the very best outcome and a profitable return. When you think about it, it's a lot like your IT network really.

Analogy can also help you clarify a technical concept to a layperson. A former state treasurer used to compare public finances with the family budget. This helped his listeners understand technical concepts like 'accrual accounting' more readily than using finance-speak.

Use proofs of authority cautiously

Arguments of authority cite external sources that support your position. This may be a law that mandates that you do things in a certain way. You may work to an industry or international standard, or follow an internal policy and procedure manual. You may defer to a boss. These are all sources of authority. Here is a university arguing from authority:

> Without timely and appropriate upgrades to the University LMS, the quality of the on-line part of the students' whole learning experience will fall below acceptable standards being established by the higher education sector in Australia and internationally.

If the reader respects the authority that you quote, your argument may carry weight. But don't rely on it to carry your whole case, as the 'someone else says so' argument will not always convince. If you cite an authority, do so clearly, make sure it is an informed and impartial source, and cross-check it with other sources.

Another form of authority to quote is precedent. The law is driven by this form of argument, which is structured into common law. Under precedent, you argue for a course of action based on similar previous actions:

> We, like many publishers have a small number of pages that distort our CTR rates. We could double CTR by removing ads from those pages, and only lose a small percentage of our revenue directly. But when we have done this in the past, although CTR and eCPM go up significantly, earnings go down.

Although this example cites a precedent, notice that it is also combined with a consequence argument. You will often find that some of the categories overlap in particular circumstances.

Perhaps the most high-minded argument is to invoke the authority of a principle. This is where writers advocate an action simply because it conforms to an endorsed abstract idea such as democracy or social justice:

> In addition, compulsory voting effectively closes the SES (socio-economic status) gap that operates in most (industrially advanced) voluntary systems. By ensuring that voting participation is not confined to the more prosperous members of society, compulsory voting serves to protect such important democratic values as representativeness, legitimacy, accountability, political equality and minimisation of elite power.

You might think that principle is a powerful argument, but it is often the least effective in the workplace. Think of the advertising for an energy-efficient laundry appliance. What will garner the most sales—the claim that it will save you money by using less electricity (consequence) or that it is good for the environment (principle)? When arguing by principle, make sure your audience will be strongly committed to it.

Select proofs of definition sparingly

The final group of rhetorical proofs are arguments by definition. Sometimes you can try to define your way out of a corner by playing around with the accepted meanings of words. Here is the confectionery industry arguing for the nutritional value of junk food using proofs of definition:

> 'Junk food' is a contradictory term. All food by definition has some nutritional value. Confectionery is a source of carbohydrate, protein

> and fat—all essential macronutrients. Some confectionery products also contain levels of micronutrients that make positive contributions to the diet, such as the minerals and antioxidants in chocolate.

This example shows how hard definition can be to pull off. If you are attempting it, define your terms clearly and objectively, and don't shift your definition midstream.

One of the most manipulative arguments is the 'persuasive definition'. This embodies the case you are making in the very name you give to something. A classic example is the use of the word 'reform' by political spin doctors. When arguing for a particular policy in taxation or economics, they will label it 'tax reform' or 'economic reform'. These are not objective definitions because the word 'reform' carries positive connotations of improvement or correction. This assumes the case instead of making it. Persuasive definitions can certainly be effective, but they are not entirely ethical.

Another dubious proof of definition avoids accountability by arguing that a situation is not your responsibility. You might refuse to help a colleague, for example, because a problem she raises is the responsibility of the sales department, and you are in finance. Sometimes this is valid, but don't overdo it. Government agencies use this argument too often, and it always looks as though they are passing the buck:

> The second issue raised in your letter concerns the portfolio of the Minister for Transport. We have therefore forwarded your concerns to the Minister for her consideration and reply.

The final argument of definition is another old public-sector chestnut, although large corporations also use it when they have something to conceal. This is the argument of process. You reason that you are acting validly because you are following an appropriate procedure. Here is a bureaucratic classic:

> This problem has been recognised and is being addressed through a strategic, whole-of-government approach involving several key agencies.

Unless your reader supports the process you are citing, don't run with a process argument. You don't want to give the impression that your only solution is to form a committee.

Use the proof analysis checklist to see which arguments will work for your case. Sharpening your proofs will also help you test the strength of your conclusions.

Avoid poor or false arguments

It is also worth bearing in mind some of the common fallacies that too often arise when an argument is weak. Being caught out using these can be particularly damaging to your ethos. Here are 10 to avoid:

Fallacy	Example
Playing the man	We all know that the director gets things wrong.
The straw man	This proposal is simplistic, and simplistic solutions can't work.
Red herring	The product will work for you, and it is home grown.
Poisoning the well	Here comes Neville with his silly proposal.
Begging the question	We need to cut costs so we can reduce expenses.
Appeal to the masses	Everyone knows that this won't work.
Appeal to pity	But my feet hurt, why can't I leave early?
False dilemma	You either do it my way or resign.
Generalisation	She has a fiery temper, just like all Vandemonians.
Appeal to ignorance	You can't disprove what I say, so it must be true.

6 Coherence

At a glance

The toolbox

- Work with three elements of coherence: unity, structure and flow 117
- Use the paraphrasing checklist to map coherence 118

The living language

- Understand the history of the paragraph 124
- Unify your text through tone, voice and vocabulary 125
- Use familiar paragraph structures 126
- Maximise the flow 127

Power tools

- Use the 'old before new' principle 127
- Structure paragraphs in groups 131
- Use some transitional words and phrases 131
- Bind with some grammatical flow 132

The toolbox

'Since I've become a central banker, I've learned to mumble with great coherence.' So observed Alan Greenspan, then Chairman of the US Federal Reserve, in a 1987 speech to the US Congress. The quip highlights a problem all central banks face when sending out messages on monetary policy. Markets hang on their smallest utterance, so some ill-chosen words can send stockbrokers into a selling panic or a buying spree. The Reserve crafts its words very carefully to give a general sense of the bank's direction without committing to definite action.

In this environment, it is hardly surprising that Greenspan should have likened Reserve statements to mumbling. What is more interesting is that he highlighted coherence as the compensation for this lack of clarity. This is one of the most important yet least understood skills in writing, and it is one of the few that operate at every level of a document.

Work with three elements of coherence: unity, structure and flow

At its simplest, coherence means 'sticking together', and it flows from three elements:

1. Unity in purpose
2. Transparent structure
3. Effective flow

Whether for a paragraph or an entire report, you must unify your text around a single topic, with each part relating to it. That sounds easy enough. But you cannot just throw even closely related things into a series of heaps and expect your reader to make the connections between them. Your heaps need to be arranged in some kind of order, some clear and binding structure. Thirdly, even where a pattern exists, coherence calls for close connection between adjacent parts of the text to help your reader move between them. All three elements must be present to guarantee a document will hold together.

The key to coherence lies in one of the more recent developments in writing: the paragraph. While major headings in a document might give you an outline at the macro level, the paragraph will knit your documents together. So it is no surprise that the tool that will help you improve coherence is related to the paragraph—paraphrasing.

Use the paraphrasing checklist to map coherence

Paraphrasing helps you sketch a thumbnail map of your document to analyse how well it pinpoints your purpose, charts your structure and connects each part of the text. It is particularly valuable as an editing tool once you have draft text. Summarise each paragraph's content using a phrase or a short sentence. Where you have more than one point, you may need to write more than one paraphrase. But don't over-specify the content: you are not writing a replacement paragraph, but a short summary to outline the document's topography. Then read through the paraphrases and apply the following checklist.

The paraphrasing checklist

1. What is the core message and where is it in the text?
2. Which paraphrases group together into related sections?
3. Does the overall text use a standard structural pattern?
4. Are some sections given too much space or others too little?
5. Does each paragraph or section clearly connect with its neighbours?
6. How might you restructure the text to highlight the core message, clarify the structure and strengthen the bridges between adjacent text?

Let's see how this tool can diagnose and improve a letter from a publisher to magazine subscribers.

> Dear subscriber,
>
> As a COSMOS subscriber, we know that you value an intelligent magazine that revels in the beauty and excitement of the natural world and the quest to understand its many still unsolved mysteries.

Like you, I enjoy reading COSMOS, and I believe Australia and New Zealand deserve such a publication. This is why – after years of working as a scientist and later as a successful biotechnology entrepreneur – I helped establish COSMOS.

While still young, COSMOS already shows great promise, winning a number of industry and journalism awards, receiving high praise from many quarters and attracting a healthy number of subscribers.

We know COSMOS is special and that our readers adore it. We've received many letters, emails and phone calls of encouragement and appreciation since it was launched in June last year. We've also had many readers tell us there's so much in each issue they barely finish reading it before the next one arrives.

However, COSMOS is still largely unknown: on an almost daily basis, we hear stories of people who only recently discovered the magazine. So it's going to take time for COSMOS to be as widely recognised as we'd like it to be. Until that time arrives, we've made two decisions to ensure its continued success.

The first is to expand COSMOS beyond Australia and New Zealand, taking the magazine to larger markets in Asia, Europe and North America where we believe such a title will be warmly received. The second is to give our readers more time to enjoy the content in each issue by reducing its frequency from a monthly to a bi-monthly magazine (or 6 issues a year). Publishing a bi-monthly will also allow us time to develop our website and explore other enhancements that will increase the value we offer our subscribers.

This change will have no impact on the number of issues you receive as part of your subscription – only on the interval between each issue being published and posted to you. If you subscribed for 11 issues (1 year), you will now receive those 11 issues over 2 years instead, and so on.

In the meantime, we ask your assistance in helping COSMOS to grow. Enclosed is a readership survey seeking your feedback on the magazine so that we can make it even better. We will use the results to better understand your interests and improve our magazine – without compromising our determination to deliver a visually-rich and intellectually exciting publication.

I am very committed to COSMOS and know there are thousands more potential readers out there who would enjoy it as avidly as you and I do – if only they knew about it. I ask that you help us find them, and support the magazine by recommending it to friends, family, colleagues, or to your school or library.

With your help, COSMOS can attain the success it so richly deserves.

Sincerely,
The publisher

Here is a paraphrasing of the text:

Paragraph	
1	We know you value COSMOS.
2	Australia and New Zealand deserve this magazine.
3	COSMOS has already won awards and recognition.
4	Readers give great feedback, and barely finish it each month.
5	But COSMOS is still largely unknown. So we've made two changes for it to succeed.
6	We're expanding overseas. We're moving to bi-monthly publication and increasing subscriber value.
7	This affects the timing but not the number of issues.
8	To help us grow, please complete a readership survey.
9	To help us grow, please recommend us to others.
10	With your help, we can succeed.

This letter demonstrates how crucial the placement of the core message is in unifying the text. The main point is to gain subscriber acceptance for changes to their service. But these changes aren't mentioned until the end of paragraph five in a 10-paragraph text. Having worked through half a page to reach the main point, readers must think back on what they've read for the message to cohere around that point. When readers don't understand your purpose until well into the text, they are likely to be far less receptive to your message.

Paraphrasing is also an effective way of stripping a document to its bones to reveal the underlying structure by grouping the paraphrases into related areas. The *Cosmos* letter:

- starts with some background about *Cosmos* and its track record (paragraphs 1–4)
- introduces the problem it faces and outlines a two-part solution (paragraphs 5–7)
- asks the reader for further support (paragraphs 8–9)
- rounds off with a concluding sentence (paragraph 10).

Yet there is nothing in the paragraphing or the layout to reveal this structure. It leaves the readers to nut it out for themselves. This may not be a problem if you use a standard structure—readers follow text more easily if it fits into a familiar pattern. This text, however, does not fit into any single model.

Next, check how well your paraphrases connect and flow, each to the next. In this letter, the transitions between paragraphs four and five and between seven and eight jar. This makes the flow uneven, as readers have to pause to work out the connections before continuing. Also look at the balance of information between each section. Should the introductory information take up 50 per cent? Clearly, we could merge some or all of these paragraphs and get to the point much more quickly.

Paraphrases allow you to test out other paragraph arrangements without editing the full text. Sometimes it takes two or three goes before settling on an alternative like this one:

Paragraph	
1&4	We know you value COSMOS. Our readers give us great feedback, but they say they barely finish reading it each month.
5	However, COSMOS is still largely unknown. So we've made two changes for it to succeed.
6&7	We're moving to bi-monthly publication and increasing subscriber value. This affects the timing but not the number of issues you receive.

Paragraph

2&6	Australia and New Zealand deserve COSMOS. But now we're also expanding overseas.
8&9	To help us grow, please complete a readership survey and recommend us to others.
3&10	COSMOS has already won awards and recognition. With your help, COSMOS can realise its early promise.

This version keeps most of the content but improves its coherence by re-grouping and re-ordering it. Because the core message is moved up into the second paragraph, the remainder coheres more clearly around it. But because the document doesn't follow a standard structure, the paragraphing needs to do a lot more work to reveal which parts stick together. Some headings will also reveal the structure much more clearly:

Dear subscriber,

As a COSMOS subscriber, you value an intelligent magazine that revels in the natural world and the quest to understand its many still unsolved mysteries. We've received many letters, emails and phone calls of encouragement and appreciation since COSMOS was launched. Readers have even told us there's so much in each issue that they barely finish reading it before the next one arrives!

Unfortunately, COSMOS is still largely unknown: every day we hear of people who only recently discovered the magazine. Because it's going to take time for COSMOS to be as widely recognised as we'd like it to be, I'm writing to let you know about two changes we've made to continue our success.

1. Moving to bi-monthly publication

To give you more time to enjoy each issue, we are reducing its frequency from monthly to bi-monthly. This will also give us time to develop our website and explore other enhancements that will increase the value we offer subscribers. The change will have no impact on the number of issues you receive as part of your subscription—only on the interval between issues.

2. Expanding overseas
Australia and New Zealand deserve a publication such as COSMOS. But to strengthen and sustain the magazine, we are also taking it to larger markets in Asia, Europe and North America, where we believe it will be warmly received.

How you can help
In the meantime, we ask for your assistance in helping COSMOS to grow. Enclosed is a readership survey seeking your feedback so that we can better understand your interests and improve the magazine. I also know there are thousands more potential readers out there who would enjoy COSMOS as avidly as we do—if only they knew about it. I ask that you help us find them by recommending the magazine to friends, family, colleagues, or to your school or library.

COSMOS has already won a number of industry and journalism awards, received high praise from many quarters and attracted a healthy number of subscribers. With your help, COSMOS can attain the success it so richly deserves.

Sincerely,

The publisher

With a little practice, you can paraphrase mentally, particularly with short documents such as emails. With complex or too-familiar material, use this tool to help you step back, view the skeleton of your document and see how its parts connect.

KEY TIP Compare your final paraphrases to your original structure outline. This will help you improve your planning.

The living language

Understand the history of the paragraph

What paraphrasing reveals most of all is the close relationship between document coherence and paragraphing. Despite this importance, the paragraph is a relatively recent feature of Western writing, having evolved along with the printing press. Yet its origins go back a long way. Aristotle used a 'paragraphos' to mark a break in content—probably a horizontal stroke underneath the new starting point.

The term 'paragraph' appeared in written English in the 16th century. A symbol such as a [or a § marked the start of a new point and it quickly became popular. When the printing press was invented, the paragraph was typeset to start on a new line, often indented.

The late development of the paragraph explains why it took a while for a coherent theory about effective paragraphing to emerge. Scots logician Alexander Bain, in his 1866 book *English Composition and Rhetoric,* wrote that effective paragraphs met a number of simple rules, in particular, 'unity', 'development' and 'coherence'. Each paragraph, he said, should have one unitary topic, set out in a topic sentence. Subsequent sentences should illustrate or develop this topic. Coherence means that each sentence should be logically connected to the ones next to it, as well as to the main topic.

But if paragraph theory started in Scotland, it found its real home in America. Academic John Genung's *Practical Elements of Rhetoric* reworked Bain's rules into the three principles of 'unity', 'proportion' and 'continuity'. Harvard professor Barrett Wendell elevated these to 'unity', 'mass' and 'coherence' in his 1891 book *English Composition*. An important model in American universities, this influenced the burgeoning professional community right across the country.

These three elements have remained at the core of paragraph theory ever since, and Wendell describes them best:

> (1) Every composition should group itself about one central idea; (2) The chief parts of every composition should be so placed as readily to catch the eye; (3) Finally, the relation of each part of the composition to its neighbours should be unmistakable.

Unify your text through tone, voice and vocabulary

The most important way you can unify your text, whether it is an entire document or an individual paragraph, is to have a clear purpose. Once you have a unifying topic in each paragraph, however, you can strengthen coherence by adjusting a further three elements:

1. Tone
2. Voice
3. Vocabulary

You will undo all your good work in thematic unity if you switch the tone of your text from the formal to the informal. This will draw attention to your text and away from your content:

> My first allocated task in the new position was a request to attend the annual trade show. I had a you-beaut time and saw so many whiz-bang things, that I was able to prepare a highly complimentary report about the event for the marketing team.

Secondly, you will maintain unity if your text speaks with a consistent voice or 'person'. This might be the first person (I, we), the second person (you), the third person (he, she, it, they), or the passive voice. But do not intermingle them unnecessarily. This is a common mistake in instructional text, which often jumps between all four:

> When staff log on to the server, you should always be sure that no one is able to observe the password being entered. It is the responsibility of staff to change their passwords in line with the corporation's policies every six weeks. Follow the guidelines that we make available on the intranet.

In a consistent voice, this text would read:

> When you log on to the server, always make sure no one can see the password you enter. You must also change your password every six weeks. For details, you can read the corporation's guidelines on the intranet.

Vocabulary or word choice also contributes to unity. Clear, dominant themes throughout a paragraph help to bind the text together. Sometimes you can achieve this by repeating key words. At other times, you can use closely related words or synonyms to maintain the unity.

Use familiar paragraph structures

The next development in the history of the paragraph related to its internal structure. Like paragraph theory in general, paragraph structuring evolved in US colleges through freshman courses in composition and rhetoric. Its chief proponents were Fred Newton Scott and Joseph Denney at the University of Michigan and Ohio State University. *Paragraph-Writing*, which they published in 1891, popularised the craft of paragraphing. They identified six 'means' or basic patterns for paragraphs, which they treated as mini-texts. The century of work that followed expanded their categories into something like 20 or 30 standard patterns.

Although too limiting for some, this approach does offer an accurate way of diagnosing, and often repairing, faulty paragraphs. If 30 models sounds like too many to remember, here's a short list of 10 that mostly covers the field:

The checklist of paragraph structures

1. Statement and support
2. Question and answer
3. Problem and solution
4. Cause and effect
5. Sequence
6. Description or partition
7. Comparison or contrast
8. Definition
9. Example or analogy
10. Signpost, such as an introduction or conclusion

Most of these patterns are self-explanatory. The standard practice is to introduce each with a topic sentence and proceed in logical order. Make a statement, and then follow it with several sentences that back it up. Ask a question and answer it, or state a problem and work towards a solution. A sequence structure will often work well if you are describing a series of events or a process. Describe something by breaking it into parts and listing them one by one. You can define something, set up a comparison between two or more elements, give an example, or leave a signpost for moving between sections or to summarise and conclude.

If you are having trouble with your paragraphs, try to use one of these models to make your document clearer and more coherent.

Maximise the flow

So you've unified your topic, used consistent tone and voice, and standardised your paragraph structures. There's one piece of the coherence puzzle to come: flow. Your paragraphs and sentences might all be on the one topic, and they might very well follow a logical pattern, but if they do not connect closely to their neighbours, they will not flow easily. Readers will struggle to build bridges between them, and your coherence will still suffer. To make sure your sequencing works:

- use the 'old before new' principle
- sequence paragraphs into substructures
- use transitional words and phrases
- bind sentences with grammatical flow.

These are the power tools of coherence.

Power tools

It's no accident that Barrett Wendell used neighbourhood as his metaphor for effective flow. This final step in binding your documents is to connect adjacent sentences and paragraphs. Good neighbours generate an effortless flow. If you raise fences too high between them, you will constantly pull up your reader.

Use the 'old before new' principle

The first step in neighbourliness is to apply the principle of 'old before new'. Modern linguistics has identified this principle as one of the implicit contracts that exist between a writer and a reader. It means that your readers unconsciously expect your text to begin with information that they are familiar with before it moves on to present something new. They will first scan the text to confirm the old information, then absorb what is new. Then, once that new information is made familiar, it can lead to further new information. Readers will follow you comfortably through the chain. When you do this with skill, you can take them in any direction, as long as you build effective bridges between paragraphs.

The following diagram shows how you can link paragraphs using the 'old before new' principle:

Topic 1 (old and familiar) ....
....
.... topic 2 (new)

Topic 2 (now old) ....
....
.... topic 3 (new)

Topic 3 (now old) ....
....
.... topic 4 (new)

And so on ....
....
....

You can also vary this pattern by linking material from different parts of the previous paragraph. The variations can be endless, but they all apply the same principle of old before new.

Let's see a first-rate writer applying this principle in one of the great speeches of the 20th century. Here is the opening of Martin Luther King's 'I have a dream' speech, given at the Lincoln Memorial in Washington, DC, on 28 August 1963. The text is marked up to show the connections that form bridges between each paragraph and help the text flow.

Five score years ago, a great American, in whose symbolic shadow we stand, signed the Emancipation Proclamation. This momentous decree came as a beacon light of hope to millions of **Negro** slaves who had been seared in the flames of withering injustice. It came as a joyous daybreak to end the long night of their captivity.

But **one hundred years later**, we must face the tragic fact that the **Negro** is still not free. One hundred years later, the life of the Negro is still sadly crippled by the manacles of segregation and the chains of discrimination. One hundred years later, the Negro lives on a lonely island of poverty in the midst of a vast ocean of material prosperity. One hundred years later, the Negro is still languished in the corners of American society and finds himself an exile in his own land. So **we have come here today** to dramatize a shameful condition.

In a sense **we have come to our nation's Capital** to **cash a check**. When the architects of our republic wrote the magnificent words of the Constitution and the Declaration of Independence, they were signing a **promissory note** to which every American was to fall heir. This note was a promise that all men would be guaranteed the unalienable rights of life, liberty and the pursuit of happiness.

It is obvious today that America has defaulted on this **promissory note** insofar as her citizens of color are concerned. Instead of honoring this sacred obligation, America has given the Negro people a bad **check**; a check which has come back marked 'insufficient funds'. But we refuse to believe that the bank of justice is bankrupt. We refuse to believe that there are insufficient funds in the great vaults of opportunity of this nation. So **we have come to cash this check**—a check that will give us upon demand the riches of freedom and the security of justice. **We have also come** to this hallowed spot to remind

America of the fierce urgency of **now**. This is no time to engage in the luxury of cooling off or to take the tranquilizing drug of gradualism.

Now is the time to make real the promises of Democracy.

Now is the time to rise from the dark and desolate valley of segregation to the sunlit path of racial justice.

Now is the time to open the doors of opportunity to all of God's children.

Now is the time to lift our nation from the quicksands of racial injustice to the solid rock of brotherhood.

We can analyse the flow by separating the old and new elements.

Paragraph	Old	New
1	A great American (The venue is the Lincoln Memorial)	Five score years ago Negro
2	one hundred years later Negro	we have come here today
3	we have come to our nation's Capital	to cash a check promissory note
4	promissory note check we have also come	now
5–8	Now	

These markers at the start and end of each paragraph bind the text together and help it to flow seamlessly. But looking a little closer reveals the same principle operating within each paragraph as well. The themes that link the paragraphs are echoed from sentence to sentence, further increasing coherence and rhetorical power. Key words such as 'Negro', 'one hundred years', 'note', 'promissory', 'cash', 'check', 'America', 'justice' and 'now' recur throughout, forming a thematic spine. You can apply exactly the same techniques to bind your own text and make sure that it flows.

Structure paragraphs in groups

Where your content doesn't easily fall into an old-before-new pattern, you can return to the second principle of coherence: structure. Bind a group of paragraphs by using a pattern that links them. There are 10 standard models that work well in the workplace, forming mini-documents within a document:

The subsection checklist

1. Statement and support
2. General to specific
3. Question and answer
4. Problem and solution
5. Cause and effect
6. Sequence
7. Description or partition
8. Comparison or contrast
9. Definition
10. Example or analogy

For example, an analytical document such as a report or a submission will often use a statement and support substructure across several paragraphs. This gives the main information in one paragraph, then follows up with the details. A web-based information document can turn to a Q&A structure, while proposals or memos might discuss a problem and solution or a cause and effect over several paragraphs. Where these fit with your content, these patterns can bind your documents together at the substructure level, flowing clearly from one paragraph to the next.

Use some transitional words and phrases

You can also make the connections between paragraphs and sentences more obvious by using transitional words between them. These are most often adverbs and conjunctions. If your sentences don't seem to flow one to the next, use one of these to make the relationship clear. There are about 1000 in all, but they fall into 10 common categories:

The table of transitional words

Transition type	Transitional words
Addition	and, also, in addition, what's more, besides, furthermore, as well as, another, next, following, or, since, as, so
Comparison	also, both, and, in comparison, together, each, similarly, likewise, as well as, in the same way, consistent with, equally, matching
Contrast	but, however, although, in contrast, nevertheless, on the other hand, than, while, despite, even so, still, yet, instead, opposing, unlike
Cause and effect	as a result, because, for, since, then, thus, consequently, it follows, so, therefore, in effect, hence, due to, owing to
Emphasis	of course, above all, indeed, surely, more important, in fact, actually, equally, significantly, increasingly, notably, by all means, without doubt
Example	for example, in particular, for instance, specifically, in other words, such as, namely, in this case
Qualification	at the same time, although, after all, and yet, certainly, doubtless, even though, granted, of course, yet, no doubt
Sequence	first, second (etc.), before, next, later, once, presently, meanwhile, initially, after, then, finally, afterwards, in the past, during, immediately
Space	at the front, at the back, in the centre, to the right/left, nearby, above, below, beyond, far away, ahead of, close to, next to, opposite, between
Summary	in summary, in short, so, thus, as a result, in conclusion, therefore, to sum up, in closing

Transitional words are extremely useful, but beware of overuse. They are the easiest way to connect sections, but also the clumsiest. If you rely on them to do all your bridge-building, your reader will become more conscious of the bridge than the shores on either side.

Bind with some grammatical flow

You can reduce the clunkiness of too many transitionals with the grammatical techniques of reference and ellipsis. Reference is particularly powerful in workplace writing, where the same nouns and noun phrases tend to turn up again and again. You can use them in full, or substitute a pronoun or demonstrative:

- Pronouns—he, him, she, her, it, they, them, his, her, its, their.
- Demonstratives—this, these, that, those, here, there.

These references help to establish where the old or familiar information lies, promoting both comprehension and flow.

The last power tool is what linguists call ellipsis. In speaking and writing, we do not always use a full grammatical structure or explanation, but leave out parts that our audience can fill in. The letter to the editor below discusses the editorial practice of newspapers filling in the ellipses of quoted speech.

> SIR: The plethora of parentheses [square brackets] in your publication is approaching plague proportions.
>
> Almost every line [in the paper] is littered with annoying explanations for those of us [readers] unable to comprehend simple sentences [without superfluous clarifications or complications].
>
> Had your subeditors been around in the days of [the playwright William] Shakespeare they would doubtless have given us lines like: 'A horse! A horse! [I am willing to exchange] My kingdom for a horse!'
>
> Or in [British wartime Prime Minister Winston Spencer] Churchill's era: 'Never [before] in the field of human conflict has so much [deep gratitude] been owed by so many [besieged British citizens] to so few [brave RAF fighter pilots].'
>
> If things [these persistent parentheses] get much worse [than they are now], I [the writer] shall [be compelled to] stop reading your [the editor's] paper.
>
> Even my dog finds it [the paper] hard to digest. He [the dog] is choking on the brackets[[]]!

Don't fill in every detail for your readers where they can easily work it out for themselves. This will make your text efficient as well as improve its coherence.

7 Design

At a glance

The toolbox

- Choose a legible font 135
- Give your text room to breathe 137
- Align the text carefully 138
- Maximise the contrast 139
- Prefer bold for emphasis 139

The living language

- Combine writing with design 140
- Keep up to date with design techniques 141
- See design as part of delivery 142

Power tools

- Set your page grid 143
- Add plenty of white space 145
- Use headings and numbering to show the structure 145
- Use bullets for sentence lists 146
- Expand the use of tables 147
- Make your data clear 148

The toolbox

What is a chapter on design doing in the middle of a book on writing? Workplace writers seldom used to worry much about the appearance of their words on the page. Either their documents were typed in standard formats, or they used a printer. Those days are gone. Technology has brought the tools of the typesetter to every workstation. Design is now something you need to know.

Of course, you probably always had an opinion about which font your organisation should use, or whether you liked its logo. But now you're being asked to typeset complex documents and even to print, bind and distribute them yourself. How do you know which is the right font to choose, or how many headings are best, or how to lay out a page? Professionals are increasingly responsible for making documents look good as well as read clearly. And in many cases, you can no longer achieve one without the other.

Let's begin with some basics of typography. To make informed choices about how to set your text, look at the six elements below:

The type checklist

1. Font type
2. Font size and style
3. Line length and spacing
4. Alignment
5. Contrast
6. Emphasis

Choose a legible font

A font is a group of typefaces that have similar letter shape, height, weight and other features. There are something like 60,000 fonts you can choose from, but which should you use? Start by considering the two broad types of fonts: serif and sans serif. The serif fonts have small 'caps' and 'feet' at the ends of most letters, and their lines vary in thickness:

Times New Roman is a serif font.
Book Antiqua is a serif font.
`Courier is a serif font.`

The sans serif fonts do not have these features:

Lucida Sans is a sans serif font.
Myriad is a sans serif font.
Arial is a sans serif font.

The traditional approach in typesetting is to use serif fonts for body text. The serifs arguably aid reading by helping hold the reader's eye on the line. Walk into a bookshop and pick up any book, and it will almost always use a serif font. Pick up your newspaper, and you will see that it uses a serif font. Typewriters also used serifs.

But if serifs are more readable, why did we invent sans serif fonts? First, for variety. If you use only one serif font, text can look rather boring. Well-designed reports often use a serif font for their body text and a sans serif font for headings and titles. Sans serif text is perfectly readable in short bursts, such as a single line. It is also fine in large print, such as on road signs or in large-print books. In the computer age, sans serif text is also common as a screen font. Because the resolution of the average computer screen is limited, the serifs and thinner lines of serif fonts are less prominent when text is read on screen. As a result, many websites use a sans serif font for their text.

When you have chosen the font, what is the right size to use? For most workplace purposes, you will want to use a type size between 10 and 14 points. Generally, pitch your body text at around 12 points for a serif font, and 10 or 11 points for a sans serif font. For larger headings and subheadings, you can go up to 12, 14 and even 16 points. If you have a lot of larger block quotations, you could make these one point smaller than your body text. Don't stray outside these parameters for most documents.

While varying fonts between body text and headings is standard, try not to go beyond two fonts in most documents, as you will start to lose visual coherence. Also try to pick a font that matches your corporate voice and readership. If yours is a fairly conventional organisation, go for a classic font such as Times New Roman or Garamond. If you want to convey a more modern look, you might pick a more recent font such as Georgia. In either case, avoid anything with fancy scrolls, along with calligraphic fonts unless you are using them for a specific effect.

Give your text room to breathe

Many workplace writers have never thought about the length of the text lines they use, which is probably why they often use overly long lines. In the old school of book publishing, the rule of thumb was that any line of text should be no longer than two and a half alphabets, or 65 characters, long. This was mainly applied to books, with their fairly narrow pages. In a workplace document, you can get away with a slightly longer line—up to 70 characters, and perhaps a tad more. But by the time you are using more than 80 characters on each line, you are asking your readers to work extra hard to hold their eye steady as they move across the page. Have you ever skipped lines as you were reading? It was probably because of their length.

Closely related to line length is the amount of space, or leading, between each line. You need to give the text some space to breathe or your readers will find it hard to distinguish between different lines. But leave too much space, and the opposite will occur—your reader will have to jump between lines rather than glide, and this is less accurate and more taxing for the eyes. A good balance is to make your line spacing at least two points larger than the size of your font. So if you are using a 12-point font, set your spacing to 'at least 14 points' in your word processor:

> Here is some text in 12-point Garamond. It has a reasonable line length, without too many characters, but the spacing between the lines is two points below the font size. The letters are starting to overlap and clash.

> Here is a similar block of text with the same 12-point font and line length. Its line spacing is double the point size of the font. This wastes paper and is not easy to read.

> Here is some text with the same 12-point font and line length as the previous two examples, but with better line spacing set to 'at least 14 points'.

Align the text carefully

Once you have the right font, size and spacing, you next need to decide what alignment you will use as your standard. There are four options:

Left Left justification aligns text flush on the left margin, keeping the right edge uneven. This is the way most typewriters used to set text because it was all they could do. As a result, the business world got used to left justification. It remains a safe standard to use in your documents because it will automatically mean that the spaces between your words are even, which aids readability.

Full Full justification automatically aligns the text flush with both the left and right margins. This creates more formal blocks of text, which look neat and clean. The main problem this presents, however, is that the word processor automatically adjusts the spaces between words, which can cause uneven spacing and wavy white lines down the page. These 'rivers and lakes' can reduce legibility. If you have a fairly narrow line width, it is probably safer not to fully justify your text, particularly within a table.

Centre Centre justification for body text is not a good idea because your reader's eye has no fixed anchor point at either end of the line. You will quickly tire their eyes and their patience. Reserve centre justification for short bursts of text.

Such as in headings.

Right You will seldom use right justification, except in a table where you want to bring two columns of text or figures into closer relationship. Because we read from left to right, moving the left anchor point will annoy your readers.

Maximise the contrast

Contrast refers to the difference between the colour of your text and the colour of its background. This is very important to legibility because the more contrast you have, the easier it will be for readers to distinguish your words. The maximum contrast comes with black text on a white page. Be very careful if you use colour for your fonts or background. If you reduce the contrast too far, you stand a chance of reducing your readership as well.

Similarly, avoid large blocks of text that are 'reversed out' with a white font on a black or coloured background. This can work well as a design element in short bursts, such as a heading in a large font size. But over a longer block it starts to become counterproductive.

If any of your readers have a visual impairment, don't mess with the contrast. If you are presenting your writing direct to the public, such as through a website, you will certainly have readers with weaker eyesight, so don't play around with their eyes. Avoid certain combinations that cannot be read by those with colour blindness: red text on a green background or yellow text on blue. If you have a lot of readers with poor eyesight, use a large font size, a clean font style and well-balanced spacing.

Prefer bold for emphasis

When pen and ink were the dominant workplace technologies, there were only a few ways to draw attention to aspects of your document. You could use capital letters or underline words for emphasis. These conventions carried over to the typewriter and dominated for decades.

Capital letters slow down reading. When the eye scans a word, a reader does not interpret one character at a time but rather recognises the overall pattern. A word such as 'corporation', for example, has an even number of letters that do not rise or descend, divided by two letters that do. With capitals, CORPORATION loses this pattern and reading slows down. This is why capitalisation was reserved mostly for headings or small amounts of text. In the digital age, capitalising whole words has a further unwanted effect. In emails on a screen, IT LOOKS

AS IF YOU ARE SHOUTING AT THE READER. While you may sometimes want this effect, for the most part avoid it.

Likewise, underlining has almost passed its use-by date. It used to be the most common way to set apart headings, to indicate that a title referred to a publication or work of art, and sometimes even to reinforce a point in the text. As with capitalisation, this came partly at the expense of legibility, as underlining interferes with a reader's sense of letter shapes. We used to have little choice, because a typewriter had nothing else to offer. Now we are better off using italics to indicate a book title or an act of parliament, to highlight a scientific name or to signal a foreign or unfamiliar word. Reserve underlining for its new function of showing a live hyperlink such as a website or email address: www.plainenglishfoundation.com.

Be miserly with italics apart from the purposes it has taken over from underlining. The sloped italic characters are less easy to read than standard Roman characters. Because of this, avoid using italics in body text, especially when quoting whole clauses or sentences. When you are quoting text within a paragraph, enclose it in quotation marks. If you have a block quote, start it on a new line and indent the left margin to show it is a quotation. Indenting, italicising and enclosing in quotes all at the same time is a clear case of overkill.

Where you need some emphasis to set apart headings, bold is the new black. It preserves the shape and legibility of characters better than other options while drawing attention to what you want to emphasise. However, because the thicker letters are harder to read than normal type, avoid using bold for slabs of text.

The living language

Combine writing with design

Even this cursory look at typography shows just how involved simple choices of type can become. You can do so much more with type now than 10 or 20 years ago. Only in the last few decades have books on writing begun to catch up.

Look at any of the writing texts published 50 years ago, and you won't find design or typography mentioned as part of the craft. One hundred years ago, type design was so far separated from writing that it was something that sweaty men in printers' shops took care of, much like any craftsman. There were masters of the craft, of course—mostly working in the compositors' rooms of good book printers—but design was not something the writer was much involved in.

Then business machines came onto the scene, rapidly replacing handwritten text. The typewriter sparked a revolution, but it had major limitations—not least in the number of copies it could make. If you needed to send a report to several readers, you had to place sheets of carbon between a number of pages, with the typewriter creating fainter and fainter impressions as it slammed against the rolled-up wad. After seven copies, you had to start typing again. Readers knew their place in the pecking order by the faintness of the copy they received.

Only a few decades later, a one-person small business with a single PC can type and print letters in bulk, using mail-merge software to print and collate thousands of names and addresses. You can scan any original document and send it anywhere in the world. Instantly. You can design your own letterhead and brochures, reach millions through your website, and conduct business from the other side of the planet, all the time doing your own typesetting and page design, binding and printing. The quality gap between the small office user and the major printing press is getting narrower every year. The quantity gap is close to being closed.

Keep up to date with design techniques

The pace of change has been so rapid that the techniques of design professionals have been struggling to keep up. It took until the 1970s for 'information design' to gain currency as the umbrella term for an emerging set of practices, initially denoting the equal importance of writing and presentation in effective documents. NATO hosted a conference in 1978 in the Netherlands, which gave birth to the *Information Design Journal*. In the same year, the United States National Institute of Education launched the Document Design Project, which produced foundation references such as its *Guidelines for Document Designers*.

In the 1980s, Edward Tufte published a series of books on the display of information, and Richard Saul Wurman coined the term 'information architect'. By the 1990s, professional associations for information design were being formed, and the Society of Technical Communicators in

America set up a Special Interest Group on information design that attracted 2700 members in the first three years. Technology had been demanding a new set of skills to realise its full potential, and those skills meant a merger between the visual craft of designers and the literary craft of writers—along with a healthy level of technical savvy.

This combined focus, and the experience of working with entirely new media such as websites, extended the concept of information design itself. Within a few years it came to signify not just the combined writing and layout of a document, but an entire process of information-planning, project design, content collection, page design, text drafting, and document testing with real audiences. Information design in this broader sense has expanded the contexts within which writers operate. Writing in workplaces will become an increasingly collaborative enterprise, not just with colleagues in the communications department but also with your readers. Just as plain English is breaking down barriers by narrowing the gap between officialese and everyday language, so too information design is narrowing the distance between businesses and customers, agencies and clients, writers and readers.

The Plain English movement itself was initially silent on the question of design. Ernest Gowers' *Plain Words*, published in the 1940s, contained nothing on the subject. As a result, Plain English has attracted some criticism from information designers, but in truth its exponents have been doing their own catching up with the importance of visual elements. No major text on plain English today ignores design or usability.

See design as part of delivery

In a sense, information design is the latest version of a very old rhetorical concept: delivery, the fourth canon of classical rhetoric. For rhetoricians such as Cicero and Quintilian, once you had learned how to generate arguments (invention), structure them (arrangement) and express them well (style), you needed to work on conveying them to an audience (delivery). In ancient times, this meant vocal delivery because oratory was the dominant form of public exchange. So the ancient rhetorical texts gave advice on tone of voice, vocal strength and accompanying gestures.

Then came paper, the book and the printing press, and business was no longer done so regularly through oration, except in institutions such as parliaments and law courts. The document has become the common medium for information exchange, but we should still work on its tone, its visual strength and its design gestures, just as ancient speech-makers used to do for an oration.

Document design offers the best methods for delivery in the contemporary world. You will increasingly need to handle graphics as much as grammar, spacing as much as style, page layout as much as punctuation. In the professional workplace, today's writers need to employ an unprecedented range of writing and design skills.

Power tools

Once you have control of your type, the next step is to understand some principles of page layout. This is more than just an aesthetic nicety: it goes a long way to establishing your credibility with readers. The look of the page is what gives readers their first impression. If it is well composed and attractive, they will be more receptive to your words. If the text is dense, disjointed or unappealing, your content will have to work extra hard. Work with five specific elements when composing your pages:

The page design checklist

1. Page grids
2. White space
3. Headings and numbers
4. Bulleted lists
5. Tables

Set your page grid

Choosing a clear and readable type is one thing. You will also have to decide how you are going to arrange your text on the page. Designers talk about setting the page 'grids', the blocks of space that will hold text, and where and how they will integrate graphic elements. You will also need to decide where to set headers, footers and page numbers.

The standard grid in workplace writing is a single rectangle on an A4 page with a margin on four sides and page numbering at the bottom. Graphs or tables are most often placed with text running before and after but not around:

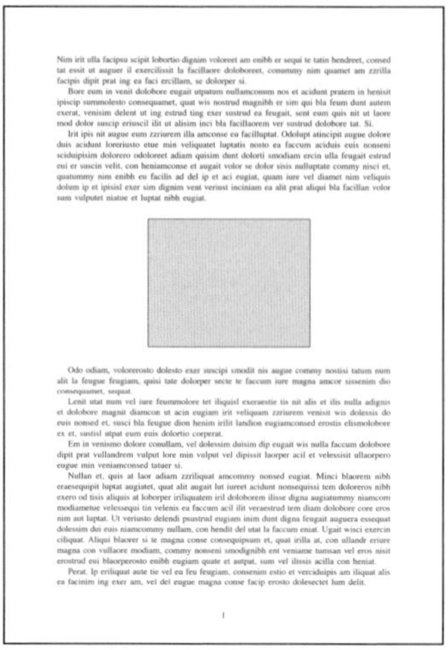

While this may be your most common page size and layout, don't feel it is the only one you can use. Often a two-column format will work well for documents such as newsletters, annual reports or information documents like policies and procedures:

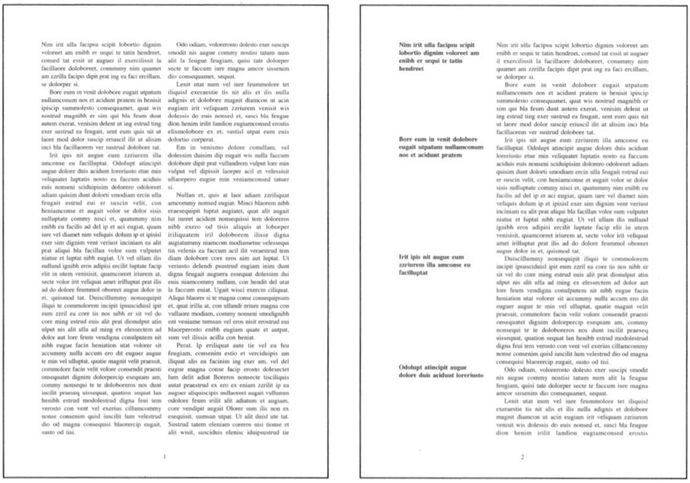

The final question with page design is how to position graphic elements. You might place them across a whole two-column grid or within each column. You might reserve a column for graphics, or set a grid across the bottom of each page:

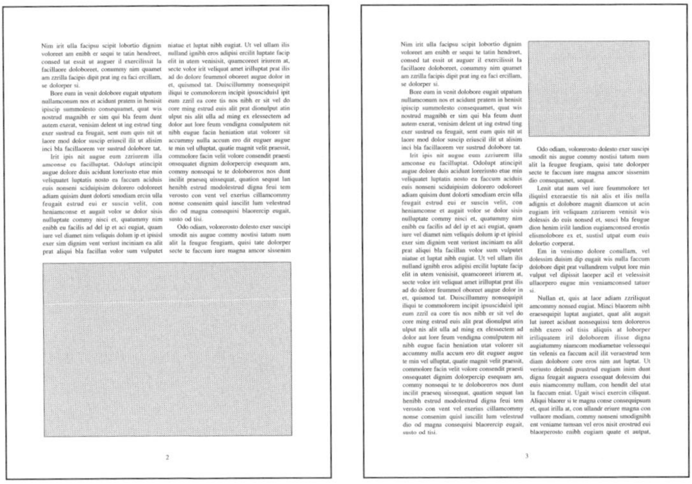

Add plenty of white space

Perhaps the most common error that workplace writers make with document design is to crowd too much material onto the page. Allow enough space between your text and the edges of the page, and your readers will be drawn into it. When you set the text too close to the edges, readers can feel daunted by what looks like a tough mental task. It is hard to measure exactly how much white space you should leave, but try to keep at least 25 mm as the minimum margins on the left and right of an A4 page, with a little more than this at the top and bottom of each page.

Of course, generous white space runs up against considerations of cost. The wider the margins, the more pages you will need to carry the same text. While you won't want to be profligate with space, keep to these minimums to strike an effective balance. If you are working with pre-set margins that are a little too cramped, you can compensate to some extent by the way you place headings, tables, graphics and bulleted lists throughout the text.

Use headings and numbering to show the structure

Headings are an important element because they contribute equally to the structure and to the design. They give you some visual interest but also help to break the text into sections and guide your reader through the document. To use them effectively, you will need to develop an effective structure in the first place, breaking your text into orderly parts.

Of course, overdoing the headings can be counterproductive if it ends up confusing your readers. Most documents will only need one level of heading to mark divisions in the content. In this case, a major heading per half page is a reasonable rule of thumb. In longer reports, you may also want to add some subheadings to break down your content further. In this case, make sure you distinguish clearly between the different levels of heading by using different point sizes, perhaps a different font, and emphasis such as bolding.

Heading 1

Heading 2

Heading 3

Numbering can also help to guide your readers through a document, particularly when combined with headings. Readers will gain the most benefit from numbering at the highest end of the heading hierarchy, which gives them a quick snapshot of the overall structure. If you want to use numbering beyond that, generally restrict it to the second level. Avoid decimal numbering that runs to three or four levels, such as 1.2.1.1, 1.2.1.2, 1.2.1.3, as this quickly becomes hard to follow.

Use bullets for sentence lists

With a sentence containing a list, either of single words or longer phrases, try to format it using bullets instead. Select a standard bullet, indent it to match your paragraph indent, and indent the text slightly after the bullets. This makes a lot of sentences much more accessible, and it is a great way to add some white space. Compare these two versions:

> Good performance management comes from a transparent process, two-way communication between managers and staff, and fair, equitable and confidential treatment of employees.

Good performance management comes from:

- a transparent process
- two-way communication between managers and staff
- fair, equitable and confidential treatment of employees.

As with headings, however, don't overdo your bullets. Some organisations make every paragraph a bullet in an effort to make them punchier. This unfortunately comes at the expense of integrated paragraph structures and effective flow. It also wastes space. Mostly keep your paragraphs in conventional format, and use bulleted lists where they are appropriate to the content. If you find yourself wanting to use a whole page of lists, or a list within a list, try to convert them into other elements such as tables.

Expand the use of tables

You might associate tables with numbers more than text, particularly if this was the first way you encountered them in technical documents. Yet the ease with which you can now incorporate tables into a word-processed document has forced a rethink of exactly what constitutes a table. No longer does it need to be a box with a frame around it, with labels at the top of the columns and rows and numbers in between.

If bullets are the device to turn to for a sentence list, consider a short table when the list has two or more elements running through it. It is particularly effective when one of the elements relates to stages in a process or a chronology. Compare, for example, the following two versions.

> If you have not received your authority to fundraise by 28 February 2007 and the Department has not asked for additional information, then you may assume that your application has been approved. In such circumstances, fundraising appeals may be undertaken in accordance with the provisions of the Act, the Regulations and the Conditions.
>
> However, if you have not received your authority or any other request for additional information from the Department two weeks before 28 February 2007 it is suggested that you telephone, facsimile a letter or send an email to the Office of Charities and inquire about the status of the application.

By	If this doesn't happen	Take this action
14 February	You have not received your authority to fundraise or a request from us for further information.	Contact us by phone, fax or email to check on the status of your application.
28 February	You have not received your authority to fundraise or a request from us for further information.	You can assume your application has been approved, and you can start to fundraise in line with the Act, the regulations and the conditions.

All these elements of page composition are particularly important in informational documents. Analytical documents usually have some built-in variation, moving from descriptive information to analysis. When you are writing a more descriptive document, such as a procedure or an instruction, you do not have this variation, but are often piling fact upon fact. Design becomes a much more important tool for maintaining interest.

KEY TIP Use prose for analysis and design to convey the facts and figures.

Make your data clear

With clear typography and page design under your belt, a final design consideration is whether to add any further graphic elements. The tools at your disposal today are extremely sophisticated: most word-processing programs are fully integrated with a related spreadsheet that can generate all types of graphs and charts. You can also scan and paste in almost any picture or drawing, and build diagrams without specialist software. The most common six graphics are:

The graphics checklist

1 Tables
2 Charts
3 Graphs
4 Drawings
5 Photos
6 Diagrams or maps

Although these are an easy way of adding visual interest to your documents, do not introduce them just for the sake of their appearance. Add them only when they will do a more effective job at presenting your content than words would do on their own. Each has its strengths and weaknesses, so be aware of which one to turn to for a specific purpose:

Graphic element	Situation
Tables	Presenting small sets of data (up to 20 elements)
Graphs and charts	Presenting more complex data, or to show trends
Tables and charts	Presenting a sequence of events
Tables, charts or diagrams	Presenting a process
Photos or drawings	Showing a physical object
Photos or maps	Showing people, places or situations
Charts or diagrams	Showing the structure of something

In a series of influential books in the 1980s, Edward Tufte at Yale University helped to drag information graphics out of the doldrums. Rather than seeing them merely as a way to liven up dull sets of data, he argued persuasively for some key principles of graphic excellence:

- Have a reason for showing the data.
- Show the data clearly.
- Don't distort the data with graphics elements of different proportions.
- Draw attention to the data, not to the graphic.
- Reveal the data at different levels, from an overview to the details.
- Maximise the data–ink ratio by culling anything not related to the data.
- Show the data in a relevant context.
- Label everything clearly.

Above all, turn to a graphic not for its visual appeal alone but because it is able to integrate the purpose, the data and the design into an effective whole.

Expression

8	Tone	153
9	Grammar	169
10	Words	188
11	Clutter	205
12	Verbs	222
13	Sentences	241

Tools covered in this section

The tone scale	155
The tone checklist	164
The open-class words	171
The closed-class words	171
The table of officialese words	191
The table of officialese phrases	192
The Fry readability graph	199
The Flesch reading ease formula	202
The key words tool	207
The grammatical clutter checklist	215
The hidden verb tool	225
The passive voice	229
The verb index	239
The sentence length average	244
The four rhetorical sentence structures	245
The four sentence types	252
The five sentence patterns	253

8 Tone

At a glance

The toolbox

- Test the tone of your text 154
- Strike a balance of formality 155
- Don't overdress the text 156
- Maintain a professional tone 158

The living language

- Set your tone to communicate rather than to impress 158
- Resist the language of power 160
- Don't swing too far to the informal 162
- Take care with email tone 162

Power tools

- Work with seven elements to adjust your tone 164
- Put people in your prose 166

The toolbox

The linguist M.A.K. Halliday once said that for anyone interested in language, there is no such thing as boring speakers. You simply stop listening to what they are saying and start analysing how they are saying it. If you do this regularly you will discover that, while their words are crucial to their meaning, elements such as the tone of voice, expression and gesture are just as important.

When you write, by contrast, your tools are much more restricted. You are usually communicating with someone remote from you and must rely on printed words alone to convey your tone. Never underestimate the difficulty of using a visual medium to convey sound. As William Zinsser put it, this 'may seem absurd: readers read with their eyes. But actually they hear what they are reading—in their inner ear—far more than you realise.'

Unfortunately, many workplace writers are deaf to the actual sound of their words. As a result, they tend to overestimate their ability to convey nuance. A music-tapping study by Elizabeth Newton illustrated this effect by asking participants to tap out the rhythm of a well-known song and estimate how easily listeners would identify it. The tappers estimated that half of listeners would be able to tell the song from their tapping. The real figure was around 3 per cent. The tappers had the full experience of the music resounding in their heads, so the taps appeared accurate to them. The taps themselves were unintelligible.

Similarly, when you write you can hear the stresses, the rise and fall of pitch, the careful placement of emphasis, and you assume that your readers will hear them as well. Have you ever written what you thought was a witty email, only to find that a reader took offence? Chances are that the tone you heard was not actually conveyed by your words. Learn to listen to your text as your reader would. Read it aloud if you must, but make sure you are certain how it will sound before sending it.

Test the tone of your text

To help you attune your ear, compare the tone of your writing with the following scale:

The tone scale

	Tone	Text
1	Text language	Thx 4 yr txt ;-)
2	Informal	Got your note and liked it.
3	Chatty	Thanks for your note. I've read it with interest.
4	Formal yet friendly	Thank you for your letter and the comments you make.
5	Official	I have received your letter and noted the matters you raise.
6	Officialese	Receipt is acknowledged of your recent communication, whose contents have been noted.
7	Legalese	Acknowledgement is hereby made of your communication (hereinafter the 'letter') by the undersigned who has apprehended its matter.
8	19th century	Your esteemed favour to hand of the fourth ultimo; the contents of same have been duly appraised.
9	Ceremonial	Let it be hereafter promulgated that said missive has been gazetted and cognizance raised pursuant to its substance.
10	Biblical	I receiveth unto me thy epistle, and its wisdom escapeth me not.

Where does your writing score? Are you at the heavy end of the middle, somewhere between official and legalese? If so, consider whether you might be able to lighten your tone to somewhere around the 'formal but friendly' level. On the other hand, does your text sit low down on the tone scale, somewhere closer to informal? Might this be a bit too informal for your readers?

Strike a balance of formality

Striking the right tone is all a matter of balance. You don't want to be too formal and overdressed, but neither do you want to be naked. You wouldn't head out for a day on the beach in a business suit, and you wouldn't wear your bathers to work. Listen carefully. Listen out loud. Like those music tappers, you might not be conveying the tune you think you are.

Romesh certainly discovered this when he applied the tone scale to his writing. He works in a government agency processing applications for a welfare benefit. Applicants commonly do not send in all their supporting information by a legally mandated deadline, and they miss out as a result.

Romesh is genuinely sympathetic, but his hands are tied. Yet this is how he conveyed his sympathy in a form letter:

> Here in relation to this matter, as the documents were submitted subsequent to the 28 day closing date, s.22(a) requires the application to be assessed without reference to them. As this is a legislative requirement, this office cannot have any regard to this documentation in its determination.

Romesh was used to officialese, so to his inner ear this sounded warm and sympathetic. When asked to read it aloud, he was shocked at just how cold it really was. He quickly placed it at level 6 on the tone scale and rewrote it to capture the tone he had intended:

> Unfortunately, you submitted the documents after the 28-day closing date. This means that we have to assess your application without referring to them. This is a legal requirement set by section 22(a) of the Act.

KEY TIP Internal documents should be no higher than 5 on the tone scale. With documents for the public, aim at 3 to 4.

Don't overdress the text

Here is an extract from a local government letter that scores a 6 on the tone scale. The edited versions become increasingly lighter in tone. Which version best maintains its content and professionalism while also having a human touch?

	Tone	
6	55 words Officialese original	It should be noted that Council endeavours to expedite the process of approval by preparing a summary of formal submissions that have been received with respect to applications of the nature indicated by your correspondence, however submissions are able to be reviewed in complete form by Council members prior to a final decision being made.

	Tone	
5	42 words Official	I should note that Council tries to expedite the process of approval by summarising submissions received about projects of the type raised in your letter. However, every submission can be reviewed in full by Council members before a final decision is made.
4	32 words Formal but friendly	Please note that Council tries to expedite the approval process by summarising the submissions it receives about these projects. However, Council members can review all submissions in full before they make their final decision.
3	22 words Chatty	Please note that we summarise submissions to expedite the approvals. Council members can always look at the submissions before their final decision.
2	18 words Informal	We summarise submissions to speed things along, but members can always have a gander at the full thing.

Selecting the best tone is not a matter of correct or incorrect grammar. All of these versions are in grammatically acceptable English. But varying the tone changes their impact, readability, clarity and efficiency. These can make all the difference to the success of your text.

This sample comes from a letter written to Vera, a member of the public who had complained that her submission was not given enough consideration before the council ruled on a development. She felt that council members ought to read her entire text rather than a summary prepared for them by council staff. The level 6 tone of the response attempted to convey that the process was proper, but it backfired. Vera felt she was being given the bureaucratic brush-off. A level 4 tone would have been far more effective.

Too many workplace documents need to make the same shift of about two points on the tone scale. This will also improve efficiency by up to a third without sacrificing content. If you feel your readers would object to level 4, level 5 should be a safe benchmark. In many cases, you will be able to write at level 3, but by this time you will be trimming a level 6 text by close to 50 per cent, and that risks losing content and striking too informal a note. This risk increases as you move down to level 2, which most workplaces could not use.

Maintain a professional tone

Police in the Kingswood area of Bristol in the United Kingdom found this out the hard way when they used a level 1 tone to connect with local youth. They thought they would reach their intended audience by using what the *Guardian* newspaper described as an 'Ali G-style text message terminology'. They put up placards reading:

> Du ur olds knw whr U r o wot ur doin coz D bil wl tel em
>
> D bil cum arnd hre n wl vzit ur olds if ur messin bout

The community reaction was severe. A local charity director commented that 'the Police seem to be falling over themselves to appear trendy when the simple truth is a sign written in plain English would get the message across just as well, if not better'.

There is a minimum expectation of formality whenever a professional writes to the public, and crossing the line into informality risks rejection, even if the language would be acceptable in other contexts. Unfortunately, professionals tend to err too far on the other side of formality, and write too high up the scale towards officialese and legalese. Use the tone scale as a ready reckoner of your current tone and a reference point for where you should pitch your text.

The living language

Set your tone to communicate rather than to impress

Given the drawbacks of a heavy tone, why is it still so prevalent? The answer is in part historical. The institutions that established our public language deliberately chose an elevated style to reflect their social and political status. The languages of the church and the law, of the universities and of the trade guilds, were all pitched to elevate their importance. When Sir Thomas Elyot wrote the first educational text in English in 1531 to train those working at the court of Henry VIII, his dedication set much of the style to follow:

> I late consideringe (moste excellent prince and myne onely redoughted sovereign lorde) my duetie that I owe to my naturall contray with my faythe also of aliegeaunce and othe ... I am (as God juge me) violently

> stered to devulgate or sette fourth some part of my studie, trustynge therby tacquite me of my dueties to God, your hyghnesse, and this my contray. Wherfor takinge comfort and boldnesse, partly of your graces most benevolent inclination towarde the universall weale of your subjectes, partly inflamed with zele, I have now enterprised to describe in our vulgare tunge the fourme of just publike weale.

This overdressed text used many then new words drawn from French, Latin and Greek. Elyot and other officials tried to enrich the English language, but the effect of such efforts was also to separate the language of our institutions from the language of the people. This had its detractors almost from the start. Thomas Wilson in 1553 made the case for 'Plainnesse' and against what were called 'inkhorn' terms:

> Among all other lessons this should first be learned, that wee never affect any straunge ynkehorn terms, but to speak as is commonly received: neither seeking to be over fine, nor yet living over-carelesse, using our speeche as most men doe, and ordering our wittes as the fewest have done. Some seeke so far for outlandish English, that they forget altogether their mothers language. And I dare sweare this, if some of their mothers were alive, they were not able to tell what they say: and yet these fine clerkes will say, they speake in their mother tongue ...

Unfortunately, the institutions that became home to the professions tended towards Elyot rather than Wilson, overdressing their language in robes far more formal than their tasks required. This is as much the case in the corporate sector as it is in government. Many companies cling to the belief that a formal style will lift their status in their readers' eyes. Yet how, as a customer, would you react to being spoken to in this tone:

> A number of means are employed to maintain security; however, the Internet is an inherently insecure medium of information exchange, and it is incumbent upon the customer to take reasonable precautions as well. Apart from keeping confidential any password that is obtained in relation to a registration account for using parts of this website (e.g. the discussion forums), the customer should ensure that an antiviral application is in use on any computer that is employed for accessing the website; the customer should keep all virus definitions updated; and should ensure that the computer's operating system and applications are updated with any security patches immediately those become available.
>
> (107 words)

Here is a version that tries for a more human touch while retaining a professional tone:

> Unfortunately, the Internet is inherently insecure. While we use a number of methods to maintain security, you should take reasonable precautions as well. Keep confidential any password you choose for this website, and run an antiviral application on any computer you use to access our site. Please also update your virus definitions and your computer's operating system and applications with security patches as soon as they are available.
>
> (67 words)

The shift here is about two points on the scale, from almost officialese to the formal but friendly level. The second version is around 40 per cent shorter and far more readable. It informs customers of their obligations much more clearly and persuasively. Instead of being lectured at by a faceless institution, the reader should now feel part of a human dialogue.

Resist the language of power

Companies are generally more amenable to lightening their tone when selling a product, and much more resistant to it when setting out the costs and obligations they impose in return. Here, for example, is a phone company being upbeat about its service:

> Put simply, 3 is Australia's first 3G mobile telecommunications company. We were the first to bring you live, face-to-face video calling, as well as other ways to make more of your mobile, like watching full-length music videos and getting mobile Internet broadband speeds.

The tone is 3 to 4 on the scale, and the writing is direct, light and energetic. But here's the tone the company switches to when describing what it will charge:

> When you are roaming overseas and send an SMS back to Australia, you will be charged the standard SMS rate as per your current plan and, on top of this, an additional flat fee will be charged as determined by our roaming partner.

While not quite at level 6, the voice has still shifted to a heavier pitch. Too many companies adopt this two-tone strategy, being human and direct when selling, then more officious and bureaucratic about costs, contracts and warranties.

Nowhere is this more apparent than in the language of the law. Often, the tone is about as light as a verbal cudgel. Here is part of a letter from a child support agency to a company it (erroneously) believed was about to employ someone who owed child support. The company knew nothing of the case, but the stick came out anyway.

NOTICE TO PAY MONEY DIRECTLY TO THE CHILD SUPPORT REGISTRAR PURSUANT TO SECTION 72A

Child Support (Registration & Collection) Act 1988

I DO BY THIS NOTICE REQUIRE Company XYZ being a person

(a) by whom money is due or accruing, or may become due to; or

(b) who holds, or may subsequently hold, money for or on account of; or

(c) who holds, or may subsequently hold, money on account of some other person for payment to; or

(d) who has authority from some other person to pay money to

JOHN SMITH

. . .

TO PAY TO THE REGISTRAR, out of each payment you are liable to pay to the child support debtor, an amount of $0.50 cents in every dollar, such amount to be paid to the Registrar no later than seven (7) days after you become liable to make payments of money to the child support debtor until the debt referred to above is satisfied.

WHERE A PERSON without reasonable excuse, refuses or fails to comply with this notice that person is guilty of an offence under subsection 72A(2) (a copy is included at the end of this notice) and liable to a penalty of $1,000.00. Subsection 72A (2) is an offence of strict liability.

This text is clearly a level 7 in tone. Lawyers and courts use it when making demands of people or companies, particularly when they might have broken the law. It is a language of power, a bullying tone intended to frighten its reader. In this case it was addressed to an innocent third party whose cooperation the agency needed to secure. It had the opposite effect.

Don't swing too far to the informal

Fortunately, there is a counteracting trend to lighten the tone of our public language. But, as with all change, early adopters sometimes take it too far. Some companies are experimenting with a highly informal style. The mobile phone company Virgin, for example, writes at level 2 to its younger audience about the safe use of chat services:

> **Be careful**: Remember, someone you meet may have a creepy identity crisis and claim to be your 16-year-old chicky soul mate, when in fact they turn out to be a 40-year-old male freak-azoid ...

This risks coming across as trying too hard. Kids are particularly suspicious of adults aping a cool style. You'd need to be certain that your customers really do use terms such as 'chicky soul mate' and 'male freak-azoid'.

Take care with email tone

Another factor helping professionals to lighten their tone is the email. This has been both a blessing and a curse. The immediacy that it provides means that many people treat emails as speech, and let go of the more formal tone of official documents. But they may move too far down the tone scale for a professional environment, and once their message is sent, it can reach thousands, even hundreds of thousands of people. Jonas Blank learned this the hard way when he was working as a summer associate for a law firm and wrote the following email to a friend:

> Congrats on the CFA. I'm sure you're about to make VP any day now.
>
> I'm busy doing jackshit. Went to a nice 2hr sushi lunch today at Sushi Zen. Nice place. Spent the rest of the day typing emails and bullshitting with people. Unfortunately, I actually have work to do—I'm on some corp finance deal, under the global head of corp finance, which means I should really peruse these materials and not be a fuckup ...
>
> So yeah, Corporate Love hasn't worn off yet ... But just give me time ...

Before he knew it, Jonas' email had circulated worldwide and he was lucky to keep his job.

The immediacy of email carries further dangers. Rather than pausing before responding to a message, you may leap onto the keyboard in the heat of the moment. The trouble is that your first response is not always the wisest. A marquee supplier in New Zealand found itself the subject of worldwide attention when a blunt email to a customer went into mass circulation. When a couple decided not to use the company's service for their wedding, they sent a polite email explaining why. The company's office manager lost control of her tone:

> Thanks for your reply. Your wedding sounded cheap, nasty and tacky anyway, so we only ever considered you time wasters.
>
> Our marquees are for upper class clients which unfortunately you are not. Why don't you stay within your class level and buy something from payless plastics instead?

The couple forwarded the email to some of their friends, and within hours it had circulated throughout the corporate world, eventually reaching tens of thousands of people in Australia and New Zealand and attracting extensive news coverage. The company lost business through the damage to its reputation, and the office manager lost her job.

Studies show that people routinely overestimate how well they can communicate via email. A journal of the American Psychological Association reported in 2005 on five separate studies testing the gap between the ability of readers to understand the humour or sarcasm in a short email and writers' confidence that it would be understood correctly. In one study, writers expected they would be understood 98 per cent of the time, when this was the case only 84 per cent of the time. Another study found the gap was 78 per cent versus 56 per cent. So take particular care with your email tone. Your reader may not hear it the way that you do.

Power tools

Work with seven elements to adjust your tone

While the tone scale gives you a ready reference point to attune your ear, sometimes shifting your tone is a lot harder than it sounds. You can hear the difference once the text is edited, but what do you look for when revising?

Research shows that seven elements seem to have a particular impact on tone.

The tone checklist

1. Personal pronouns such as 'I', 'we' and 'you'
2. Active rather than passive voice
3. Simpler words
4. Humanising words such as 'welcome' and 'please'
5. Informal elements such as contractions
6. Shorter sentences
7. Less clutter

Let's put these to work in transforming the tone of a text from an energy utility authorised to certify that electrical, gas and plumbing products meet particular standards. The readers of this document are manufacturers considering whether to obtain certification from the utility. Yet the company is selling its benefits in a level 6 tone:

> To give confidence to the view that the certified product continues to comply with certification requirements, and to support the renewal process attached to the certification, product is subjected to a regular product verification audit (PVA) and a review of the measures to control quality of product. Such audits are not designed (or funded) to provide

an exhaustive check of the product but, rather, a limited and largely visual review against the current technical specifications. It is incumbent upon the *Certificate Holder* to ensure the product remains unchanged and to seek formal application if a modification or addition is required. The Annual renewal fee for each Certificate that *AGA* invoices for at the start of each financial year includes an amount for a routine PVA (exceptional and failure audit costs excluded).

(131 words)

Let's see how this fares with the tone checklist:

	Element	Sample
1	Pronouns	None
2	Active voice	Passive expressions such as 'is subjected' and 'is required'
3	Simple words	Unnecessary officialese such as 'it is incumbent upon'
4	Welcome words	None
5	Informal elements	None
6	Short sentences	Average sentence length 33 words
7	Lack of clutter	Plenty of redundant phrases, such as 'give confidence to the view that ...'

The text scores poorly against all seven elements, so it's no wonder the tone is so formal—which gives us some hints on how to improve it:

To give you confidence that your certified product continues to comply with certification requirements, we conduct regular product verification audits (PVA) and review quality control measures. This also helps you when you need to renew the certification. Our audits don't check the product exhaustively but do review the product visually against its technical specifications. You must always ensure that the product does not change and formally apply for certification if it does. Our annual renewal fee for each certificate covers the cost of a routine PVA. We invoice this at the start of each financial year.

(96 words)

The revised passage is now at level 4 on the tone scale. It preserves the content of the original while improving efficiency by a quarter. Let's see how the seven elements changed:

	Element	Sample
1	Pronouns	Nine uses of 'you', 'your', 'we' and 'our'
2	Active voice	All verbs now in the active voice
3	Simple words	Words simplified where possible
4	Welcome words	'Please'
5	Informal elements	Probably not appropriate and are not needed
6	Short sentences	Average sentence length of 16 words
7	Lack of clutter	Text is 25 per cent shorter

When you conclude that your document is not pitched at the right level, look to adjust these seven elements. The following chapters will give you further tools for doing this.

Put people in your prose

It's no accident that the first item on the list of tone elements is the pronoun. Probably the most powerful thing you can do to adjust tone is to restore people to your writing. This is usually not difficult in the workplace. You write about clients, customers, colleagues, the public and yourself. Including them humanises your writing, and this flows through to tone.

To use pronouns effectively, be aware of the grammatical 'person' your text uses:

Person	Pronouns
First person	I, we, us, our, my
Second person	You, your
Third person	He, she, it, they, their, its

When choosing which 'person' to use, think about how you want to position your relationship with your reader. When you need to maintain a greater deal of detachment, use the third person. This distances you by referring to things 'over there', as if from an independent vantage point. The point of view you are establishing for yourself is that of an observer rather than a player in the action. You can still use pronouns, but also the actual name and titles of the people and organisations that are the actors in your workplace drama.

When you want to establish a more direct relationship, you can use both first and second person. This reveals the underlying dialogue between writers and readers more clearly. As a result, the tone becomes more inclusive and even less formal. This is appropriate when writing to customers in letters and emails, or in internal information documents such as procedures and policies. It is not always possible to use the first person singular ('I') because you are writing as part of a broader organisation. You can, however, safely opt for the first person plural ('we').

Here is an extract from an internal corporate memo about financing for an IT project. Where and who are the people in this mini-drama?

> In relation to this engagement, a number of processes were undertaken to ascertain the most suitable methodology of financing the infrastructure component of IntraConnect, on the proviso that the financing arrangement be of the nature of an operating lease or some other form of off-balance-sheet arrangement for Best Bets. In accordance with the operational period proposed for the IntraConnect service, the original project was expected to be financed either on a 6-year or 10-year term, with the 6-year option containing provisions for the extension of contract terms.
>
> (90 words)

There are neither people nor pronouns in this passage, and the writer is plodding along in the passive voice: 'were undertaken', 'was expected', 'be financed'. This is an attempt to keep a professional distance, but it goes too far. It is also partly dishonest, because the writer was in fact a player in the story. Here is the same text with its people restored:

> We assessed the best way to finance the infrastructure for IntraConnect using an off-balance-sheet arrangement such as an operating lease. This assumed Best Bets would finance the service for 6 or 10 years, in line with IntraConnect's proposed operating period. Under the contract, we could extend the 6-year option to 10 years.
>
> (52 words)

We still have an institutional voice here, but it is far more human than the original, achieved by using active voice and just two pronouns and one organisation name. Simplifying and shortening the text helped as well. It is now clearer, easier to read and over 40 per cent more efficient. It certainly doesn't sound too informal or unprofessional.

So Thomas Wilson's advice from 1553 still holds true today: 'speak as is commonly received: neither seeking to be over fine, nor yet living over-carelesse'. While workplace writing for many years was pitched in an over-fine tone, you should not replace this with one that is over-careless. Try not to stray from the middle range of the tone scale.

9 Grammar

At a glance

The toolbox

- Overcome your grammar phobia 170
- Remember the major word classes 171
- Learn which proper nouns still take a capital letter 172
- Prefer concrete to abstract nouns 173
- Use verbs to make your writing precise 173
- Stick mainly to the simple tenses 174
- Embrace modal auxiliary verbs 175
- Avoid the verb 'to be' 175
- Add adjectives and adverbs for detail and colour 176
- Use a balanced proportion of the open-class words 178

The living language

- Understand the difference between grammar and usage 179
- Resist attempts to fix the tongue 180
- Use a more modern grammar 182

Power tools

- Use pronouns to tighten your expression 183
- Understand determiners to help those using English as a second language 184
- Use conjunctions for effective joinery, even at the start of a sentence 185
- Use single prepositions rather than wordy phrases 186

The toolbox

Overcome your grammar phobia

You may have taken a deep breath as you turned the page to read this chapter. There's no use denying it: as a topic, grammar rates right up alongside a colonoscopy. This might be because of the way the old school used to teach it—in a dull, rigid, even moralistic fashion. This often involved simplistic rules such as the prohibition on the word 'got', a rule intended to encourage kids to expand their vocabulary. Children developing language skills use a narrow range of verbs, and 'got' is often overdone: 'I got up and then I got to school and then we got to the pool and I got to swim the relay ...'

But the old school had a powerful way of enforcing its point. Some teachers forced an entire class to write the word 'got' on a piece of paper, then marched them out into the school yard, dug a hole, lined them up, and buried their pages in a mass grave. The psychological message was pretty clear to a 10-year-old—get your grammar wrong and you'll be buried alive!

The problem with those old, simplistic rules is that nobody updated them. If they were ever justified in primary school, by the time you are in university or the workforce there are indeed some valid uses for the word 'got'. But many professionals cling to the ban, often without knowing its original point, let alone when they should discriminate.

More recent generations of graduates face an even worse problem. When education authorities twigged to the problems with old-school grammar, they removed it from the curriculum altogether. So our younger troops have little or no grammar and sometimes enter the workforce believing it is obsolete. As a result, they are ill-prepared for workplace writing, because they do not have any practical tools to evaluate their work. To their great frustration, they soon find themselves working for older managers who edit their writing using the rigid rules of the old school.

This grammar generation gap is costing workplaces a packet because it causes conflict and inefficiency without improving the final product. In these circumstances, grammar offers, as it always has, a practical way of helping you to assess your writing. It is simply the conscious study of how we combine words into meaningful sentences. We wouldn't send people out to be practising chemists without teaching them to distinguish between an element and a compound. Yet we've been sending graduates into the workforce with small understanding of what makes up a sentence, let alone what makes one effective.

Remember the major word classes

We will lay some foundations by looking at the basic labels that describe what words do in a sentence. Modern grammars identify eight main classes, grouped into two—open- and closed-class words:

Open classes	**Closed classes**
Noun	Pronoun
Verb	Preposition
Adjective	Conjunction
Adverb	Determiner

The open classes are the content words that generate the core meaning of every sentence. I could use these words to describe what is happening now:

> are holding reading book will rapidly explain enjoyment usefulness grammar offers

This is not a grammatically complete statement, but you probably got the joke. That means that the core meaning of my text succeeded. To complete the sentence, we need to add some functional closed-class words. These form the scaffolding that supports the open classes:

> you and a which the and that

We need these words to complete the statement:

> You are holding and reading a book which will rapidly explain the enjoyment and usefulness that grammar offers.

The other reason we separate these groups is that open-class words have open-ended membership. When we add new words to the language, they tend to come into one of the open classes. The closed classes, on the other hand, are rather resigned to their lot in life and have largely been the same for centuries.

We will work mainly with the open classes because they are the most important to your style. Unfortunately, they aren't always easy to define.

You can identify them partly by their form and partly by what they tend to mean. But you will also need to look at the way a word functions in a sentence. Sometimes, the same word can have different functions:

Hand me the *report* (noun—an object)

We must *report* to management (verb—an action)

We'll begin with these two parts of speech—nouns and verbs—as they are at the heart of every sentence. A noun names a person, creature, place, thing, activity, condition or idea. When infants begin to speak, their first words name the world around them, often starting with nouns like 'mama' or 'papa'. There are several ways we can classify these naming words, but for professional writing the most important categories come in pairs.

Learn which proper nouns still take a capital letter

The first pairing resolves one of the most frustrating grammar arguments in the workplace: when to use a capital letter. These first came into English to mark the start of a chapter, and then to show the start of a sentence. Then in the 16th century, the suggestion emerged that we use capitals to distinguish 'important' nouns such as names. The trend became so popular that over the next 100 years, some writers were capitalising every noun. By the 19th century, however, capitalising mania had narrowed down to the start of sentences and for proper nouns that name one unique person, place, publication, title, date or institution:

Australia continues to reject the *Kyoto Protocol.*

Jonathan Creek will not address the shareholders.

We assess our graduate intake in *November* each year.

Common nouns, on the other hand, do not take a capital letter because they name a general, rather than a unique, class of thing.

Our *students* intend to apply to several *universities.*

Small *business* is struggling to pay *taxes* and *charges.*

Our *managers* supported the new government *structure.*

When you are writing about people, institutions or positions in a plural sense, such as *students*, *managers* and *universities*, you don't need a capital. Nor do you need to capitalise a word such as *government* when it is not referring to one specific government, or when it is describing another noun.

But just when you think you have a handle on capitalising nouns, they are currently going through another shake-up. As with the trend to minimise punctuation, we've been using fewer capitals in recent years. We now tend to reserve them for the full title of an organisation or position, and use lower case in a short title that derives from it. So it is 'Minister for Health' in the full title, but 'the minister' for the shortened title. Needless to say, ministers don't always agree with this trend.

Prefer concrete to abstract nouns

The second pair of noun types is far more important for the effectiveness of your writing. Concrete nouns name physical, material things:

> The proposal is to lay 1000 km of *pipeline*.
>
> *Amanda Smith* will conduct our assessment.

Abstract nouns, on the other hand, name phenomena, such as concepts, processes, emotions and ideas, that have no physical qualities.

> The *proposal* is to lay 1000 km of pipeline.
>
> Amanda Smith will conduct our *assessment*.

If you use a high proportion of abstract nouns, your writing can have a dense, vague and abstract quality. If you include a higher proportion of concrete nouns, the writing will usually have more vividness and energy.

Use verbs to make your writing precise

The second most important part of speech is the verb. At its simplest, a verb is a word of action. After infants start naming the world around them, they begin to use verbs to interact with it: 'give', 'want', 'come', 'like'. Verbs are the engines of your sentences, propelling readers through your writing while telling precisely what is happening.

Most verbs specify the action a particular noun is doing, often to a second noun:

The company *employs* new graduates every February.

Phonetica regularly *advertises* its new line rental rates.

The nouns 'company' and 'Phonetica' are 'doing' the verbs 'employs' and 'advertises'. So far, so good. But verbs have extra layers of complexity that the other word classes can only dream about.

Stick mainly to the simple tenses

First, verb forms change to convey not just the action, but the time it is happening in. English has evolved a complex structure of 'tenses' that break time into precise portions.

Tense	Example	Time frame examples
Present		
Simple present	I consider	Action happening now
Present continuous	I am considering	Action happening now and ongoing
Present perfect	I have considered	Past action, possibly over a number of points in time, which can continue into the present
Present perfect continuous	I have been considering	Action happening continually from the past to the present and possibly ongoing
Past		
Simple past	I considered	Past action, often as a single event
Past continuous	I was considering	Action over a span of time in the past
Past perfect	I had considered	Action during a past period that stopped in the past, but sometimes also continues
Past perfect continuous	I had been considering	Action happening continuously in the past
Future		
Simple future	I will consider	A future action, often as a single event
Future continuous	I will be considering	A future action over a span of time
Future perfect	I will have considered	A future action completed by a particular time

Tense	Example	Time frame examples
Future perfect continuous	I will have been considering	A future continuous action completed by a particular time

The strength of this part of our grammar is that you can be ultra-precise about when the action you are reporting takes place. But don't over-complicate your tenses without cause, and stick mainly to the simple tenses in each time frame.

Embrace modal auxiliary verbs

The precision of verbs doesn't stop with tense. We can add some supporting verbs to supply even more information. The first of these are the modals, words such as: 'can', 'could', 'may', 'might', 'must', 'shall', 'should', 'will' and 'would'. These never stand alone, but are used to indicate the mode of another verb: how or under what conditions—of permission, possibility, ability, necessity, likelihood or obligation—the main verb's action happens.

Our staff *must* attend training sessions.

The new procedures *should* reduce waiting times in our stores.

Modal verbs are your friends. They give you great scope to qualify the action in your writing. You can use them to be a bit more diplomatic, or to modify something you might not be sure about.

Our staff *could* attend training sessions.

The new procedures *might* reduce waiting times in our stores.

Avoid the verb 'to be'

There are three other supporting verbs, but these have a double life. They can support another verb but can also function independently. As support verbs, 'to do' helps make questions, 'to have' forms the perfect tenses, and 'to be' forms part of the passive voice.

Did you review the customer complaint?

I *have* reviewed the customer complaint.

The customer complaint *was* reviewed.

The first two are essential to our grammar when we need to ask questions or adjust tense. But beware of the verb 'to be'. This is the most overdone verb in the English language. Most people don't even recognise it as a verb, simply because they intuitively grasp that it doesn't represent action. Yet it functions in our grammar like any other verb, working its way through all the tenses:

Person	Present	Past	Perfect	Future	Continuous
I	am	was	have / had been	will be	am being
You	are	were	have / had been	will be	are being
He/ she	is	was	has / had been	will be	is being
It	is	was	has / had been	will be	is being
We	are	were	have / had been	will be	are being
They	are	were	have / had been	will be	are being

The action this verb represents is the rather abstract action of 'existing'.

The new policy *is* a vast improvement.

The customer *was* late with his payment.

Unlike modals, the verb 'to be' is not your friend and it will deaden your text. Kill 'to be' wherever you can and replace it with something more vigorous. Which verbs sound more vital and alive to you?

am was were be being is are

assess review consider write present speak

Nouns and verbs are the core of our grammar. Just about every sentence boils down to things doing actions. Our next two parts of speech are also important because they give us more information about these first two.

Add adjectives and adverbs for detail and colour

An adjective is a describing word that supplies more information about a noun. It tells us what kind of noun it is, how many there are, or which one it is. Most commonly, adjectives come immediately before the nouns they qualify.

Corporate leaders gave their views about the *white* paper.

The *new* procedures have produced *minor* changes in *operational* statistics.

Adjectives can also come after some verbs, particularly the verb 'to be':

I am *happy*.

I remain *upset*.

Adjectives have an obvious practical function, but they can introduce a subjective element that is not always appropriate for workplace writing:

The customer is a *hysterical* man with an *appalling* attitude.

Of course, adjectives can for the same reason give your writing some life and colour, so try to strike a balance. Under-use leaves your text dry and bloodless.

Just as adjectives qualify nouns, most adverbs modify verbs, although they can modify other words as well. They usually tell us how, when, where, why and for what purpose an action is happening. Unlike with adjectives, however, you have a lot more flexibility about where you place an adverb. Sometimes it can come before, and sometimes after, the verb.

The new approach *effectively* eliminated pay roll errors.

The 2005 level increased *slightly* in 2006.

The key to placing adverbs is to throw emphasis where it best supports your meaning. Notice that moving the adverb can change the sense of the sentence.

The new approach eliminated pay roll errors *effectively*.

The 2005 level *slightly* increased in 2006.

All these versions are grammatically correct. They just say different things.

Like adjectives, adverbs add life and colour, so much so that officialese shuns them. You can read hundreds of pages of an organisation's writing without encountering a single adverb of quality. Officialese authors would rather write inefficient phrases such as 'provide consistency in the administration of' instead of 'administer consistently', and 'on an annual basis' instead of 'annually'.

Use a balanced proportion of the open-class words

Now let's apply all of this to a practical purpose: evaluating your writing. The open-class words are important not just because they are the core meaning words, but also because by changing their form you can change them from one part of speech to another.

Verb	Noun	Adjective	Adverb
to decide	decision	decided	decidedly
to consider	consideration	considerate	considerately
to identify	identity	identifiable	identifiably
to approve	approval	approved	approvingly
to succeed	success	successful	successfully
to provide	provision	provided	provisionally
to suggest	suggestion	suggestive	suggestively
to expect	expectation	expected	expectedly
to respond	response	responsive	responsively

Such shifts are the key to unlocking your writing style. Dead and dreary workplace writing tends to use a high proportion of nouns and verbs, few adjectives, and almost no adverbs. More importantly, abstract nouns outweigh concrete nouns, and the verb 'to be' is run almost to death. Let's look at a sample, focusing solely on the open-class words:

> The division understands that the terms and conditions of appointment were
> noun verb noun noun noun aux
>
> discussed by the Board in a thorough manner and it was noted that the
> verb noun adjective noun aux verb
>
> consultant was remunerated preparation fees.
> noun aux verb adjective noun

This is a total of eight nouns, seven verbs and auxiliary verbs, two adjectives and no adverbs. Read it aloud and you can hear how dull it sounds. Now level the playing field:

> The division understands that the Board thoroughly discussed contract
> noun verb noun adverb verb adjective

conditions, and noted that the company paid the consultant preparation fees.
noun verb noun verb noun adjective noun

Now we have a more even balance: six nouns, four verbs, two adjectives and one adverb. We've got rid of three instances of the verb 'to be' and reduced the proportion of abstract nouns. Read it aloud and hear the shift in tone.

This is ultimately the point of learning about grammar. It can help you to adjust the balance between different kinds of words and tilt your writing in different directions. The style you choose will depend on your audience. If you are writing a technical paper for a scientific journal, you will have a higher proportion of abstract nouns and more instances of the verb 'to be'. If you are writing about the same subject to the public, you will need to reduce these elements. The first approach isn't wrong, nor the second one right. Each uses a style that will do the job for its intended readers. Knowing your grammar will help you understand what makes up each style.

The living language

Understand the difference between grammar and usage

The flexibility of our grammar makes our language very adaptable, and English speakers are constantly pushing its boundaries to meet their needs. We've always been open to new words, and when we first coin or borrow them, they tend to come into the language as nouns. If they pass the test of time, we then start to use them as verbs, before working them into adjectives and adverbs as well.

Sports commentators are very good at introducing these changes. During the 2004 Olympic games coverage, there was a mild outcry over the use of the word 'medal' as a verb, as in 'the relay team should *medal* in this event'. One commentator observed that a competitor's form had been so good 'she ought to *podium* tonight. Remember that she *silvered* at the Sydney games.'

These usages sound like fingernails down a blackboard to some, but there is nothing theoretically wrong with them. They are perfectly feasible in our grammar, and apply a process that has been going on for centuries. One generation's barbarism becomes the next generation's common usage. This is the essential difference between grammar, the study of the underlying systems of rules that govern a language and usage, the acceptability of certain words and styles of expression to a particular community. It is also where the difference lies between descriptive grammarians who track the language as it is actually used, and prescriptive grammarians, who insist that it adhere to certain rules. The old school was prescriptive and tried to dictate usage. This was always going to fall out of step with language as it evolved.

Think about some noun–verb shifts that have happened in your recent memory. The noun 'text' for most of its life referred to written or printed words, often with the sense of an original or authoritative source. Then came the mobile phone, and suddenly we needed a verb to convey the action of sending text by instant message service. Among the mass of users, the verb 'texting' has gained rapid currency and acceptance. For many, this can't possibly be correct grammar simply because it is unfamiliar. Yet it follows conventions that we've used in every age.

It is hard to predict which words will catch on and which ones won't, and the experts regularly get it wrong. The willingness of writers and speakers to reshape our language is the great glory of English. It is why, when we cast back even a few hundred years, English starts to seem rather foreign.

Resist attempts to fix the tongue

The constant flux of English also gave rise to the prescriptivism of old-school grammar, to the belief that we should set the tongue in a fixed position. One of the first to argue that English needed to be fixed in place was Jonathan Swift, who lobbied for the need to 'correct', 'improve' and 'ascertain' (meaning to fix by rules) the language so that it would be 'more durable than Brass and such as posterity may read a thousand years hence'.

The real world was not having a bar of it. English flowed on, on the tongues and through the pens of its users, a dynamic and evolving language. But Swift's ideas did not die entirely, and support grew within the school system for instruction in formal grammar. A spate of works emerged to lay down what correct English should be, and many of the rules of the old school were born. A seminal text was Robert Lowth's *A Short Introduction to Grammar* (1762), which first recorded the old school's pet prohibitions: you can't end a sentence with a preposition, or say 'different to' instead of 'different from', or use two negatives because they cancel each other out. Lowth's book went through 22 editions in 40 years and influenced grammar texts for the next two centuries. It was embraced particularly by a rising middle class wanting to improve its social position. Knowledge of 'proper' grammar became a touchstone of social status.

When trying to improve and fix the language, our grammarians turned to another language as their ideal model: Latin. This is understandable, as grammar, originally a Greek discipline, had been passed down through Latin scholars such as Donatus and Priscian. After the Dark Ages, grammar was re-established in England in the 16th century by Erasmus, who prepared a work on the parts of speech of classical Latin with William Lily, the headmaster of St Paul's School, London. Before long, Henry VIII decreed this to be the Latin grammar text for all schools.

So it is not surprising that when Enlightenment grammarians such as Lowth turned to codifying English grammar, they tried to fit it into the mould of Latin. English was described in line with the cases and inflections of the language of Rome, even though our tongue had abandoned most of them.

Perhaps the best example of the inappropriateness of the Latin model is the split infinitive. The infinitive form of a verb in English uses the word 'to' combined with the verb—'to go'. In Latin, the infinitive uses only one word—'amare', for example, means 'to love'. The prescriptive grammarians reasoned that the infinitive should be one unit in English because that's how it was used in Latin. A rule was born that it was not correct to place an adverb between the two parts, as in 'to boldly go'.

Three centuries later, workplace managers adhere to this rule religiously without understanding that there is little technical basis for it. It even features in the affairs of state. In the 1860s, the British government telegraphed its American ambassador about a treaty it was negotiating with the US. It said that the draft terms were acceptable, but that it would 'under no circumstances endure the insertion of an adverb between the preposition and the verb'.

Use a more modern grammar

Inevitably, in the 20th century there emerged a new generation of grammarians wanting to put the discipline on a more rigorous footing. They established what is now called linguistics, which has flourished into sub-branches such as transformational grammar and psycholinguistics. These offer far more sophisticated accounts of our grammar than the traditional categories, and they have forced traditional grammar to smarten up its act. One of the results is the falling influence of the old school.

At the same time, grammar came under attack in the curriculum itself, as the educational theories of the 1960s swung the pendulum against it. In the US, the National Council of Teachers of English commissioned Charles Carpenter Fries to prepare a new work on grammar. He modestly concluded that the new 'scientific' grammar he proposed was comparable to Harvey's work on the circulation of the blood, and likened traditional grammar to the outmoded practice of 'bleeding' patients.

These trends meant that grammar was cut from the curriculum, and two generations of professionals have now entered the workforce without it. This happened right around the English-speaking world, from the UK and the US to Australia. The result is that two generations in the workforce adhere to the old school, while the two following generations are rather grammar phobic.

For both groups, grammar provides an objective framework that can help increase clarity and precision. It has already returned to the school curriculum, and you should learn to wield it in your writing. You don't need to master linguistics, just the basics of traditional grammar—sharpened up and well rid of the old-school rules.

Power tools

When you need to adapt your style to different audiences, most of the adjustments you will make will be to the open-class words. It is worth understanding the closed-class words, however, to reach an advanced level of control over your writing.

Use pronouns to tighten your expression

Pronouns are the stand-ins of grammar. When the real stars are off getting their hair and make-up done, pronouns can take the place of a noun or a noun phrase.

Pronouns are one of the few areas where English retains something of its old case system. This means that we use some forms when they are doing an action: 'I', 'you', 'he', 'she', 'it', 'we' or 'they', but we use different forms when they are receiving the action: 'me', 'you', 'him', 'her', 'it', 'us' or 'them'.

> *I* am confident *we* will continue to work with *him*.
> *I* am disappointed that *you* will not help *me* with this problem.

In Old English, nouns used to change their form depending on whether they were the noun 'doing' or 'receiving' an action. This gradually dropped out of our grammar except in their pronoun substitutes. The other place we've kept the distinction is the case of question pronouns such as *who* (doer) and *whom* (receiver). Increasingly, however, *who* is becoming common for both situations, but only time will tell whether this will flow through to other pronouns as well.

The main danger with pronouns is that on their own they do not tell your reader which noun they are standing in for. To use them effectively, you need to make sure the context reveals their meaning. If you are writing a letter and your signature is on the bottom, then you can safely use the word 'I'. If you are writing on behalf of an organisation, you might use the word 'we', and address your reader as 'you'. But danger lurks when the pronoun reference is not so obvious:

> Guilt, vengeance and bitterness can be emotionally destructive to you and your children. You must get rid of them.

Because of this danger, many workplace writers avoid pronouns. They are worried about being misunderstood, so they repeat nouns or noun phrases over and over. The effect becomes stupefying, as it lengthens sentences unnecessarily and reduces readability. As long as you are careful with your pronoun references, you will find them immensely useful for tightening your style.

Understand determiners to help those using English as a second language

Determiners are a loose group of associates linked only in that they all specify, or determine, the scope of a noun. They function a bit like adjectives, except that they take a fixed form and cannot change into nouns or verbs. Determiners are not a high priority to learn about if English is your first language, because you will have internalised the rather complicated rules that govern them and will use them without conscious effort. If English is not your first language, however, you may find these rules frustrating, as some of them are unsystematic, and you have to learn them by rote.

The best examples are articles, which help to pin down a noun when there is no adjective. Sometimes. In other cases, we don't use them at all. The definite article is 'the', and the indefinite articles are 'a' and 'an'.

> *The* customer did not follow *the* usual procedures.
>
> Increased workload presented *a* major problem for *the* team.

If you have a colleague using English as a second language, chances are you will have to correct their errors with articles, but will struggle to explain why. Turn to some of the specialist resources in the Further Reading section for help.

Some determiners overlap in form with the pronouns. Demonstrative determiners, possessive adjectives and indefinite determiners direct sentence traffic or qualify nouns in other specific ways:

> I am still waiting for *that* policy manual.
>
> The Customer Service representative will respond to *this* letter after she has assessed *these* issues.
>
> We received *your* email discussing *their* concerns.
>
> *Some* participants will not respond to *each* question.

The overlap between determiners and pronouns causes a great deal of grammatical confusion. Indeed, pick up two grammar books and you will often find competing systems of classification. It pays not to get too hung up about which word is which, and to focus on the practical implications for your writing. For native speakers of English, the use of determiners is largely internalised, so just follow your ear to guide you. The other word classes are more important for improving your style.

Use conjunctions for effective joinery, even at the start of a sentence

More functionally important are conjunctions, joining words that show the relationships between words, phrases and clauses. We can divide these into two groups. Coordinating conjunctions join things of roughly equal status: 'and', 'but', 'or', 'yet', 'nor', 'for' and 'so'. Subordinating conjunctions link a main item to a subordinate one. There are more of these because they show the more complex relationship between things:

Relationship	Example
Time	before, when, whenever, after, until, till, since, as soon as, while
Place	where, wherever
Cause	because, as, for, due to, since
Condition	if, although, unless, or, as long as, however, once
Comparison	as, than, like, as if, as though, whereas, while
Purpose	so, lest, to, whereby
Result	so, so that, such, that, in that, in case
Preference	sooner than, rather than, but
Exception	except, except that, but

Understanding the range of conjunctions will help you to draft more complex sentences with precision.

The aspect of conjunctions that gets all the attention in the workplace is the old-school rule that you can't start a sentence with one. Like the 'got' prohibition, this is a primary school rule designed to teach children to write more sophisticated sentences. Yet great writing breaks it all the time:

> And God saw every thing that he had made, and, behold, it was very good. And the evening and the morning were the sixth day.

No one would accuse the King James Bible of being ungrammatical, yet it often puts conjunctions at the start of sentences. This is not something you generally want to do, but sometimes it is just right to draw attention to something of importance. Here is an engineering firm livening up its description of a panel simulator for railway signalling:

> Working together to understand the objectives, the company believed it could create an excellent panel simulator to simulate the signalling operation. But we took it further. The simulator now includes everything a real signal operator uses.

Use single prepositions rather than wordy phrases

Prepositions help to show the relationship of a noun to another word or group of words, usually a verb. Some—'to', 'by' and 'for'—have very general applications. Others come out when we need to show spatial relationships: 'in', 'at', 'to', 'from', 'into', 'off', 'over', 'between', 'near' and 'beside'. The third type can indicate time: 'after', 'at', 'before', 'since', 'during', 'until' and 'past'.

English has tended to develop prepositions in a haphazard way. Some verbs use them and some verbs don't, and the usage doesn't follow a straightforward pattern:

> Draw a picture (no preposition).
> Draw *down* some funds.
> Draw *out* an argument.
> Draw *up* some plans.

As with determiners, native speakers of English have already internalised which prepositions to use. Non-native speakers will need to turn to some specialist references and get set for some rote learning.

In the workplace, there are two aspects of prepositions to watch for. First, always try to use a precise preposition rather than a long-winded phrase. Compare these versions:

> I am writing *in relation to* your proposal.
> I am writing *about* your proposal.
>
> I need to finish the document *in order to* make my decision.
> I need to finish the document *to* make my decision.

Second, be prepared for one of the myths of the old school—that you cannot end a sentence with a preposition. Winston Churchill is said to have reacted to a clumsy change along these lines by saying it was 'the sort of English up with which I shall not put', which is how that sentence would have to be expressed to conform to that rule. The argument against prepositions at the end of sentences was based on the definition contained in the word itself. 'Pre–position', it was argued, means that they must come before the word they qualify. While this is mostly the case, prepositions in English can and do come in other parts of a sentence, and always have.

KEY TIP Double-check any grammar 'rule' that someone learned at school.

10 Words

At a glance

The toolbox

- Make the most of the largest language 189
- Choose the shortest words that match your meaning 190
- Simplify long words when you can 190

The living language

- Understand the origins of 'Englisc' 195
- Know the influence of French in officialese English 196
- Strike a balance between authority and readability 197

Power tools

- Measure your readability 198
- Apply the Fry readability graph 199
- Write below grade 10 for a public reader 202
- Aim at grade 12 readability for a more educated reader 203
- Beware of the limits of readability tools 204

The toolbox

Make the most of the largest language

English is big. Very big. The sheer size of its vocabulary gives our language great power and scope, but it is also why so much can go wrong when you write at work.

There are about 200,000 English words in common use, yet this represents only a fraction of our total word stock. Webster's *Third New International Dictionary* lists 450,000 words, while the *Oxford English Dictionary* finds over 600,000. And that's just a straight word count. Think of all the words with more than one meaning. 'Stock', for example, can be something you use in a soup, a pole that helps you ski down a mountain, goods that you shelve in a store, shares you own in a company, a timber frame that holds people for punishment, a plant of the genus *Matthiola*, or a description of your ancestry. If you count every meaning as a separate word, then add all the scientific terms and brand names, our language grows exponentially.

A large word stock makes English a tasty language, but for practical purposes, how many words do we actually use? In 1930, Cambridge University Professor C.K. Ogden came up with what he called Basic English, a vocabulary of just 850 words. This was enough, he argued, for people new to the language to express themselves after 30 hours of learning.

At the other end, we know that classics of literature such as the works of Shakespeare or the King James Bible use thousands of words, although even the experts don't agree on exactly how many. Some put Shakespeare's vocabulary at around 16,000 words, while others count as many as 30,000; estimates on the Bible vary from 7000 to 10,000 words. This only goes to show that people who are good with words often can't count, or at least have trouble agreeing on what a word is.

So we can't be exact, but we can safely assume that in our workaday writing we wield several thousand words, many with more than one meaning, others with identical meanings, and still more that overlap in meaning. If, for example, you are writing about the launch of a new product, you might talk about when it will 'start'. You could equally use 'commence', 'begin', 'embark', 'get underway', 'activate', 'initiate', 'inaugurate', 'found' or 'launch'. You might speak of an 'opening', 'inception', 'onset', 'set-up', 'origin', 'genesis' or 'introduction'. Which is the best word to use?

Choose the shortest words that match your meaning

Use two simple tests when choosing your words: first, look for the word that conveys your meaning most exactly. This will narrow the field. Second, pick the shortest of the remaining alternatives. The word that passes both tests will give you precision and power.

The first test sounds simple enough. Is there any viable difference in meaning, for example, between 'correspondence' and 'letter'? Does one convey your intentions more exactly? If you are writing to a customer, you will want to refer to the previous correspondence if this involved a mix of letters, faxes and emails. Here the word 'letter' does not convey the whole meaning. If, on the other hand, you are replying to one letter, just call it a letter and your word choice will be short and precise.

We like to think that the long words are essential to our content, and there certainly are technical words you need to keep. But don't overdress the rest—it will only impair communication. How many of us, for example, have read this kind of language in a policy document:

> Approval of sick leave is subject to the provision of satisfactory supporting evidence. A staff member wishing to utilise sick leave shall normally inform their supervisor of their intention to do so by 10:00 a.m. on the day of utilisation. Supporting evidence may be required for absences greater than one (1) day; and/or where the staff member has exceeded three (3) single days sick leave in any one (1) year.
>
> (70 words)

The content here is not difficult, but the word choice complicates the text unnecessarily: 'provision', 'utilise', 'inform', 'intention', 'utilisation', 'required', 'absences', 'exceeded'. All have shorter alternatives that will do the job just as effectively:

> If you need to take sick leave, you should normally tell your supervisor by 10:00 a.m. on the day you are ill. We may need you to give us supporting evidence if you are away for more than one day, or for more than three single days over one year.
>
> (50 words)

Simplify long words when you can

The rule of thumb for many workplace writers seems to be that if there is a short word that conveys an idea and a long one that does the same job, go for the long one because that will sound more impressive. Of course, if that is your purpose, you may achieve that with the longer words. But if your intention is to inform or persuade a reader as efficiently as possible, then the most impressive word will not always be the best.

Let's look at some examples of overdressed words in the professions:

Officialese	Everyday expression
additional	more, extra
approximately	about, around, roughly
ascertain	find out
assistance	help
commencement	start
concerning	about
demonstrate	show
discontinue	stop, end
endeavour	try
enumerate	count, list
facilitate	help
forward	send
hereunder	under, below
identify	find, name, show
immediately	at once, now
indicate	show
inequitable	unfair
legislation	law
locate	find
methodology	method, approach
notify	tell, inform
notwithstanding	even though, despite
numerous	many
otherwise	or
particulars	details
prioritise	rank
purchase	buy
regarding	about
remuneration	pay, wages, fee
remainder	rest

Officialese	Everyday expression
represents	is
request	ask
subsequent	next, later
sufficient	enough
terminate	stop, end, finish
undertake	do, agree, promise
upon	on
utilisation	use
whilst	while

Few of these words have any technical meaning, and the everyday substitutes are much sharper. Of course, if we were only using a few words at a time, the gain in efficiency would be small, but over a whole document it adds up. You can see this more clearly when moving from words to phrases:

Officialese	Everyday expression
20 jobs on a full-time basis	20 full-time jobs
according to our records	our records show
assist in the resolution of	help resolve
at the conclusion of	at the end
at this stage / at this point in time	now
due to the fact that	because
expenditure that is of a capital nature	capital expenditure
for the purpose of	for
has the capability to	is able to, can
have a liability to	must
in a situation where	where, when, if
in a timely manner	on time, promptly
in accordance with	in line with, under
in addition to this	also
in advance of	ahead of, before
in conjunction with	with
in order to	to
in recent times	recently
in relation to	about, for, to

Officialese	Everyday expression
in the absence of	without
in the amount of \$x	\$x
in the event that	if
in the immediate future	soon
in the normal course of events	normally, usually
in your correspondence dated 16 March	in your 16 March letter
is of the view that	thinks, believes, considers
is reliant upon	relies on
is responsible for managing	manages
it is anticipated that this will resolve	this should resolve
it is incumbent upon you	you must
it would be appreciated if	please
on a quarterly basis	quarterly
over a four-year period	over four years
prior to the commencement of	before starting
the purpose of this report is to outline	this report outlines
the risks associated with	the risks of
the vast majority of	most, almost all
to the extent that	if

Here, you are not just shortening words, but shedding them. There is a direct relationship between shorter words, improved readability, and greater efficiency. Let's look at a paragraph typical of a government department replying to a member of the public:

> *In accordance with your* request, and in *consideration of the* fact *that significant time has elapsed, it is incumbent upon you* to *facilitate the identification* of the certificate. It *would be appreciated if* you would *ascertain and forward* this information *in a timely manner.*
>
> (44 words)

The italicised words do not have technical meaning that makes them essential, but they generate a stuffy, formal, bureaucratic tone. All this passage means is:

> To meet your request, and because of the delay, we need you to find and send us a copy of your certificate as soon as possible.
>
> (26 words)

This keeps its content while maintaining a professional tone. Of course, there is nothing grammatically wrong with the original, but the ornate dress impairs its purpose. As Ernest Gowers put it in *Plain Words*: 'good English can be defined simply as English which is readily understood by the reader. To be clear is to be efficient; to be obscure is to be inefficient.'

KEY TIP Keep a list of formal words and their everyday equivalents to simplify your style.

Recent decades have seen growing evidence of the inefficiency of much writing in the professions. The edited passage above is 40 per cent shorter than the original. Think about the documents in your own workplace. Imagine reading up to 40 per cent fewer words every time. Then add up all the people who read your documents. The time savings can be enormous.

Despite these benefits, for many workplace writers letting go of the big words is tantamount to giving up their authority. Yet there is another kind of power to embrace: the power of short words. Great writers and effective leaders have always known this. This is why Winston Churchill in 1940 took time out—in the middle of the Battle of Britain—to write a memo to all civil servants imploring them to adopt a simple style:

> Let us have an end to such phrases as these: 'It is also of importance to bear in mind the following considerations ...' or, 'Consideration should be given to the possibility of carrying into effect ...' Most of these woolly phrases are mere padding, which can be left out altogether, or replaced by a single word. Let us not shrink from using the short, expressive phrase, even if it is conversational.

The living language

If the benefits of a simpler style are so obvious, why isn't there a lot more of it about? To understand this, you need to know something of the history of our language. Officialese has been deeply entrenched in our institutions, not just for decades but for centuries.

English is something of a mongrel tongue: part Germanic, part French and part Scandinavian, with words drawn from as far afield as Hindi, Persian and Pawnee. Yet the language of the professions privileges the Latinate French of the 11th century. We too often reject the real-world mongrel in favour of a highly primped French poodle. The poodle might impress, but the working dog will get the job done.

Understand the origins of 'Englisc'

English was originally a Germanic language, originating from parts of what are now Denmark and northern Germany. It was born out of a military power vacuum. The Romans ruled the Celtic speakers of Britain for over 300 years, but when the legions withdrew in AD 410 the Celts were suddenly vulnerable to the Picts and the Scots on their borders. They had probably relied too much on the Romans for both statecraft and military muscle, for their solution was to invite the Jutes over to drive out their enemies.

In return, the Celts offered the Jutes the Island of Thanet off the coast of Kent. The Jutes decided they liked the look of the rest of Kent as well, and started to remove the Celts by force. Word got around, and in the decades to come, the Jutes were joined by Saxons in the south and the west. By the middle of the sixth century, along came the Angles on the east coast. It is hard to be exact about who settled where and when, but what is clear is that the invaders referred to their mutually understandable dialects as 'Englisc', and by around AD 1000 to their land as 'Englaland'.

Then the invaders were themselves invaded by the Danes. In a series of raids during the ninth century, 'Englaland' was reduced to a part of Wessex, and the language looked like being overrun. Then, the Saxon King Alfred put together some 2000 men and, if we are to believe their account of it, routed a Danish force of 5000 who were in a superior position on a hillside. This led to a treaty and the division of Britain into English and Danish areas, but the see-sawing conflict continued, melding languages and dialects. Our vocabulary bonanza began, and persists today in the speech and accents of northern (Danish) and southern (Saxon) England.

Know the influence of French in officialese English

'Englisc' had survived its first five centuries of conquest in part because it shared common roots with the languages of the invaders. But the next invader spoke a different tongue, and it is the one that gives us our officialese. Norman French evolved from the language of the Gauls, but was highly influenced by Latin. After the Danish line of kings had petered out in England, the Saxon Harold claimed the throne. His second cousin, William, Duke of Normandy, also claimed the title, and in 1066 William triumphed at the Battle of Hastings.

The Battle of Hastings greatly reduced the English nobility, and William ruthlessly finished the job. He replaced everyone in positions of power in the aristocracy, the church, the military, the government, the law and the academy with French-speaking supporters. By 1072, only one of the 12 English earls was an Englishman, and he only lasted another four years.

The Doomsday Book records that over half the country was put into the hands of just 190 men, and half of that was given to just 11, few of whom spoke a word of 'Englisc'. The result was that French swiftly supplanted English as the language of record, the law, the academy, the local administration, and high culture. Yet over 90 per cent of the population continued to speak English, setting a sharp divide between the language of power and the common tongue.

Numbers, of course, would eventually tell, particularly after King John lost Normandy to Phillip of France in 1204. A hundred years of war with France gave English the opportunity it needed to restore its social status. Over the next two centuries, those in positions of power increasingly came to see themselves as English, and restoration of the language followed. In 1362, the Chancellor for the first time opened the Parliament in English. The proceedings of the Sheriff's Court in London used English from 1356, and the *Statute of Pleading* of 1362 made English the official language of all pleadings, debates and judgments throughout the realm.

By 1388, reports from towns and guilds to Parliament started to appear in English. When Henry IV deposed Richard II in 1399, the proceedings were in English. When Henry V wrote to his subjects of his success at Agincourt, he did so in English. He had already decreed that the Signet Office, the centre of government administration, use English.

The main engine of government paperwork, the Chancery, then had the task of standardising written English.

By the time of Chaucer, English was very different to the language of the Anglo-Saxons. It was suffused with about 25 per cent French vocabulary. Three centuries of official French had flowed into all walks of life, and remain with us today. Yet our institutions did not relinquish the language of power lightly. Officialese uses as much as 50 per cent Latinate French, and this is the root cause of all those long words. Their use has been passed down through our institutions, not just decade to decade, but century to century.

This is why the worst of our professional writing lives in our oldest institutions: in government, law, the academy and commerce. Their French poodle diction is well out of kilter with the living tongue, and that's why it communicates so poorly.

Strike a balance between authority and readability

The language of the Norman conquerors is certainly alive and well in this regulation explaining a worker's allowance:

> For the purposes of section 5(10) of the *Accident Compensation Act 1985*, the prescribed rate for an allowance for accommodation paid or payable to a worker by that worker's employer for accommodation expenses necessarily incurred by the worker in the course of his or her employment where the worker is absent from his or her headquarters overnight is $130.00 in respect of every night for which the worker is absent from the headquarters.
>
> (73 words)

Look at all the French-derived words asserting status and authority: 'purpose', 'section', 'accident', 'compensation', 'prescribed', 'allowance', 'accommodation', 'employer', 'expense', 'necessarily', 'incurred', 'course', 'absent', 'quarter' and 'respect'. Invariably they are also the long ones. By simplifying the vocabulary, we can express the same text as:

> Under section 5(10) of the *Accident Compensation Act 1985*, the allowance that an employer must pay to a worker for overnight accommodation that the worker needs while working away from head office is $130 a night.
>
> (36 words)

Notice we haven't thrown away the French words altogether. We need to keep 'section', 'accident', 'compensation', 'employer', 'allowance' and 'accommodation'. Many French words did not have equivalents in Anglo-Saxon, or replaced the Anglo-Saxon word completely. But we overdressed the poodle with 'prescribed', 'expense', 'necessarily', 'incurred', 'course', 'absent' and 'respect'. In striking a better balance, we have improved readability and conveyed the content in half the words.

Power tools

Measure your readability

Understanding the history of English can help you let go of long words you don't need and make your writing more efficient and readable. Great writers have always understood this. You can certainly find plenty of short words in Shakespeare:

> Shall I compare thee to a summer's day?
> Thou art more lovely and more temperate:
> Rough winds do shake the darling buds of May,
> And summer's lease hath all too short a date.

Almost 85 per cent of the words here have only one syllable, yet no one would accuse Shakespeare of 'dumbing down' his text.

Of course, that's all very well if you are Shakespeare. For lesser mortals, knowing when you have the balance right is easier said than done. This is why scholars have invested nearly a century of effort in developing readability tools to tackle the task. Their promise is a seductive one: an objective, consistent measure of how easy a text will be to read.

Over 1000 studies have looked at just about every conceivable element of language and 'correlated' each with the results of comprehension tests for particular texts. They established that two factors are strongly associated with reading difficulty:

1. The average length of words
2. The average length of sentences

The intuitive explanation for this finding goes something like this. When people read, they do not interpret one character at a time, one word after another. Rather, they mentally snatch groups of words. When writers use too many long words, and combine them in long sentences, those mental snatches get harder to lift. This asks our readers to bring greater skill, higher concentration and more time to their reading. If they cannot or will not do this, our readers may not get our meaning.

Apply the Fry readability graph

You can see these two elements at play in the Fry readability graph, named after its author, Edward Fry, director of the Reading Centre at Rutgers University in the US. Fry estimates the average length of words by counting the number of syllables or beats in each. His 1977 graph plots the number of syllables per 100 words on one axis, and the number of sentences per 100 words on the other. The point at which these two intersect tells us the approximate grade level a reader would need to read a passage once and understand most of it.

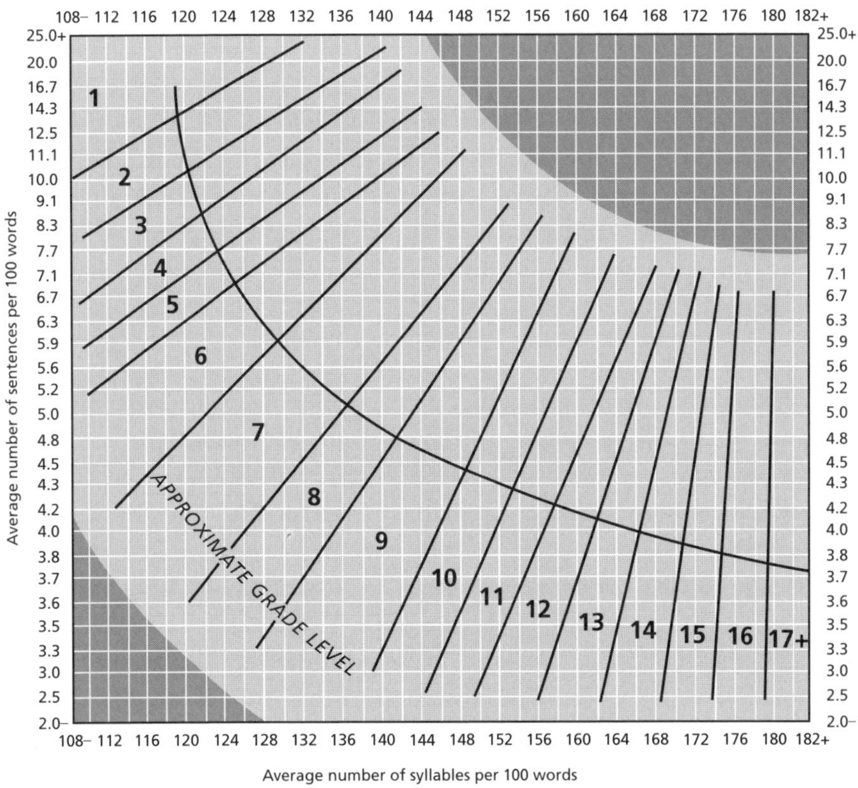

Note that the grade level does not represent the age of your reader. Grade 12, for example, represents 12 years of education, which means a 17- or 18-year-old just finishing high school or starting university. This is about the level of style that a newspaper such as the *Australian*, the *Age* or the *Sydney Morning Herald* writes to. This also strikes a good balance for most workplace writing.

How to use the Fry graph

1	Select three passages from different parts of a document.
2	Count 100 words from the beginning of a sentence. Don't include tables, bulleted lists, charts or headings.
3	Count the number of sentences in the sample to the nearest decimal place.
4	Count the number of syllables or beats. For example, 'grade' has one beat, 'tested' has two beats, and 'considered' has three. If you are unsure, speak the word aloud. Mark all of the syllables, and count them. For numbers and initialisations count one syllable for each letter or number.
5	Calculate the average sentence length and syllables for all three passages. Plot the average on the Fry graph and find the grade level for the document.

Let's apply the Fry graph to a common type of document from the world of accounting. For brevity, we will take just one extract, but when applying this to your own work, you should use three 100-word passages to get a statistically valid average. The text is from a covering letter to an audit report sent by an accounting firm to a client to explain the limits of its work.

> We have performed the procedures agreed with you as detailed in the written instructions of 1 May 2006 and described hereunder with respect to the company's procedure in relation to the authorisation of capital expenditure in connection with the James Place project. Our engagement was undertaken in accordance with Australian Auditing Standards applicable to agreed-upon procedure engagements. The responsibility for determining the adequacy or otherwise of the procedures agreed to be performed is that of the directors. The procedures performed were solely performed to assist you in ensuring the authorisation of capital expenditure in relation to James Place project was correctly adhered to.
>
> (104 words)

You probably found yourself tuning out as you were reading. Give it another go. How many times do you have to read it until you are certain of what it is saying? Perhaps you experience the same thing at work, having to read and reread documents before you are sure of their content. The chances are that your reading skills are not at fault, but that the writer's expression was far more complex than the subject demanded.

There are just short of four sentences per 100 words in this passage and over 190 syllables, which is actually off the graph altogether. This places the text at grade 17+, meaning a reader needs at least 17 years of education—a postgraduate reading level—to be sure of understanding it after reading it once. This doesn't suggest you can't understand it without a doctorate, but that you will spend more time and concentration than you need to in doing so. It is likely that the busy company directors the letter was written for would skim through it and miss some or most of its meaning. The writing is not doing its job.

Fortunately, the Fry rating also points out how you can improve the readability of the letter, by simplifying some words, shedding syllables and breaking up sentences:

> We have reviewed the way the company authorised capital spending on the James Place project to help you assess whether it used the correct process. The audit method, which we describe below, was in line with your written instructions of 1 May 2006. Our work complies with Australian Auditing Standards for a procedure engagement. This means your directors will need to judge for themselves whether the methods we agreed to were adequate.
>
> (72 words)

How much easier is this text to follow? On the Fry graph, the number of syllables per 100 words is now 157, within 5.5 sentences. Instead of falling off the scale, the text scores grade 11, making it clearer and more accessible for the client. There is an important qualification covering this audit work, and if the directors did not understand it they might have made a poor decision in response. This kind of example explains why the Royal Commission investigating the collapse of the insurance giant HIH called for plain English to be mandatory in audit reports. The text being about one-third shorter cannot hurt either.

Test the Fry graph method with a document of your own and see where you score. If, like many professionals at work, you find you are writing at grade 15 or over, it's time to work on your readability. Just how far you take this will depend on who your readers are.

Write below grade 10 for a public reader

If you are writing for the public, you should probably aim below grade 10 readability. This is about the level that news services such as United Press International and Associated Press in the US have used as their benchmark. With the help of readability experts such as Rudolph Flesch, American newspapers during the fifties and sixties reduced the average reading grade for front-page stories from grade 16 to grade 11. This helped them boost circulation, advertising and profits.

Flesch was among the first and perhaps the most influential of the readability experts, and his 1949 study *The Art of Readable Writing* set out a simple formula to assess readability. Some find it easier to use than the Fry graph because you don't need to refer to a graph for your score.

> **Reading ease** = 206.835 minus (1.015 × average sentence length) minus (84.6 × average syllables per word)

This gives you a number you can then place on a scale of difficulty:

Reading ease score	Style	Estimated reading grade
0 to 30	Very difficult	Postgraduate
30 to 50	Difficult	Grade 13 to 16
50 to 60	Fairly difficult	Grade 10 to 12
60 to 70	Standard	Grade 8 to 9
70 to 80	Fairly easy	Grade 7
80 to 90	Easy	Grade 6
90 to 100	Very easy	Grade 5

Flesch's work kicked off several decades of readability work in the American military, which had an understandable need for clear instructions for operating equipment. Here readability is more than a matter of workplace frustration—if readers get it wrong they can die. The army found that the average soldier had grade 9 reading skills, so it needed to pitch its texts at that level.

An adapted version of Flesch's work, the Flesch–Kincaid formula, is still the official readability standard in the US armed services, the Internal Revenue Service and the social services administration. You will find a version of this within some word-processing software, but don't trust it—it can only calculate as far as grade 12.

Aim at grade 12 readability for a more educated reader

If you are writing for a reader with a university education, you can use a more complex style with some safety, but try to keep your readability to a maximum of grade 12. Your colleagues won't thank you for making the text harder than necessary to follow, but they will thank you for the productivity that readability brings.

A study by the Victorian Law Reform Commission gave two groups of lawyers different copies of the Takeovers Code: the traditional version and a version in plain English. Both were able to understand the document, but those with the more readable version did so in one-third to one-half less time than those working with the traditional text.

Here's an example of a text written for a highly educated reader on a university campus. Let's apply the Flesch formula to test whether its complexity is justified.

> A child on campus for breastfeeding purposes could be introduced to an environment not designed to accommodate their needs and potentially raise concerns surrounding safety, supervision and liability. The University's legal obligations therefore extend to ensuring that any occupational health and safety risk is appropriately addressed. If such concerns are raised they will be taken into account, after due enquiry and consideration, by the Manager/Supervisor or Lecturer/Teacher when considering a request to breastfeed on campus.
>
> (75 words)

Reading ease = 206.835 – (1.015 × 25) – (84.6 × 2.04)
= 206.835 – 25.375 – 172.584
= 8.876 (very difficult, postgraduate)

By adjusting sentence length and shortening some words, we can improve readability and efficiency:

> A woman breastfeeding a child on campus might do so in an environment not designed for their needs. This may raise concerns about safety,

> supervision and liability. The University must address any risks to health and safety. Managers or lecturers should assess these risks when someone asks to breastfeed on campus.
>
> (51 words)

Reading ease $= 206.835 - (1.015 \times 12.75) - (84.6 \times 1.64)$
$= 206.835 - 12.941 - 138.744$
$= 55$ (grade 10 to 12)

Beware of the limits of readability tools

Readability measures are a useful power tool, but they do have their limits. Their strength is that they offer an objective, consistent way of testing the likely comprehension of a particular text. This also leads to their weakness, because to arrive at a measure, we need to boil down all of the factors that might influence reading to just two elements: sentence length and word length.

To show how dangerous this can be, here is a passage that passes muster at grade 6 readability:

> Words mental when we, we one time at one higher word after tend another. We to a, demand groups read snatch of. If those don't letter interpret are too long, we snatches skill and effort.

If you apply the formula blindly, the result suggests that this should be a snack for a 10-year-old, but it's a piece of nonsense. Critics rightly point out that there is much more to comprehension than the two factors that the formulas track. You also need to take account of the content and structure, the design and layout, the grammar and syntax, the context, and the motivation of your readers, yet these are things that the formulas simply cannot put a number on. As a result, they do not always predict the comprehension of texts accurately when tested against real audiences reading documents to complete real-world tasks.

So exercise some caution when applying a readability tool. Readability experts have always admitted that the formulas are a rough guide only, not to be used mechanically. Think of a good readability score as a necessary but not sufficient condition. Effective writing will tend to score well on a formula, but that alone won't guarantee that the text will work. The formulas and graphs can only ever be one tool among many in your writing toolbox.

11 Clutter

At a glance

The toolbox

- Resist the two types of clutter 206
- Use the key words tool to identify your clutter 207
- Measure the fitness of your expression 209

The living language

- Clarify your thinking before drafting 210
- Resist the desire to impress 212
- Avoid using deceptive clutter 212
- Be aware of historical clutter 213

Power tools

- Understand the grammar of clutter 215
- Avoid prepositional phrases 216
- Simplify long-winded conjunctions 217
- Let nouns and adjectives speak for themselves 217
- Simplify your verbs and verb phrases 218
- Avoid adverbial excess 219
- Look for the dozen patterns of clutter 221

The toolbox

Resist the two types of clutter

We are bombarded by words. They rain down on us as never before, on the street, in our living rooms and in the workplace. Increasingly, we have to deflect the verbal ordnance to find the words with meaning:

> CANTEEN NEWS
> Hot Dogs $3.00—Lunch
> This week we will be making Hot Dogs for lunch.

The writer of this has a point to make, but uses too many words to make it. The lexicographer Samuel Johnson likened this to poor target practice: 'A man who uses a great many words to express his meaning is like a bad marksman who, instead of aiming a single stone at an object, takes up a handful and throws in hopes he may hit.'

While we might forgive the manager of the school canteen, we can no longer afford to forgive the workplace writer who tosses this many stones in the general direction of meaning:

> In relation to the search for possible collaborators as mentioned above, it is of interest that several subjects, all younger academics who would not at this stage have had many opportunities for face-to-face interaction with established researchers in their discipline areas, whether in their own country or overseas, allude to making regular and systematic searches of the home pages of other universities in search of details relating to staff working in the same or allied fields. Having located such people, several of the staff interviewed have gone on to make some form of contact electronically, all of them agreeing that this is less intimidating than the prospect of approaching unknown individuals either in person, on the telephone or by conventional mail.
>
> (123 words)

This is crammed with clutter, full of stones that have little hope of hitting the target meaning. They come in two forms:

1 Unnecessary detail
2 Inefficient expression

Combined, these can bury the core meaning of the passage, forcing readers to cull the words that contribute nothing, work around the repetition, separate the marginal details and identify the main point. After a painful process of reading, they might come up with this:

> Several of the younger academics reported that they regularly search university websites to identify possible collaborators working in or near their field. While only some had then contacted established researchers electronically, they all agreed that this was less intimidating than making an approach in person, by phone or through the mail. Few of these younger academics have had the opportunity for face-to-face interaction with more senior academics.
>
> (67 words—46% shorter)

Of course, the edited version has left some details out. Part of achieving efficiency is being able to scrutinise your content and cut out the parts that are not earning their keep. Did we really need 'as mentioned above', 'at this stage', 'whether in this country or overseas', 'regular and systematic', or 'searches of the home pages of'?

There is even more to trim, however, because of the second form of clutter: inefficient expression. At least another two lines of text can be tightened: 'In relation to the search' (cut), 'it is of interest that' (cut), 'details relating to' (to), 'have gone on to make some form of' (had then contacted), 'the prospect of approaching unknown individuals' (making an approach), and 'conventional mail' (mail).

You may not agree with all of these cuts or replacements, but the overall result will still be fewer yet more accurate stones cast at the intended meaning.

Use the key words tool to identify your clutter

Unfortunately, eliminating either form of clutter from your writing is not as easy as it sounds. You are usually close to your content, which makes it hard to separate what is essential from what is marginal. You will also focus on your intended message, and when you find it there, you may not notice that you have used too many words to express it.

The key words tool can help you to find the stones in your writing that are unlikely to hit a target. Start not by looking for the material you will cut, but by identifying the words in a passage that carry the core of your meaning. Once you identify these, you can more easily test whether the words in between are marginal detail or inefficient expression. Then cut what you can.

To begin with, underline the key words intuitively, without stopping to think too much about why a word seems important. Then read the words you have underlined. They won't form a grammatically complete sentence, but you should get a complete word picture of your content. The key words will mostly be open-class words such as nouns, verbs, adjectives and adverbs, although in an inefficient passage not all of these will be key. The functional words such as conjunctions, prepositions and determiners are seldom key. Of the closed-class words, usually only pronouns are key words.

Here is a passage with the key words underlined. See whether they have captured the core content.

> Whilst Management Essentials does provide courses that may be of assistance to you, my principal reason for contacting you was to initiate a process where we could collaborate and review the completeness of the programs currently available to BioGas Ltd employees who have access (and want to utilise) our products. My focus is simply to help maximise users utility from their investment. Through a process of review the outcome could vary from providing reassurance that your existing programs are of the highest quality (and value) through to arming you with questions and options.
>
> (93 words)

Turn the torchlight on the words left stranded throughout the text. Ask whether they are unnecessary detail or inefficient verbiage. Then remake the sentence with the key words:

> While the Management Essentials courses may assist you, I am contacting you mainly to suggest we review the completeness of the current programs for BioGas employees who access our products. My focus is to help users maximise their investment. The outcome might simply reassure you that your existing programs deliver high quality and value, or arm you with questions and options.
>
> (61 words—35% shorter)

The efficiency gain of more than 35 per cent speaks for itself, but the flow-on benefits are in precision, clarity and readability. There are far fewer stones, and they are now hitting their targets.

Measure the fitness of your expression

At the first few attempts, the key words tool may feel like a slow way to edit your writing. The bad news is that this is perfectly normal. If you are prone to wordiness, you need to force yourself to scrutinise your text with a more objective eye. By narrowing your focus to what is essential, the key words tool helps you to then let go of the words that aren't earning their keep. Before long, you will internalise this mental process and tighten your drafting. This will speed up editing and reduce the number of your drafts.

When you have reached this stage of drafting skill, the key words tool remains useful for two more evolved reasons: as a way of measuring the efficiency of your style, and as a way of helping others to improve their writing.

So far we've measured efficiency by looking at the before and after versions of a text and calculating the percentage reduction in length. This is a valid measure, but if we extend its logic, the most efficient passage of text would be 100 per cent shorter. The key words tool offers you a better measure of fitness: the ratio of key words to the total number of words. A fit passage will generally have around two-thirds key words.

To illustrate, let's measure the efficiency of this passage from a local council policy on road-sealing projects:

> COUNCIL POLICY
> Warrants for sealing of unsealed roads will be assessed against a set of criteria to provide a means to ranking projects in priority order. Should budget resources be available, projects will receive a recommendation in order of precedence (unless there are extenuating circumstances, such as concerns over loss of rare flora) until budget funding is depleted.
>
> The full set of criteria used to assess the merit of a warrant or proposal to seal an unsealed road are outlined in the attached Evaluation Form. Each project put forward is to be assessed. The scoring of a project against the full set of criteria will provide a means to ranking projects in priority order.
>
> (114 words, 33 key words, 29% key words)

With only 33 key words, the passage barely makes it halfway towards the two-thirds benchmark. Not only is there unnecessary detail but plenty of inefficient expression, including whole sentences that repeat essentially the same information. Not surprisingly, rewriting the text with only the key words reduces it by half as well:

> COUNCIL POLICY
> Council uses set criteria to assess and prioritise road-sealing projects. When the budget permits, projects proceed in order of this ranking until funds are depleted, unless there are extenuating circumstances, such as the loss of rare flora. The attached Evaluation Form outlines the criteria used.
>
> (48 words, 35 key words, 73% key words)

The best indicator of efficiency is not the total reduction in words but the change in the proportion of key words. Notice that the number of key words has not changed much, rising only from 33 to 35. Very often, the number of key words in your edited version will be identical to that in the original. But the ratio of key words to total words has risen from around 30 per cent to over 70 per cent, well above the two-thirds benchmark. If your key words ratio falls below 50 per cent, you have some trimming to do.

The key words measure is also a great way to explain to someone else why their writing is wordy and how they can correct it. Rather than rewriting a paragraph in your own words, mark up the key words and ask the writers to check them before editing the passage themselves. That way, they will learn not just why changes are needed but how they can make them.

The living language

While the key words tool will tighten your early drafts, it won't make them come out perfectly. You also need to be aware of the contexts of clutter—the circumstances that make you prone to inefficiency.

Clarify your thinking before drafting

Most clutter has a simple origin: uncertain or unclear thinking. A common example is the throat-clearing opening, a phrase or clause that writers use to announce their topic instead of getting on with saying what they have to say. While these can be easy to spot, coming as they do at the start of sentences and paragraphs, they are not always so easy to fix:

> In regard to the 'rights' attaching to company names and business names. Firstly, Members believe the system of registration of such names should continue and a fee for retention on the ASIC database and the business names register should be imposed. Secondly, there should be, in Members' opinion, attached to the registration of a business name and a company name an exclusive right to use those names in relation to a particular business.
>
> (73 words, 26 key words, 36% key words)

The entire first sentence here simply announces the topic when it could be better integrated with the sentences that follow:

> Members support the current system for company and business names, as well as imposing a fee to retain a name on the ASIC database and business names register. Members also believe they should enjoy exclusive rights to use any registered company or business name.
>
> (44 words, 40% shorter, 28 key words, 64% key words)

Sometimes, you can type faster than you think. If you catch yourself rattling away at the keyboard without much conscious thought, be sure to come back and review each paragraph. You may find the same concept repeated several times. This can happen if you are searching for the best way to express something, and have two or three goes at it. That's perfectly valid, as long as you then select the best version and delete the rest. Here are two sentences that say much the same thing:

> We believe the educative campaign should be web-based as most of Australian industry, and especially Members of the Association, are 'web-savvy' and prefer to receive all communications, training, correspondence, marketing material, etc., in electronic form. It is our view that very few (if any) Australian companies and businesses do not have access to the web and know how to use it.
>
> (62 words)

The writer here is using repetition to emphasise the point, but could do so more efficiently:

> We believe the educative campaign should be web-based. Like most of Australian industry, the Association's members prefer to receive all

> communications in electronic form. Few businesses would not be using the web.
>
> (33 words)

Resist the desire to impress

While clutter creeps in almost by default when you are not concentrating, at other times it is a deliberate choice with a specific purpose: to sound impressive. This is a strategy we learned at school and university, where we were rewarded for dressing up our work with bigger words and longer expressions. The habit tends to carry over into professional life:

> Leadership is a process whereby human resources are utilised to commence and generate relational activity that brings about not only meaningful change, but also to maintain what is considered important to the community. Any change of this nature can be viewed as being transformative in nature. The purpose of leadership is then the orchestration of human resources to maintain that which is important to the school community and to facilitate any desired change considered important by this community.

How long was it before you understood the passage was talking about a school community? There is no reason this could not have been written as:

> Schools show leadership when their staff interact with the school community to bring about meaningful change and maintain community priorities. This kind of change is transformative.

Avoid using deceptive clutter

From dressing to impress, it is only a short sartorial step to dressing to deceive. Here, clutter can be piled on as part of that ethically borderline form of public relations—corporate spin. Here is a press release from a large mining company trying to give the impression of action and concern when in reality it is doing very little. All it tells us is that an internal review is happening, but the details might not be released:

> BHP Billiton CEO Chip Goodyear today provided an update on progress of the review.

'The matters raised in relation to BHP in the Royal Commission are of real concern to us. Our priority is to ensure that the internal review remains focused on determining the relevant facts around that issue.'

Mr Goodyear said the internal review the company was undertaking would be thorough and its conclusions would be provided publicly as appropriate, given the matters before the Commission.

Of course, the masters of this kind of clutter are politicians, and they have turned it into a daily game. Here is an attorney general responding to a tough question about the treatment of prisoners:

> In terms of the concerns raised in relation to this matter, it should be noted that advice has been sought and is being provided by the department prior to the announcement of a decision.

There are only six key words here out of 34. When a key word ratio drops below 20 per cent, you know there is some deliberate evasion going on. All the statement means is 'I've asked my department for advice before announcing my decision.' The longer version is designed to fill up the limited time in a press conference, reducing the need to answer difficult questions.

Be aware of historical clutter

The next kind of clutter is built into the history of our language: a diverse word stock. Originally a collection of mutually intelligible Germanic dialects, English went on to merge with Danish and Norman French, as well as to pull in words from languages all over the world. This makes it a language of many synonyms, giving us at times dozens of closely related words to express a single concept. We have a habit of using them in pairs or triplets when one would do:

accurate and true
aid and abet
any and all
as and when
basic and fundamental
cease and desist
fair and equitable
give, devise and bequeath
new and innovative
null and void
over and done with
peace and quiet
pick and choose
plain and simple
rules and regulations
unless and until

If some of these pairs have a legal smell to them, that's because the language of law is particularly prone to this form of clutter. When defining its terms, the legal profession often began with an Anglo-Saxon word, such as 'goods', and then added a word derived from a French word, such as 'chattel'. So we don't just have goods, we have 'goods and chattels'. In some cases the words have distinct meanings, but there are plenty we can merge, including 'null and void' or 'give, devise and bequeath'.

Legal language has got itself into such tangles in part because of the search for precision, even at the expense of clarity. Unfortunately, the legal profession has used this trade-off to excuse some of the worst clutter to be found in print:

> The recording of informed consent may be done by way of the signature of a third party who witnessed the informed consent or by a file note of such a third party containing details of the circumstances surrounding the giving of informed consent.

Wherever you see words such as 'the same', 'of such', or 'the said', you can be sure there is plenty of repetition about. In just 43 words, 'informed consent' appears three times, 'third party' appears twice, and inefficiencies such as 'by way of' (by) and 'containing details of the circumstances surrounding the' (detailing the) clutter the text. Lawyers often argue that repetition is essential to eliminate ambiguity. But is this version any less certain?

> You can record informed consent by having a third party:
> - sign the document as a witness
> - write a file note detailing how it was given.

Recent work on plain legal language is establishing that there need not be a trade-off between precision and clarity. In fact, the more words you add, the more ambiguity you introduce:

> The TT-Line reserves the right at any time to substitute one vessel for another to abandon or alter any voyage either before the commencement or at any time during the course thereof to dispatch the vessel before or after the date or hour advertised or announced for her sailing from any port to deviate from any advertised route for any purpose with liberty to sail without pilots, to proceed via any route, to proceed, return to and stay at any ports whatsoever (including the loading port) in any order in or out of the route or in contrary direction to or beyond the port of

> destination or often for bunkering or loading or discharging cargo or embarking or disembarking passengers luggage or accompanying vehicles whether in connection with the present, a prior or subsequent voyage or for any other purposes whatsoever, and to carry the within passengers, luggage and accompanying vehicles and cargo into and then beyond the port of discharge named herein and to return to and discharge any cargo at such port, or to tow or to be towed, to make trial trips with or without notice, to adjust compasses or to repair or dry dock with or without cargo on board.

The clutter in this text would leave the passengers of this ferry service wondering if they were ever going to arrive at their destination. All it means is that the company can change its vessel, its route or its timetable whenever it wants to. But this core meaning of the text barely gets to sail out of port.

Power tools

Understand the grammar of clutter

While knowing the contexts of clutter will arm you against wordy writing, it will also help to understand what the most common kinds look like. Some writers try to learn specific words and phrases to avoid, but approaching the task this way is rather daunting. Robert Hartwell Fiske has compiled a dictionary of turgid expressions, and it contains 10,000 entries. Unless you feel like learning 10,000 examples by heart, you will need higher-level tools.

We can use traditional grammar to describe the most common patterns of workplace clutter. Inefficient expressions are usually expanded versions of grammatical elements. The five main categories are:

The grammatical clutter checklist

1. Prepositional phrases
2. Long-winded conjunctions
3. Unnecessary nouns and adjectives
4. Complex verbs and verb phrases
5. Unnecessary adverbs

Avoid prepositional phrases

The most common grammatical expansion is the prepositional phrase, a short series of words that does no more work than a single preposition:

Unnecessary prepositional phrases

in order to	replace with	to
so as to	replace with	to
with a view to	replace with	to
for the purpose of	replace with	for, under
by way of	replace with	as, by, through
through the use of	replace with	through, by
in terms of	replace with	for (or delete)
with regards to	replace with	for, to, by (or delete)
with respect to	replace with	for, to, by (or delete)
in relation to	replace with	for, to
in the case of	replace with	for, if
until such time as	replace with	until
in such a way that	replace with	so

Closely related to these are throat-clearing openings you can usually cut:

Unnecessary sentence starters

It is our opinion that
It is considered that
It was noted that
It was identified by us that
It is important to note that
I might add that
It is acknowledged that
It is appreciated that
It should be pointed out that
There is evidence that
In the context of the
In the situation where
In the event that
As you are aware

KEY TIP Don't pre-stage your point, just get on and state it.

Simplify long-winded conjunctions

In other cases, phrases are used where a simple conjunction would do the job:

Phrases to replace with conjunctions

as a result of	replace with	because
as a consequence	replace with	because
on the grounds that	replace with	because
for the reason that	replace with	because
inasmuch as	replace with	because
due to the fact that	replace with	because
in view of the fact that	replace with	because
owing to the fact that	replace with	because
in the absence of	replace with	without
in connection with	replace with	with
together with	replace with	with

Let nouns and adjectives speak for themselves

Most often, you will use an adjective when you want to detail some qualities of a noun. Be aware, however, that in some cases modifications are unnecessary, and the noun alone tells all:

Adjectival doubling-up

basic essentials
end result
free gift
new initiative
past history
personal opinion
true fact
various different
old adage
all-time record
particular thing
acute crisis

At other times, the unnecessary modification comes in the reverse order:

Adjectival excess

period of time
blue in colour
rectangular in shape
shiny in appearance
area of economics
heavy in weight
financial in nature
large in size
level of payments
volume of trade

Simplify your verbs and verb phrases

Verbs are particularly prone to clutter, mainly because our grammar allows you to pile them up in complex sequences:

> A Board appraisal *is conducted* annually, *as explained* elsewhere in this Statement, which *includes an assessment* of future requirements in relation to Board composition *based* on the above criteria and overall Board performance.

This can easily come down to:

> As this Statement *explains*, an annual Board appraisal *considers* the above criteria and overall Board performance to *assess* the future make-up of the Board.

Be careful of sentences that open with 'It' or 'There'. These often lead to an unnecessary use of the verb 'to be':

Unnecessary uses of the the verb 'to be'

It is my opinion that	replace with	I think
It is our recommendation that	replace with	We recommend
It is my conclusion that	replace with	I conclude
There has been a decline in profits	replace with	Profits declined
There was never a fall in profits	replace with	Profits never fell
The purpose of the report is to develop	replace with	This report develops
The aim of this policy is to inform	replace with	This policy informs
The reason for the situation is that	replace with	The reason is
The unit is in the process of compiling	replace with	The unit is compiling

English grammar also allows you to qualify the action you are expressing using a short modal auxiliary verb. For many writers, this is simply not fancy enough, so they dress up the modal as a longer phrase:

Unnecessary modal phrases

There is a requirement that you	replace with	You must
We are in a position to be able to	replace with	We can
It is expected that the situation	replace with	The situation should
It is estimated that x will	replace with	X might
It is not the case that x	replace with	X will not
Y is not in a position to	replace with	Y cannot
Z are prepared to issue	replace with	Z will issue
X will take steps to	replace with	X will

Avoid adverbial excess

The final form of grammatical clutter relates to the adverb. Watch out for unnecessary qualifying adverbs:

Adverbial over-qualifiers

basically
actually
really
presently
currently
relatively
comparatively
unduly
effectively

At other times, adverbial phrases become long-winded ways of expressing what a single adverb could convey:

Adverbial excess

prior to	replace with	before
in advance of	replace with	before
subsequent to	replace with	after
at the conclusion of	replace with	after
on a regular basis	replace with	regularly
on a daily basis	replace with	daily
at this point in time	replace with	now
during this period of time	replace with	during
in the near future	replace with	soon
in close proximity to	replace with	near
in the region of	replace with	nearby
adjacent to	replace with	next to
in an accurate manner	replace with	accurately
to a large extent	replace with	largely
over the duration of	replace with	during
in the first instance	replace with	firstly

Like adjectives with nouns, sometimes adverbs are used to modify verbs when the meaning is already captured in the verb:

Adverbial repetition

unexpectedly surprised
made in the past
possible in the future
actively involved
totally overwhelmed
referring back
returning again
definitely harmful

Put a string of these together and you are in danger of this kind of tautology:

> We will have to act quickly if we are to prevent the situation recurring again at some time in the future.

Look for the dozen patterns of clutter

So there are about 12 common patterns of grammatical clutter to learn and cutting them from your writing will tighten it considerably. If you are in doubt whether to keep some words, see if they match one of these patterns:

> *In relation to this,* the Scientific Committee *is of the opinion* that the southern subspecies of the moth *Phyllodes imperialis Druce* 1888 *is likely to* become *extinct in nature* in NSW unless the *circumstances and factors* threatening its survival *cease to operate.*
>
> Hauling out the stones reveals the following clutter:

In relation to this	prepositional phrase, delete
is of the opinion	verb clutter, replace with *thinks*
is likely to	verb clutter, replace with modal *may* or *will*
extinct in nature	noun clutter, replace with *extinct*
circumstances and factors	noun double, choose one
threatening its survival	noun clutter, delete *survival*
cease to operate	verb clutter, delete *to operate*

We can easily reduce the stones to those that are hitting the target meaning. Forty per cent shorter, 68 per cent key words and no grammatical clutter:

> The Scientific Committee believes the southern subspecies of the moth *Phyllodes imperialis Druce* 1888 will become extinct in NSW unless the threats to it cease.

12 Verbs

At a glance

The toolbox

- Energise your text 223
- Make your verbs precise 223
- Avoid hidden verbs 225

The living language

- Minimise the passive voice 229
- Know when to cut the passive 232
- Save the passive voice for specific purposes 234

Power tools

- Use the infinitive when the action is complex 236
- Use gerunds as alternative linking devices 237
- Measure your verbs to make them precise 238

The toolbox

Energise your text

Everyone remembers the definition of a verb: a doing word. Even if you missed school grammar altogether, you probably picked this much up somewhere along the way. But think for a moment about what flows from this definition. Doing words mean action, and action implies movement, energy and vitality. This is what verbs can bring to your writing.

Verbs are the workhorses of our grammar. When handled properly, they drive sentences along, bringing clarity in their wake. When mishandled or abused, your workhorses will become plodding nags that tread something like this:

> This Agreement details the consultation process implemented by the company to enable staff to contribute to the making of decisions affecting their health, safety and welfare and meet its duty to consult as required by legislation.

What are the main actions here? We'd expect to find them in the verbs, but there are far too many candidates: 'details', 'consultation', 'process', 'implemented', 'enable', 'contribute', 'making', 'decision', 'affecting', 'meet', 'consult', 'require'. That's 12 possible actions in a text of just 36 words. One in three words is an action or a potential action, forcing the reader to sift through the excess. The writer could have reduced it to something like this:

> This Agreement *details* how the company will *consult* staff as the law *requires*, so that staff can *contribute* to the decisions *affecting* their health, safety and welfare.

Not only is the meaning clearer, but in shedding 'process', 'implemented', 'enable', 'making', 'meet', and 'to consult', we've halved the verbiage and energised the text.

Make your verbs precise

This chapter will explain how to identify excess verbs and in doing so make your text precise and clear. Verbs are particularly important to precision because our grammar packs a lot of information into them. To illustrate, let's build up a sentence from a single verb: to assess. We can start by specifying the person doing that action:

> He assesses …
> We assess …

Notice that the verb form changes when a different person is doing the assessing. So it is already telling us two things: the action and who is doing it. Then we can add information about when this happened:

> We have assessed …

To complete the statement, we need to add what we assessed:

> We have assessed the *proposal*.

We could then build this into a more complex sentence by adding a second verb:

> We have assessed the proposal and believe you *will fund* the project.

We might also want to qualify an action using an auxiliary verb:

> We have assessed the proposal, and believe you *can* fund the project.

And finally, we could add some extra information about the funding:

> We have assessed the proposal and believe you can fund the project from your existing budget.

This final statement is precise, and its verbs convey:

- the actions
- who is doing them
- when the actions are happening
- the ability of one of the agents to do that action.

There is great economy in packing so much information into one linguistic form. When we read, we subconsciously decode all these pieces of information, and because they are commonly in the verb, that's where your reader will look for them. If your verb phrases are complicated or confused, the reader will have to work at putting the puzzle together:

> Following assessment of the proposal, it is suggested that consideration be given to the funding of this project from existing budgetary resources.

Instead of three verbs: 'assessed', 'believe' and 'fund', all accurately reflecting the actions taking place, we now have eight potential candidates for the action in the sentence:

Following assessment is suggested consideration be given funding.

It takes extra time for the reader to sort this out. We've also lost some of the precise meaning of the original. No longer does it specify who is actually doing the assessing, the believing or the funding, nor whose budget is involved. This imprecision reduces clarity.

You can avoid turning your sentences into puzzles by understanding four common verb forms:

Verb form	Example
Active verb	We *considered* your advice
Hidden verb	We *gave consideration* to your advice
Passive verb	Your advice *was considered* by us
Verbal noun	*To consider* your advice... *Considering* your advice...

Most of your verbs should be active. This means they express the action of a clause in a verb, and place the agent doing that action in front of the verb: 'we considered your advice'.

As a rule of thumb, these forms should account for at least 70 per cent of your verbs. This leaves you some scope for the other three forms where there is a valid reason for using them. But whenever they start to outnumber the active verbs, your text will become imprecise, inefficient and unclear.

Avoid hidden verbs

The first verb problem to watch for involves the balance between nouns and verbs. English has great flexibility in how it uses the open-class words—the nouns, verbs, adjectives and adverbs. The same base-word in a slightly different form could be any one of the four:

1 I consider—verb.
2 My consideration—noun.
3 A considerate person—adjective.
4 Speaking considerately—adverb.

The commonsense approach is to make sure that the actions you are writing about use a verb rather than a noun or adjective:

Our existing shareholders *approved* the merger proposal.

The main agents in this sentence are the shareholders, and the action they are doing is approving. The past tense verb 'approved' is active and the action in the sentence is clear. But when we express that action in a noun, we generate a hidden verb structure:

Our existing shareholders *expressed approval* of the merger proposal.

The action that the shareholders are doing here is still approving, yet this appears as the abstract noun 'approval'. We have 'hidden' the real action in a noun. But since the sentence cannot function without a verb, the author added the active verb 'expressed', which is redundant. The shareholders might very well be expressive people, but the verb 'expressed' will only distract the reader from their main action.

This process goes by a number of names. The official grammatical term is nominalisation because it turns a verb into a 'nominal', or noun. But since this is rather a mouthful, plain language specialists have given nominals a range of other names as well: hidden verbs, frozen verbs, smothered verbs and weak verbs.

Hidden verbs most commonly appear in pairs, most of which can be reduced to a single verb:

Hidden verb	Active verb
undertake a review	review
conduct an assessment	assess
perform an evaluation	evaluate
are having a discussion	are discussing
made a decision	decided
includes a requirement	requires
gave consideration	considered
will provide advice	will advise
hold a meeting	meet
produced a reduction	reduced

Hidden verb	Active verb
will enable an improvement	will improve
furnish an explanation	explain
are placing restrictions	are restricting
will facilitate the resolution of	will (help) resolve
is reliant	relies
included an exemption	exempted
provides consistency in the administration of	administers consistently

The active verbs in the right-hand column are sharper, more precise and more efficient. They bring together all of the information that should be in the verb. In the case of 'made a decision', for example, the action is in the past, but our grammar can't change the form of a noun to show tense. That's why we have to put in another verb, 'made', to tell the reader when it happened. When the tense and the action are separated, it takes extra time to puzzle out. Using 'decided' puts it in a single package.

Here are some hidden verbs in a workplace sentence:

> The partners *will give consideration* to the new business model after the Director of Finance *has undertaken an analysis* of the potential returns.

The main actions are 'considering' and 'analysing', but both are hiding in the nouns 'consideration' and 'analysis'. The two actions are happening at different times, but the tense information is attached to the verbs 'will give' (future tense) and 'has undertaken' (perfect tense). We can boost the energy, precision and clarity by uncovering the hidden verbs:

> The partners *will consider* the new business model after the Director of Finance *has analysed* the potential returns.

In the process we shed words that were not earning their keep:

> give to undertaken an of

Recent evidence shows that hidden verbs are a particular source of difficulty for readers. Charrow and Charrow, for example, analysed jury instructions and identified elements that contributed to poor comprehension. They found that a mere 54 per cent of jury instructions were understood—a finding with real implications for justice. Prominent on the list of causes was the hidden verb.

To help you identify hidden verbs, look for some of the redundant verbs that they commonly pair up with, words like 'give', 'undertake', 'conduct', 'provide', 'make', 'is', 'produce', 'hold', 'enable' or 'deliver'. These offer an amusing take on the professions that use them. Tax accountants, for example, do a lot of 'giving' and 'performing', government writers do a lot of 'providing' and 'desiring', and managers do a great deal of 'undertaking'. From their writing alone, you'd think that auditors were very musical:

> The committee *will conduct an audit* concerning current leave processing, but the call centre manager *needs to provide a written explanation* of the system first.

Why can't an audit committee just audit?

These pairs mostly combine verbs and nouns, but some hidden verbs occur in adjectives instead. These are attached to the 'intransitive' verbs that do not directly impact on a noun:

> The definition of 'new residential premises' *will remain unchanged* according to the proposed amendments.

The adjective *unchanged* hides the real action just as the nouns we've been looking at do. We can turn the sentence around and sharpen it:

> The proposed amendments *will not change* the definition of 'new residential premises'.

But just when you thought that all you had to look for was neat, identifiable pairs, this is not always the case. Sometimes the hidden verb occurs alone in a sentence, and sometimes in a completely different part of the sentence to its redundant partner:

> Further *diversification* in marine products *took* place in April 1990, with the *acquisition* by Yamaha of Bob McKay International Marinas Pty Ltd.

There is only one grammatical verb in this sentence: 'took'. This is not the key action in the sentence, but neither is the word 'place', which pairs with it. So we have to look elsewhere in the sentence and find 'diversification' and 'acquisition'—both complex abstract nouns. To turn them into verbs, we need to change their form and also recast the sentence:

> Yamaha further *diversified* its marine products in April 1990 when it *acquired* Bob McKay International Marinas Pty Ltd.

KEY TIP Look for words with common noun endings such as '-ment', '-al', '-ance', '-ence', '-tion', '-ity' and '-sion'. See if you can turn them into verbs.

Hidden verbs that don't come in pairs are a particular problem when the agent doing their action is missing from the sentence altogether. To turn these hidden verbs into active ones, you will need to restore the agent:

> After *considering definitions* of health information in other health information privacy legislation, the Inquiry's *recommendation was to amend the definition* of 'health information' to *include* 'genetic information about an individual in a form which *is or could be predictive* of the health of the individual or any of his or her genetic relatives'.

Who did the considering? Probably the Inquiry, but this noun and its verb are some way apart in the sentence. And who should do the amending, defining and including?

> The Inquiry *considered* how other health information privacy laws *define* 'health information', and *recommended* the government *redefine* the term as 'genetic information about individuals that could *predict* their health or the health of their genetic relatives'.

This sample demonstrates the ultimate danger of hidden verbs. They can omit or separate the agent from the action it is doing. Sentences become puzzles, and readers have to work hard at connecting the missing pieces.

The living language

Minimise the passive voice

While hidden verbs can slow down a text considerably, another verb form can bring it almost to a dead stop: the passive voice. Of all the elements of expression discussed in this book, perhaps none has such a debilitating influence on workplace writing. Not only does it reduce precision and clarity, but it dehumanises prose, reduces accountability and offers a false sense of objectivity.

To handle verbs effectively, you need to understand that English grammar privileges one particular sequence of words. Most of our statements start with a noun that is doing an action (called the subject), then give the action that subject is doing (the verb), and finally the noun that the verb is affecting (the object). The term 'subject' here differs from its more general meaning of 'topic'. In grammar, the subject is the person, place or thing that is doing the action of a verb.

The subject-verb-object pattern is the secret formula that lies at the heart of the English sentence:

This review focuses on corporate values.
subject verb object

The budget will provide $250,000.
subject verb object

The department has already sent a reply.
subject verb object

But our grammar also gives us a second option. Instead of placing the subject doing the action first, we can place the object—the passive recipient—up front:

Corporate values focuses on this review.

To clarify that it is still the review that is doing the focusing and not the corporate values, our grammar makes some adjustments. As in the case of hidden verbs, these insert some redundant words:

Corporate values *are* focuse*d* on *by* this review.
$250,000 a year will *be* provide*d* *by* the budget.
A reply has already *been sent by* the department.

This is the passive voice, and there are three changes that form it:

1. Inserting the verb 'to be'—words like 'be', 'is', 'was', 'are', 'were', 'been' and 'being'.
2. Converting the action verb into the past tense—usually ending in '-ed'.
3. Placing the subject after the verb—or removing it completely.

All three elements increase the demands you are placing on your reader in comprehending your text. People are far more used to reading a standard subject-verb-object clause, and when a text departs from it you are asking your reader to think through two or three steps to understand your meaning. Cognitive psychologists have measured this effect by testing the comprehension and timing of sentences in the active and passive voices. They found a measurable cost in comprehending the passive. In one experiment, active sentences were misunderstood only 26 per cent of the time, while the passive equivalent was misunderstood by up to 92 per cent of participants.

Often, you can spot a passive construction by scanning for the word 'by', which is commonly how a subject is tacked on after the verb:

> It *was* also *ordered by* the Judge that the costs of both proceedings *be paid by* the Estate.

These are the easiest passive verbs to activate, as all you need to do is place the subjects in front of their verbs instead of after:

> The Judge also *ordered* that the Estate *pay* for the costs of both proceedings.

Like hidden verbs, correcting passives then clears out the verbal debris:

> It was by be by

Passives become harder to correct when your drafting has left out one or more of the subjects altogether:

> It *is expected* that the introduction of new project funding arrangements will go some way to ensure the cost overruns *are addressed*. The situation will *be closely monitored*.

Who here is doing the expecting? Is this a different subject to whoever is doing the addressing or the monitoring? We simply don't know because the sentence doesn't tell us. Unless your readers are familiar with the context you are writing about, they may have no idea either:

> [Who?] expects that the new program funding arrangements will help address the cost overruns. [Who?] will monitor the situation closely.

When you draft, you will know who the agents of your verbs are, so you will tend to fill them in as you read. But unless you specify those agents for your reader, they may misread your content.

Know when to cut the passive

Given the potential the passive voice has for ambiguity, why is it so prevalent? Professional workplace writers tend to use as much as 40 or 50 per cent passive voice without batting an eyelid. What is the attraction?

First, the passive voice helps a writer to avoid responsibility. When you don't name who is responsible for a particular action, you can't be called to account for it:

> Any adverse findings of relevance will *be considered, communicated* and *acted* upon promptly.

Here we have an institution trying to sound responsive without committing itself to anything. Who will do the considering and communicating, and who will they communicate with? Will these phantom subjects also do the prompt acting? This is why the US Securities and Exchange Commission singles out the passive voice as something to avoid in financial disclosure documents:

> Plain English uses plain words—and, among other basic ingredients, the active voice. We want to promote the use of the active voice not just because it makes for punchier sentences, but because it requires a definite subject to go with the predicate. That's the only way that investors will be able to figure out who did what to whom.

Passive voice can also be a symptom of unclear and underdeveloped thinking. When you know that something must be done to solve a problem but you haven't done the hard yards to be sure what that should be, out comes the passive:

> It might *be suggested* to the Commonwealth Government that some consideration *be given to* establishing a suitable set of performance indicators that would enable the assessment of the merit of this approach.

This props up sloppy thinking and poor decision-making. If you can't nominate the actions precisely, then perhaps you should check your facts and your thinking:

> The Association should suggest that the Commonwealth establish a suitable set of performance indicators to assess the merit of its approach.

Government writing is particularly prone to the passive voice. This is historically understandable, as it flows from the notion of collective responsibility in the Westminster system. When you are a public servant, you are an officer of the Crown and not an individual. It is hard to write 'I recommend' because your writing is a collective product. But government agencies take this as a licence to overdo the passive voice:

> It *is recommended* that any proposed development *be informally discussed* with Heritage Council staff at the concept stage. Time and expense can *be saved* by discussing proposals with Heritage Council staff before detailed discussions *are made*.

The four verbs here are all in the passive voice. As so often in public sector writing, the agency itself is the real subject:

> The Heritage Council recommends that you discuss proposed developments informally with our staff at the concept stage. This can save you time and money.

Of course, government is not the only passive-voice culprit. Companies, too, speak to their customers in a passive way. Here is how one florist attempted to explain its holiday deliveries on the internet:

> Public holidays can be difficult in regards to delivery, therefore as orders *are received* for these days, they will *be evaluated* by a Flowerpoint Consultant initially, then any action, if at all, will *be communicated* to you via phone or email.

I'm sure that its customers are sitting at home simply bursting 'to be communicated to'. Putting the people back into your text immediately humanises your prose:

> Because deliveries can be difficult on public holidays, our Flowerpoint Consultants check orders received for these days and will contact you by phone or email to confirm your delivery.

The passive voice is also embedded deeply in academic culture, particularly in the sciences. It effaces the agent in the middle of an experiment to make the results sound more objective. Nobody actually poured liquid A into liquid B—*it was poured*. Sometimes, this might be valid if the agent is obvious or unimportant:

> The methods that *are used* for nutrition research include digestibility studies, where fish faeces *is collected* and *analysed* to see how well different diets and ingredients *are utilised*. The most promising diets *are* then *evaluated* in commercial farm ponds or cages.

The passive voice here becomes a marker of a particular genre and an author's status as a member of a particular profession. If your readers expect to read text in this style, then you may all have to put up with it. But when you are trying to reach a broader audience, see if you can activate your verbs:

> Scientists *are researching* nutrition by *using* methods such as digestibility studies, where they *collect* and *analyse* fish faeces to see how well fish *digest* different diets and ingredients. The most promising diets *are then evaluated* in commercial farm ponds or cages.

We haven't eliminated the passive voice here, but we have reduced it significantly.

Save the passive voice for specific purposes

Using the passive comes down to a question of balance. On average, you can use up to 15 per cent passive voice without causing too much damage. Sometimes, for example, you simply do not know what the subject is, or it could be any number of things:

> In the course of a BBC investigation the use of a secret recording must *be kept* under constant review. Specific approval must *be obtained* for each proposed case of secret recording. No blanket approval can *be obtained* for it.

Here, the text refers to a range of people working within the organisation. It would be hard to insert a subject.

At other times, the subject of a verb is so obvious and unimportant that it would distract the reader to include it:

> The Government *was re-elected* for a third term.
> In July 2002, the partnership *was incorporated* as Palmedia Ltd.

Another valid case is when you want to start a sentence with an object because it is more important to the point you are making:

> The Howard Government's industrial relations laws will *be examined* by an International Labour Organization Committee of Experts later this year.
>
> Décor Pebble *is* progressively more *demanded* by respected landscape architects and designers.

Workplace writers also turn to the passive when they feel the need for diplomacy. Here, for example, is an auditor writing a report for a client:

> Bank reconciliation should be performed regularly so that errors or misstatements are detected and can be addressed as soon as possible. Where bank reconciliations have not been performed in a timely manner significant organisational time is used investigating reconciling items.

Yet you can still sound diplomatic in the active voice:

> We suggest that the accounts officer reconcile bank statements regularly to detect errors and to avoid wasting time investigating mistakes.

The final reason for choosing the passive voice is perhaps the most sophisticated: the need to maintain linguistic flow. As Chapter 6 discussed, part of the unspoken contract between writers and readers is the principle of 'old before new'. You will draw your readers through the text if you start with information that is familiar to them before moving on to a new point. Once that new point becomes familiar, you can move on to something else.

Often, these sentence transitions line up with a subject-verb-object order, but the sequence of your topics or themes can vary from that of your grammatical agents. When this happens, you may benefit from swapping the position of subjects and objects.

> Scientists *are researching* nutrition by *using* methods such as digestibility studies, where they *collect* and *analyse* fish faeces to see how well fish *digest* different diets and ingredients. The most promising diets *are then evaluated* in commercial farm ponds or cages.

This keeps the passive verb in the final sentence for reasons of flow. It introduces the theme of diets at the end of one sentence, then picks it up at the start of the next.

If you find yourself using the passive voice, make sure it is because of one of these reasons. If not, activate your verbs.

Power tools

While you shouldn't exile passive and hidden verbs from your writing altogether, how do you know when you have the balance right? Can you measure it in an objective way? We are going to look at a short test you can apply to your documents, but first we need to introduce two more verb forms. These are the verbal nouns—a kind of halfway house between nouns and verbs. They act in part like a noun because they can become the subject or object of other verbs.

Use the infinitive when the action is complex

The first verbal noun is the infinitive. This is the base version of a verb, which is formed with the word 'to' followed by the present tense form of the verb:

> to audit
> to request

Infinitives are useful when the action you are describing does genuinely have two parts to it:

> The department *records* this information *to improve* its data processing.

They can often help to improve passive and long-winded verb structures:

> Project management was performed in-house by AME, thus ensuring the timely and efficient coordination of all activities.
>
> AME managed the project in-house *to coordinate* all activities efficiently and on time.

You can also move the infinitive to the start of a sentence:

> *To coordinate* all activities efficiently and on time, AME managed the project in-house.

But beware of the infinitive creeping in unnecessarily:

> AAMI *is required to give* you these documents before you buy insurance.

You can often replace these infinitives with an active verb and modal auxiliary:

AAMI *must give* you these documents before you buy insurance.

Sometimes you can replace an infinitive by changing the tense:

The service *continues to operate* with minimum disruption.
The service *is operating* with minimum disruption.

Use gerunds as alternative linking devices

Gerunds look the same as verbs in the continuing present tense, but they operate like nouns, and do not come after the verb 'to be'. Contrast two simple statements:

I am writing
I like writing

The first 'writing' is part of a continuous present tense verb, telling us the action that 'I' is doing. In the second, the action that 'I' is doing is 'liking', and its object is the verbal noun 'writing'. This is a noun that happens to name an action.

Like infinitive verbs, gerunds can be useful when the action does have two parts:

This *proved* useful in *encouraging* students to come forward.

Sometimes, however, you can delete the first verb and turn the gerund into the active verb:

The agency *is faced* with the prospect of *running* over budget.
The agency may *run* over budget.

Gerunds are especially useful as an alternative linking device between clauses. They give you some variety instead of using straight conjunctions all the time.

It is best to be explicit, setting the minimum expectation we need.
It is best to be explicit and set the minimum expectation we need.

You can also begin a sentence with a gerund as a modifier, but be especially careful because it has potential for ambiguity:

Plunging 100 metres into the gorge, we saw Tuross Falls.

When authors overuse verbal nouns, it usually means that they were not focused when drafting:

Human resources managers have a responsibility to ensure that individual files are kept.
Human resources managers must keep individual files.

This document aims to provide assistance in applying the requirements to ensure the workplace remains discrimination free.
This document demonstrates how you can keep our workplace discrimination free.

Measure your verbs to make them precise

When you are comfortable with all these verb forms, you can then measure how effectively you are using verbs. The first step is to take a sample passage and count the verbs in various forms. You can then calculate some ratios and compare the results with two simple benchmarks: the percentage of passive voice, and the percentage of active verbs out of all verb forms. It helps to apply some symbols to mark up verbs as you go:

Verb form	Mark
Active voice	<u>provide</u>
Passive voice	is provided (marked with an inverted V over "provided")
Hidden verb	provision (marked with a V over "provision")
Verbal noun	it <u>attempts</u> <u>to provide</u> (with a slash through "provide") or <u>providing</u> (with a slash through "providing") this service <u>makes</u> us happy

Calculating the verb index

1 Select a 100-word sample

2 Mark up the verb forms

We asked staff to explain the process. They told us it was done electronically. However, we found no evidence that the report was automatically generated, nor was there any evidence of manual generation. It should also be noted that no hard copies of the report could be produced. Staff should give consideration to manually producing the report to ensure it exists.

3 Count the verb forms in each category

Total verb forms:	16
Active verbs:	6
Passive verbs:	4
Hidden verbs:	3
Verbal nouns:	3

4 Calculate the percentages of both passive and active verbs and compare against the benchmarks.

Passive verbs as a percentage of active and passive verbs = 40%
Benchmark = 15%

Active verbs as a percentage of all four verb forms = 37.5%
Benchmark = 70%

This verb count is too high, almost double the benchmarks. When you edit:

- target the passive and hidden verbs first, then the verbal nouns
- convert as many as you can into active verbs
- clarify the action by inserting missing subjects as you go
- reduce the total number of verbs.

Here is the same text edited to sharpen the verbs:

> Staff explained that [they] processed the [data] electronically, but we found no evidence that [the system] generated a report either automatically or manually. Staff could not produce any hard copies and should generate the report manually.
>
> Passive verbs as a percentage of active and passive verbs = 0%
> Benchmark 15%
>
> Active verbs as a percentage of all verb forms = 100%
> Benchmark 70%

To test how you are using verbs, score your writing against these measures. If you need to, change the balance between different verb forms to maximise clarity and keep your sentences moving at a brisk pace.

13 Sentences

At a glance

The toolbox

- Focus each sentence with one idea 242
- Maintain an average sentence length of 15–20 words 244
- Vary your sentence lengths 244

The living language

- Add a rhetorical touch 245
- Use parallelism for rhythm and balance 246
- Emphasise a point through repetition 247
- Use apposition for variety and emphasis 249
- Insert parentheses with caution 250

Power tools

- Vary the sentence types in your documents 252
- Understand the parts of a sentence 252
- Use fragments for emphasis 254
- Don't overdo the simple sentence 255
- Use compound sentences for elements of equal weight 256
- Write mainly in complex sentences 256
- Limit the number of compound-complex sentences 257

The toolbox

Focus each sentence with one idea

We all know what a sentence is. It's that thing that starts with a capital letter and ends with a full stop. Sentences can be short. They can also meander along, snaking their way down the page on an extended journey that turns first in one direction, then another, setting just the right rhythm for rocking us to sleep. And we've all heard of the things we aren't allowed to do in a sentence, such as starting with a conjunction or ending with a preposition like 'up'.

All of the sentences in the previous paragraph are grammatically correct, even though some of them break the rules of the old school. But were they effective? Given the huge variety in sentence form and length, how can you judge your sentences? The golden rule is that each sentence should support and clarify its intended meaning, and the most reliable way to achieve that is to keep each idea in a sentence of its own. Let the complexity of each idea determine the length and structure.

To illustrate, let's see how one writer started with a simple idea, but then tried to cram too many extra points into the same sentence. The core concept was very straightforward:

> We should involve marketing in the development phase for this product.

The writer then added a qualification in the middle of this statement:

> We should involve marketing, who will eventually have to sell the product, in the development phase.

Although there are now two elements, they are really part of the one coherent idea, because one part explains the other. Then the writer identified the owner of this opinion:

> The director of finance continues to believe that we should involve marketing, who will eventually have to sell the product, in the development phase.

The third element adds a second qualification, but it is still straightforward and holds well enough to the sentence as part of the same idea. But we are getting close to the limit, which means we should give our readers a pause before moving on. The writer kept going:

> While acknowledging the problems and delays that the company has experienced in the past, the director of finance continues to believe that we should involve marketing, who will eventually have to sell the product, in the development phase.

The acknowledgement of past problems introduces a new, albeit connected, idea. The sentence is starting to become unwieldy. Readers must now juggle four concepts, which requires more concentration than the content demands. But our writer wasn't finished yet:

> While acknowledging the problems and considerable delays that the company has experienced in the past, the director of finance continues to believe that *we should involve marketing,* who will eventually have to sell the product, *in the development phase* and that non-inclusion in this regard represents a significant gap in the development methodology.
>
> (53 words)

Most readers would start to skim this sentence. The message is not complex, but the mechanics that convey it bury the main point, and readers have to sift it out. When that happens sentence after sentence throughout a document, your writing becomes heavy-weather reading. It is better to break this information into two sentences and bring the main point up front:

> The director of finance believes that we should involve marketing, who will eventually sell the product, in the development phase. He acknowledges the previous problems and delays, but feels that without marketing there would be a significant gap in the process.
>
> (41 words)

We have now given the reader enough pause to absorb one main idea before moving on to the next. Yes, they are related, but placing them side by side in a paragraph is enough to show that relationship. Our original 53-word sentence is now a much more digestible two sentences averaging just over 20 words. Both versions are grammatically correct, but which one would you prefer to read? Which one uses the sentence structure to reflect the content more closely? Using one idea per sentence—even when that idea has several parts to it—is the first step in making your sentences readable and clear.

Maintain an average sentence length of 15–20 words

There is an easy benchmark you can use to force yourself into separating your ideas: average sentence length. Some of the huge databases of contemporary English texts show that the average sentence in English comes in at around 18 words. This seems to be about the right size to complete one thought and let your readers pause before moving to the next. But, as every statistician can tell you, averages need to be applied with caution.

Applying any kind of mandatory length to an individual sentence is fraught with danger. A sentence should be as long as it needs to be. Some might be six words long. In other cases, particularly if your content is more complex, or if you need to include a subsidiary point, you will want to go over 18 words—perhaps even stretching towards 35 words. But these are probably the comfortable limits: few sentences shorter than five or six words, and as few as possible above 35.

With this range in mind, an average benchmark for sentence length can then become useful when you are looking at an entire document. Your average should fall somewhere between 15 and 20 words. Below 15 words as an average and you risk falling into a 'me-Tarzan-you-Jane' style that will appear overly simplistic. Over 20 words, and certainly above 25 words as an average, and you will make your writing very dense and unappealing. Workplace writers do just that by averaging between 22 and 30 words per sentence in most documents.

KEY TIP Read your sentences aloud. If you need to take a breath, you need to break up the sentence.

Vary your sentence lengths

Although a 15–20 word average is fundamental to writing well, you should also vary your sentence length to maintain your readers' interest. Any document will become dreary if its sentences are of roughly the same length, even if that length is in the right average range. Here is a paragraph with four almost identical sentences:

> As trade globalisation gains pace, so do the number of countries where consumer products are manufactured. Monitoring the production process requires on-the-spot presence to optimise the choice of a local

> supplier. Besides production capacity, a large number of aspects have to be taken into consideration. Selecting the right vendor is one of the most important conditions for successful sourcing.
>
> (59 words: 16, 15, 14, 14, average 15 words)

The text quickly becomes monotonous. Vary the sentences:

> As trade globalisation gains pace, so do the number of countries that manufacture consumer products. Yet to find the best local supplier, you will need an on-the-spot presence to monitor production capacity, as well as the many other aspects that need to be considered. Selecting the right vendor means you will source successfully.
>
> (53 words: 15, 29, 9, average 18 words)

When assessing the effectiveness of your sentences, look at both the average length and the distribution. Calculate the percentage of sentences that are 10 words or more above the average for a piece, and the percentage of sentences that are five words or more below the average. Are you using too many under-average sentences? Are you using too many long ones, or too many close to the average? If so, then mix it up.

The living language

Add a rhetorical touch

So you've overcome the first challenge, and are using a short average sentence length with variety. This will make your sentences clear and readable, but it won't make them great. For that you will need to add some rhetorical touches—a few simple devices that will help your sentences sing. Classical rhetoricians were the first to wrestle with this problem, and they identified some common 'schemes' that bring life, rhythm and interest. There are dozens of these, but the four of most use to workplace writing are:

1. Parallelism
2. Repetition
3. Apposition
4. Parenthesis

Use parallelism for rhythm and balance

Parallelism uses either related pairs within a sentence, or a series of related words and phrases. This is a common situation in workplace writing, where you will often need to list or compare related things:

> Our stationery products range from pens and pencils to compasses and clips.
>
> The major challenges we face are cost increases, sudden changes in demand and renewed pressure from competitors.
>
> Before we can extract the metals, the ore must be crushed, washed and sifted.

Parallel structures such as these bring a steady rhythm that is pleasing to read as well as practical. To work well, the related elements must use grammatically parallel forms: 'pens and pencils', 'compasses and clips' (all related concrete nouns); 'crushed', 'washed', 'sifted' (same verb form); 'cost increases', 'sudden changes', 'renewed pressure' (all adjective–noun structures).

Here is some text that lists a parallel series of actions but misses its rhetorical opportunity.

> FORGACS has Teamed with ADI on the Navy's Amphibious Ship Building Program with plans to fabricate major ship blocks at our Tomago Shipyard to be barged to our Cairncross Dockyard in Brisbane for final assembly into completed ship form.

The parallels here aren't introduced with similar forms: 'to fabricate', 'to be barged', 'for final assembly'. A revised version strengthens the rhythm:

> FORGACS has Teamed with ADI on the Navy's Amphibious Ship Building Program *to fabricate* major ship blocks at our Tomago Shipyard, *to barge* them to our Cairncross Dockyard in Brisbane, and *to assemble* them into completed ship form.

Using this kind of balanced structure is particularly helpful when you have to write a longer sentence because the parallels will keep your reader on track.

To reinforce the rhythm, try to keep your parallel items of roughly equal length. Where you can't avoid listing items of varying length, order them by increasing complexity, with the shorter words or phrases at the start of the list and the longer ones at the end:

> The company also operates HouseWorks, specialising in selling an affordable range of furniture, contemporary styled homewares and related decorative items for the home.

A final kind of parallelism is antithesis. This is also common in workplace content, where you need to contrast different things:

> Although this employee is punctual, he usually does not get down to work until an hour after arriving. Although courteous to managers, he has a record of abusing more junior staff. Although he meets all his given deadlines, the quality of his work varies greatly.

The use of parallel forms here reinforces the contrasting elements and lifts the sentences musically above the workmanlike.

Emphasise a point through repetition

Closely related to parallelism is repetition. When you use parallel forms, there will often be some repeated element, such as the word 'although' in the previous example. Devices like this offer a heightened rhetorical effect that makes them both useful and dangerous. They are useful because they can add emphasis where you need it, particularly in speeches and presentations. They are dangerous because overuse can sound forced or become inefficient. Generally, reserve schemes of repetition for an important point.

The first two schemes of repetition will no doubt be familiar to you from school: alliteration and assonance. The first repeats consonants in successive words, while the second repeats vowel sounds. These are an easy way of bringing some music to your sentences.

> Our products range from pens and pencils to compasses and clips.

> We've been trying to get the project approved, but the wide, slow wheels are turning ever more slowly.

Alliteration and assonance have two main benefits: they sound pleasing, and they can reinforce the meaning with matching sounds. Too many workplace writers avoid these effects because they associate them with poetry and literature. Not only does this rob you of some powerful tools, but it condemns us all to read dull and dreary documents all day long.

The next form of repetition is climax. As the name implies, this sentence structure builds intensity towards a key point at the end. It works best in longer sentences, particularly when they list a number of elements reaching a conclusion:

> To avoid going into administration, all we need are more customers, more cash, more turnover, more competitiveness, more profits—a more viable business.

Climax makes good use of the parts of a sentence that attract the most interest: the start and the end. The pause at each sentence break gives your readers more time to absorb the information there. Don't waste these positions by burying your key points in the middle. And don't reduce the number of these opportunities by writing too many long sentences.

The next four forms of repetition make excellent use of these opening and closing slots. They repeat a word or group of words at the start of a series of clauses (anaphora), at the end of a series of clauses (epistrophe), at the start and finish of a single clause (epanalepsis), or at the end and start of adjoining clauses (anadiplosis). While the Greek words for these schemes sound rather forbidding, you will recognise the forms themselves.

> The company secretary was responsible for the annual return. The company secretary was aware of this responsibility. The company secretary should be held to account. (anaphora)
>
> Remember that success in real estate flows from position: high occupancy rates flow from position; above average rents flow from position; strong resale value flows from position. (epistrophe)
>
> Customers generate customers, investment generates investment, profits generate profits. (epanalepsis)
>
> Poor service means our customers are dissatisfied; dissatisfied customers mean falling sales; falling sales mean pressure on profits; pressure on profits means unhappy shareholders. (anadiplosis)

Advertisers commonly use these forms because the repetition helps the line to stick in your mind. While you will want to use these cautiously in some workplace documents, they are particularly useful when selling your services to clients, such as in sales letters, websites, brochures or advertisements.

Where you are writing an oral text, such as for a speech or for a presentation, rhetorical repetition really comes into its own. Two more forms you can try out are antimetabole and chiasmus. They are both less complex than they sound, and they are responsible for some of the most memorable lines in the political speeches of every age.

Antimetabole repeats but reverses the same words in successive clauses. As a summary statement, it will often stay in your reader's mind long after they have finished 'listening':

> Ask not what your country can do for you; ask what you can do for your country.
>
> Some companies provide a service to make money; we make money to provide a service.

Chiasmus doesn't repeat or reverse the same words, but rather an entire grammatical structure.

> Production felt the product was flawed. Marketing knew the customer didn't care.
>
> Your children never stop growing. Neither should their bank balance.

Rhetorical forms of repetition are a special effect that provide rhythmical and contextual highlight. Use them sparingly, and do not take them as a licence to repeat words unnecessarily. Strategic use will give you a reputation for a fine turn of phrase.

Use apposition for variety and emphasis

Like repetition, apposition is a form of emphasis. It reinforces a point by immediately restating, detailing, commenting or qualifying it. The most common form is in a balanced sentence separated by a colon or a dash, which places two roughly equal elements side by side:

> The chemical can be extracted in three forms: as powder, in granules or in small tablets.

Often apposition uses the dash to emphasise a point or to build to a climax:

> The Minister replied that waiting lists are difficult to calculate—but that's not the issue.
>
> We can decorate your awnings with any colour, pattern or picture—whatever your heart desires.

These are extremely useful sentence schemes. They work well with workplace content and give you some extra variety and interest.

Insert parentheses with caution

Parenthesis is the most common of the rhetorical forms in professional writing but also the most poorly handled. Well used, it breaks up the monotony of standard sentence patterns by inserting a secondary element in the middle. This interrupts an incomplete thought to add supporting details or an aside. In the workplace, you will certainly need to qualify many of the statements you make. But just as you would not welcome too many interruptions to your schedule, neither will your readers welcome constant interruptions to their reading.

Parentheses work best with small additions or qualifications. Here is a sentence that tacks on a minor final detail that attracts far more attention than it deserves in the final sentence slot:

> This presentation is now available for your viewing by clicking on the Video Streaming Link on the left-hand side of this website and is titled 04-05-06 Career Planning for Engineers.

The title is much better incorporated into the main sentence:

> This presentation, titled 04-05-06 Career Planning for Engineers, is now available for you to view by clicking on the Video Streaming Link on the left-hand side of this website.

You can adjust the weight of an interruption by using three grades of punctuation marks: brackets, commas and dashes. Where the interruption is for a minor point, you can drop back from commas to brackets. When you want greater emphasis, move up to the dash. Commas mark more of a middle-strength interruption.

Of even more powerful rhetorical value are parentheses that include complete comments or asides. These can switch your point of view, not just to qualify, but to colour the way your reader will understand the information in the main clause. They are often best set off with the more powerful punctuation of the dash:

> Ms Smith has written directly to the Minister—for the third time in as many weeks—about the slow progress in her case.

While parentheses are useful devices, when they start to dominate they become counterproductive:

> *Whilst I regard the prosecution case,* on the record, *as powerful,* supporting in that sense a conclusion that the outcome in the conviction and sentencing of the appellants did not involve any ultimate miscarriage, *for three reasons I join in the conclusion that a retrial should be had.*

The italics shows the main point that a reader will have to sift out of the interruptions. This is typical of much legal writing, where sentences make labyrinthine twists and turns before (finally) completing a point.

Be particularly cautious about separating the subject of a sentence from its verb by inserting a lengthy parenthesis:

> *ADGP understands this initiative,* ABHI, which includes healthy lifestyles, supporting the early detection of lifestyle risks and chronic disease, supports lifestyle and risk modification, and encouraging active patient self-management of chronic disease, *will fall strongly in the domain of the Divisions Network.*

So don't be afraid to intrude, but don't overdo it. As with any special effect, overuse will weary or annoy your readers. Start using these devices cautiously and carefully, in the first instance by recognising a scheme where you naturally tend to use it. As your awareness and confidence grows, they will help you to take your writing ahead of the ordinary.

Power tools

With such a wide range of sentence lengths and rhetorical schemes at your disposal, there is no excuse for drab or monotonous writing. But wait, there's more. So far we've looked at sentences fairly intuitively and with a minimum of grammar. It's time for some power tools to help you understand how sentences work at a technical level.

Vary the sentence types in your documents

The next way you can bring variety to your writing is by using more than one type of sentence. Functionally, sentences tend to do one of four things:

1. Declarative—make a statement.
2. Interrogative—ask a question.
3. Imperative—issue a command.
4. Exclamation—express emphasis or surprise.

Most of your sentences will be declarative, but interrogative and imperative sentences are a great way to engage your readers by addressing them directly:

> Always address an item correctly when preparing mail for postage. Why is this important? If you don't follow the post office's 'clean mail' guidelines, it can delay delivery and attract extra fees.

Exclamations, however, need handling with far more caution. If the pun is the lowest form of wit, then the exclamation is the lowest form of emphasis.

> Which option should we adopt? The second one, I hope! It's the best option!

Your sentence structure and schemes should give you enough scope to reinforce your content without having to signal it with a breathless exclamation mark at the end.

Understand the parts of a sentence

Next, it's time to look at the sentence by breaking it down into its parts: the phrase and the clause. A phrase is a sequence of two or more words that expresses a single unit of meaning. Phrases echo the major word classes by falling into five main types:

The Property Development Corporation,	a leading property developer,	*should enter*
noun phrase	adjective phrase	verb phrase

a series of agreements	as quickly as possible	before the new financial year.
noun phrase	adverb phrase	prepositional phrase

The two most important types are noun phrases and verb phrases because they form the kernel of every clause:

The Property Development Corporation should enter a series of agreements.
noun phrase verb phrase noun phrase

The other types of phrases generally act as modifiers, in this case qualifying and adding further details about the nouns and the action.

Clauses are formed by combining words and phrases into specific patterns. Here are the five most common patterns that form the kernels of every English sentence:

Pattern 1—S V

At their simplest, clauses contain a subject and a verb:

The new machinery failed.
subject verb

Pattern 2—S V O

More commonly, however, a verb will act directly on another noun or noun phrase:

The new machinery surprised the foreman.
subject verb object

Pattern 3—S V dO iO

Sometimes the object comes in two parts, one as a direct and the second as an indirect recipient:

The new machinery presented a challenge for the foreman.
subject verb direct object indirect object

Pattern 4—S V C

At other times, we can add an adjective or a noun after a linking verb to complete a clause:

The new machinery seems useless.
subject verb complement

There are only about a dozen of these linking verbs in English, but they are common enough for this to be a regular pattern. Examples include: 'to be', 'to look', 'to seem', 'to appear' and 'to become'.

Pattern 5—S V Av

The final basic pattern completes a clause for some verbs by adding an adverb:

The new machinery failed again.
subject verb adverbial

The two most important elements in every clause are the subject and the verb. Depending on what kind of verb it is, the clause will finish in different ways—with an object (or two), an adverbial or a complement. Each of these patterns is a basic clause, and if it can stand alone it is also a simple sentence. We can then combine clauses into five more complex patterns:

1 Fragment
2 Simple sentence
3 Compound sentence
4 Complex sentence
5 Compound-complex sentence

Use fragments for emphasis

You have probably been pulled up by the grammar-checker in your word-processing software, which identified a sentence as 'fragment, consider revising'. This means you have written an incomplete sentence that may therefore be unclear:

For the third year in a row

Here we have an adverb phrase, telling us the time-frame in which something happened. A subject and verb are missing from this sentence, along with any object or complement. To make a sentence, we need to add most of these elements:

For the third year in a row, the Division failed to meet its sales target.

Now the phrase is integrated into a complete sentence in which the subject, verb and object are clear. Notice, however, what happens when we reverse the order and keep the adverb phrase as a fragment:

> The Division failed to meet its projected sales figures. For the third year in a row.

Here the sentence pause between the main clause and the fragment reinforces the failure. This is where the fragment comes into its own as a rhetorical device. It is not grammatically complete, but has considerable bite when used consciously and judiciously.

Don't overdo the simple sentence

The next level up is the simple sentence, an independent clause that uses one of the five basic patterns:

> Our analysts are watching very carefully.
> subject verb adverbial

Simple sentences will always be a part of your writing, but they should never dominate your style. Allowing them to do so will generate a kind of baby talk. The investment division of a major bank was apparently advised to do just that to improve the readability of its documents. You can only wonder about its credibility after clients digested this kind of writing:

> The market is holding up better than expected. The gloomy predictions of the last few months have not happened. These predictions might happen in the next few months. We are of the view that this is unlikely. Our analysts are watching very carefully. We will immediately act on any trend. You can be reassured. We will act if we need to.

While a fiction writer might use this breathless effect to build tension in a scene, in the workplace too many simple sentences become annoying. Vary the clause combinations:

> The market is holding up better than expected. Although the gloomy predictions of the last few months have not yet happened, they might do so over the next few months. We think this is unlikely, but our analysts are watching very carefully. You can be reassured that we will act immediately on any trend if we need to.

Save your simple sentences for emphasis and effect, particularly within a longer passage, and as a way of highlighting a key piece of information. They work particularly well at the start or end of paragraphs.

Use compound sentences for elements of equal weight

The next level of complexity in the sentence coordinates two or more independent clauses, either in sequence as a balanced sentence, or nested one within another as an interrupted sentence. We can represent these using the symbol 'I':

I , I , (I) ...	balanced
Ia—I—Ib , (I) ...	interrupted

The most common balanced sentence connects two simple sentences that carry content of equal weight:

> You can choose to sign an authorisation to disclose this information, but you can later revoke that authorisation in writing.

The second form of compound sentence inserts one independent clause into the middle of another, forming an interrupted compound. Be careful with this form of parenthesis, particularly if the interruption goes on for too long. Longer clauses work better in balanced parallels than in parentheses:

> *The power of our award-winning web development team,* on top of the first-rate content written or revised by the fully qualified medical staff at our Station Street office, *will build you a client-friendly site.*

Write mainly in complex sentences

The next sentence combination sequences an independent clause (I) with one or more dependent ones (D), in one of three core combinations:

I , D , (D) ...	leading
D , I , (D) ...	delayed
Ia—D—Ib , (D) ...	interrupted

The leading sentence structure works best when you want to start out with your main point but then add some qualifying detail:

> The Inquiry recommends broadening the definition of 'health information' to include genetic information, based on the definitions of health information in other health information privacy legislation.

This makes good use of the opening slot of the sentence, particularly in a topic sentence at the start of a paragraph. But just as too many simple sentences start to become monotonous, so do too many leading sentences. Mix them up with some delayed sentences that reverse the pattern and start with a dependent phrase or clause:

> Notwithstanding this criticism, His Honour acknowledged that experts are aligned to the party engaging them.

Apart from bringing variety, delayed sentences can help you to link your sentences by pointing to what was in the previous one and connecting it with the next. They also provide important information about time frame or point of view:

> Unfortunately, the last batch to come off the line was overbaked.

> At the start of every month, we intend to compare our budget against actuals.

The rhetorical effect of a delayed sentence can also be to build interest and tension, particularly if you use a series of parallel dependent clauses to reach a climax:

> Operating in over 25 countries, employing more than 15,000 people, providing support services to hundreds of thousands, we are the global leader in our field.

Limit the number of compound-complex sentences

Keeping within the benchmarks for sentence length will mainly mean writing simple, compound and complex sentences, but there will be times when you need to use an even more elaborate pattern, combining two or more independent and one or more dependent elements. This is the realm of the compound-complex sentence, and the variations are endless.

The chief failing of many workplace sentences is unnecessary use of compound-complex structures. By the time you get to three independent clauses, some of which have dependent clauses attached, often parenthetically, you are asking a lot of your reader. It takes a great deal of skill to make such sentences work.

More likely, compound-complex sentences will sprawl across the page, tacking together point after point, stopping for interruptions along the way, then marching on again without pause for breath or thought until another point occurs to the writer and they keep going, somehow, but without any rhetorical schemes to guide their reader, and certainly without much justification from their content, with the final result that they will put their reader to sleep.

As with everything we have looked at in this chapter, variety is the key. Use some short sentences. Mix them up with some sentences of middling length or longer. Add some rhetorical touches such as parallelism and repetition, omission and apposition. You can even pause, if you have something to pause over, by using parenthesis. While doing all this, use some delayed sentences. You can also write some simple sentences. Or even fragments. Use an imperative sentence to engage your reader. Your documents will also benefit if you mix in a balanced compound sentence.

Structure each sentence to convey its content, but also integrate it carefully with the sentences that surround it. This will ensure that you write with clarity, but perhaps also with that elusive quality of excellent prose: music.

Review

14 Punctuation 261
15 Style 280
16 Editing 297
17 Proofing 313

Tools covered in this section

The comma checklist	263
Two guidelines for apostrophes	268
The quick guide to hyphenation	273
The guide to dashes and slashes	274
The four principles of style	281
The style checklist	283
The shortened forms checklist	284
The capitalisation checklist	285
The numbering checklist	287
The sample style sheet	294
The four elements of editing	299
The editing checklist	301
The levels of editorial intervention	307
The proofing checklist	316
The top 10 proofreaders' tips	323
Proofreading marks	325

14 Punctuation

At a glance

The toolbox

- Use five guidelines for commas 262
- Use semi-colons or bullets for sentence lists 266
- Get your apostrophes right 267

The living language

- Understand some punctuation history 270
- Balance the rhetorical and grammatical functions of punctuation 271

Power tools

- Join and separate with hyphens, dashes and slashes 272
- Use colons for introduction and apposition 275
- Use brackets for less important parenthetical elements 276
- Terminate with full stops or question marks and avoid exclamation marks 277
- Prefer single to double quotation marks 278

The toolbox

Contrary to a growing popular belief, punctuation is important. An unpunctuated passage can give you one meaning:

> A woman without her man is nothing.

Then some punctuation will turn it around:

> A woman: without her, man is nothing.

Without punctuation, you cannot distinguish these meanings easily on the page.

In Canada recently, a comma cost a company $2.13 million. It had signed an agreement that:

> shall continue in force for a period of five (5) year terms, and thereafter for successive five year terms, unless and until terminated by one year's prior notice in writing by either party.

One party to this deal, Rogers Communications Inc, thought it meant the contract would run for five years before termination. The other party, Aliant Inc, argued successfully that because of the second comma, the 'unless' clause could kick in straight away. The difference meant the deal could be cancelled, although this was not the original intention. Rogers had to pay an extra $2.13 million for utility poles as a result.

Use five guidelines for commas

While most comma errors will be less spectacular than this, it pays to understand the comma. It is probably the most complex of the punctuation marks, but you can start by applying a simple pause test. Read this sentence aloud, or sound it out in your head, and see where you pause in your reading:

> If you have any questions about our service, please contact Dr Smith.

Did you pause at the comma? It's a safe bet that this is also where the comma will help to convey your grammatical meaning. This is an 'if ... then' statement: *if* you have questions, *then* contact us, and the comma separates the two effectively.

The pause test is more reliable in shorter sentences. In complex sentences, it can and will let you down. Read this text aloud and listen for the pauses to help you place the commas:

> During the audit of employee benefit expenses audit found that the system was focused on management accounting and not financial reporting.

How many commas do you need in this sample? One or two? There is clearly a pause after 'expenses', but is there also a pause after 'accounting'? Some will say yes and some will say no, and that's when you should turn to some more technical guidelines to supplement your ear:

The comma checklist

1. Use a comma after an introductory item.
2. Consider commas to list three or more items in a series.
3. Use commas around parenthetical elements.
4. Do not use commas with restrictive elements.
5. Generally use a comma before a conjunction that links independent clauses.

1. Use a comma after an introductory item

This is the most straightforward use of the comma:

> In November 2005, the committee agreed to a review.

> When agreement is not reached, there are various mediation options you can pursue.

Often, these are adverbial phrases that give extra information about timing. They can also form a more complex clause.

> When more than a dozen packages were returned with evidence of tampering, the only course of action was to recall the entire product line.

These commas signal to your reader that the main clause is coming up ahead, and that they are starting the sentence with a secondary piece of information. This will help them get the structure of the sentence right on first reading.

You might want to depart from this guideline if the introductory item is short, but it is far safer to include it to prevent ambiguity. Compare these versions with and without the commas:

> Further, violence may erupt between fans if they are not kept apart.
>
> From 2002, overseas students will constitute 60 per cent of fee-paying places.

2. Consider commas to list three or more items in a series

Commas can also help you separate more than two short items listed in a sentence.

> These insured the integrity of key operations such as enrolment, billing and cash collection.

American usage generally includes a second comma before the final conjunction, but British and Australian usage leaves it out. Often called the serial comma, this generates a great deal of debate. Use your judgement and don't be afraid to add a second comma if it clarifies the meaning, particularly if the last item is a double:

> The department checked revenue rulings, business rules, and technical and procedural instructions.

It can also be useful for separating three or more complex items.

> The utility reports on daily and monthly water quality, water usage and storage, and overflows and bypasses.

If the items in a list become more complex than this, it is better to move onto the heavier semi-colon to separate them.

3. Use commas around parenthetical elements

When you add words that are not essential to the primary meaning of the sentence, you should mark them off from the main clause with commas. If you remove the parenthetical elements, the sentence still makes sense:

> The IT Advisory Group, which meets monthly, will discuss the establishment of intensive support services.

Here the commas signal to the reader that we're pausing now, considering something secondary, then returning to pick up and finish the first thread.

4. Do not use commas with restrictive elements

Beware that often what seems parenthetical may be restrictive, defining the subject of a sentence. If you remove this element, the sentence no longer makes sense. The commas in this example should be removed:

> Any company, that does not comply with the new conditions, will be in breach of the law.

Make sure you learn this difference, as misunderstanding it can change the meaning of a sentence completely. A training manual for wartime pilots used the more insulting of these two:

> Pilots whose minds are dull do not usually live long.
> Pilots, whose minds are dull, do not usually live long.

This is also the rule that the grammar-checker in your word processor uses to tell you when to use 'that' and when to use 'which'. This says you should use 'that' for a restrictive element, but 'which' for something parenthetical. That's why it wants you to put a comma before every 'which' in your sentence—it assumes that what follows is parenthetical. It's a useful rule of thumb, but don't follow it religiously. The grammar-checker would lead you into this sort of nonsense:

> All land in NSW is taxable, except for land, which is exempt.

If you like, you can keep the grammar-checker happy by using 'that':

> All land in NSW is taxable, except for land that is exempt.

5. Generally use a comma before a conjunction that links independent clauses

An independent clause can stand alone as a sentence or join with other clauses. Use a comma when you link two independent clauses with conjunctions, particularly if they have different subjects.

> The customer service officer explains the fees, but the client often does not listen.

> The manager was on sick leave, so I rescheduled the visit for the following week.

The comma here signals to your reader that you are going to complete one idea, then start a connected one that is also reasonably independent. For many of us, this runs counter to the old-school rule never to put a comma in front of a conjunction. Instead, we often use a comma splice, putting in a comma alone:

> The market strategy quantifies possible demand, the penetration of that market is realistically assessed over a long period.

This is asking a little too much of a comma, so help it out by using a conjunction as well. The 'no comma with a conjunction' rule may have been useful at primary school, but it should never have been raised to the level of catechism.

Combining the pause test with these five guidelines should resolve well over 90 per cent of your comma placements. For any uncertainty that remains, breaking up or recasting the sentence should do the trick. The handful of comma dilemmas left over are unlikely to be of any consequence.

Use semi-colons or bullets for sentence lists

Semi-colons are the ageing divas of punctuation. Once one of the most common marks, they are getting harder and harder to find. This is mainly because average sentences are getting shorter; when we wrote in long snaking paragraphs with only a single full stop, there was a much greater need for the semi-colon to provide some internal structure. In recent times, we tend to break these structures into separate sentences.

One remaining use for the semi-colon is to link two independent clauses without a conjunction when the connection between the two is closer than a sentence break would indicate:

> The market strategy quantifies possible demand; the penetration of that market is realistically assessed over a long period.

This will be relatively rare, as you will more likely use two sentences or a comma and a conjunction.

You will more commonly use semi-colons in a complex sentence list, when the heavier mark adds value:

> Our customer profile for this vehicle found that: most purchasers are women between 18 and 35 years old; these customers return their cars for servicing according to the recommended schedule; most feel uncomfortable with the service personnel, especially when they enter the workshop floor; and over one half do not continue with the marque when they come to upgrade, citing their service experience as a factor.

Yet even here the semi-colon's use is declining as bullet points take over more of this role:

> Our customer profile for this vehicle found that:
>
> - most purchasers are women between 18 and 35 years old
> - these customers return their cars for servicing according to the recommended schedule
> - most feel uncomfortable with the service personnel, especially when they enter the workshop floor
> - over one-half do not continue with the marque when they come to upgrade, citing their service experience as a factor.

Initially, we punctuated bullet lists using semi-colons as well. More recently, we've realised that the bullets now do the punctuating, so you don't need the semi-colons. Reserve them for a conventional sentence list within a paragraph.

Get your apostrophes right

The punctuation mark that causes the most confusion has been doing so for centuries. The apostrophe emerged in English during the 16th century to mark the omission of letters—'I bid thee think on't, Sir!'—but also the plural of some imported nouns—'three comma's'. Its third function, to show possession, was by no means common until well into the 18th century, and not broadly mandated until the 19th. The second function has since been abandoned except by errant greengrocers advertising 'banana's' and 'tomatoe's', or by music stores selling 'CD's'.

The confusion over the apostrophe arises because we have two elements—the apostrophe and the letter 's'—that we ask at different times to perform three different functions: indicate omission, possession and number. When you deal with these one at a time, there is little problem. But when you have to show two or more elements in the one word, conflict arises. This means that most cases will fall easily into one of two areas, but there are a few exceptions you just have to learn by rote.

1. To mark the omission of letters and numbers

The first area is the easiest. When you leave out letters or numbers, use an apostrophe to show where something was cut:

the class of '99	the class of 1999
don't	do not
it's	it is or it has

This brings us to the first exception: *it's* versus *its*. The first is a contraction, and the second a possessive pronoun. Although possession usually uses an apostrophe, the contraction needs the apostrophe more, so we leave it off the pronoun to distinguish between them. An easy way to think of it is that if you can spell the word out, use the apostrophe.

2. Possession by a noun

The second major use of the apostrophe is to indicate ownership. When nouns are singular, show possession by adding an apostrophe and the letter 's':

the plaintiff's response
the customer's complaint

But here we have a problem, because we also use the letter 's' to indicate whether something is plural. To show both ownership and plurality, add the 's' first, then the apostrophe:

the plaintiffs' response
the customers' complaint

Where a word doesn't use the letter 's' to form a plural, treat it like a regular singular noun:

the children's toys

The golden rule with apostrophes is to indicate whether a noun is singular or plural first, and only then whether it owns anything. Applying this principle will prevent mistakes such as these:

Each of the MP's received the papers in electronic form on CD's.
The 1970's saw the emergence of stagflation.

The nouns in these cases are plurals that don't possess anything. No apostrophe is necessary.

The final area of the apostrophe creates the most confusion of all: what to do when a singular name ending in 's' possesses something. The punctuation authorities are heavily divided on this case. Some argue that, for simplicity, always add an apostrophe and then an 's', just as you would for any other singular noun:

Neil James's book
John Keats's poetry

Others argue that, while this is generally acceptable, depart from it when it would sound awkward, or when the word involves a historical figure:

Menzies' prime ministership
Jesus' disciples

To further complicate matters, institutions are increasingly leaving the apostrophe out of their spelling:

The Allied Services Corporation
The Department of Community Services staff

The argument here is that what might seem to be possession is just as arguably descriptive, functioning rather like an adjective. This reasoning also leads to modern forms such as:

drivers licence
six weeks time

In Australia, the Geographical Names Board in 1966 ruled along these lines that placenames would no longer take an apostrophe despite any possessive origin:

St James Station
Kings Cross

This kind of complexity leaves you wondering whether it might not be simpler to abandon the apostrophe altogether, or perhaps to prevent anyone with a name ending in 's' from owning anything. But if we are stuck with complexity when punctuating possession for names ending in 's', at least it is only one case. For the most part, you can resolve apostrophe placement using the two more consistent guidelines.

The living language

Understand some punctuation history

The role that punctuation plays in grammatical clarity was originally not its highest priority. Our earliest writing lacked any punctuation at all, including the most basic form: spaces between words. When writing was done on clay tablets, inscribed in stone or scratched on papyrus, the letters were run together: Claystoneandpapyruswereexpensiveafterallsok eepingcostsdownfaroutweighedtheneedsofreaders.

Punctuation began with the Greek dramatists in the fifth century BC, who separated words using dots and symbols to show who was speaking and how long each speech would be. These lengths were called commas, colons and periods. They referred to the text itself, which was enclosed by either a low, middle or high point.

The major gong for inventing a punctuation system usually goes to Aristophanes of Byzantium, who ran the Library of Alexandria in the second century BC. He developed a system of points with the functions of the comma, semi-colon and full stop that indicated the relative length of text involved. But he added more sophisticated separators to show the relationship between individual words, including the virgule or forward slash, the hyphen, the apostrophe and the quotation mark.

Unfortunately, most of Aristophanes' innovations did not catch on. Latin authors in later centuries used dots as separators, along with large letters to indicate new sentences, but not much of his word punctuation. It was left to monks such as Jerome and Alcuin between the fourth and eighth centuries AD to evolve the system of points, and their focus was still at the sentence level, to help priests and monks to read and chant scripture aloud.

For several centuries, then, the main purpose of punctuation was its rhetorical duty. It showed readers how to pronounce the text off the page, where to breathe and to pause, so that actors could get their lines right and priests wouldn't stumble over the Word of God.

Only with the rise of the printing press did the second major purpose of punctuation emerge, as increasingly text was produced to be read silently. In the 15th and 16th centuries, the Venetian printers Aldus Manutius and grandson revised the punctuation marks we have today, including commas, semi-colons, colons, full stops and brackets. By the

17th century, apostrophes, dashes, exclamation marks and quotations rounded out the set.

The rise of the printing press elevated the grammatical role of punctuation over its initial rhetorical role. This was particularly important for English as it was evolving. Old English built into the endings of words indications about their relationship. We gradually lost these case endings, but as a result the order of the words became much more crucial for conveying meaning, along with some punctuation. Yet English writers were still attached to the Latin practice of using punctuation to mark rhetorical pauses more than grammatical structures.

The two trends divided along geographical lines, with the British retaining more of this rhetorical focus, and the Americans applying more rigorous systems to the grammatical function. They occasionally trade insults. Eric Partridge lamented the 'simple, almost mechanical routine that American schools recommend'. The Americans, on the other hand, conclude with the *New Yorker* that the British lecturing the Americans about punctuation 'is a little like an American lecturing the French on sauces'.

Balance the rhetorical and grammatical functions of punctuation

In reality, the grammatical duty constitutes as much as 80 per cent of the punctuation tasks you will face at work. It is worth learning some guidelines for these and settling disagreements quickly. There is nothing more frustrating, when several staff work on the same document, than one person putting in a comma, the next taking it out, and the next one restoring it. The guidelines in this chapter will give you an objective reference point, but this doesn't mean you can't sometimes finesse your text for rhetorical impact. Never become a slave to a guideline.

Wherever you fall on the rhetoric–grammar divide, one trend has affected both over the last century: the gradual reduction in the range and volume of punctuation marks in professional documents. This was partly driven by the shortening of sentences, as time-stressed workplaces made their documents more punchy and readable. The trend accelerated with advances to word-processing technology, because punctuation is harder to distinguish on screen than on the page. There is no reason that the full set of marks that worked well for the linotype printing press and the typewriter should be the same ones to suit the digital age. As a result, we have continued to simplify punctuation.

Some see this as a decline in standards, but punctuation has always adapted to contemporary technologies. Marks such as the virgule disappeared for a while, then returned as the forward slash when a new use suggested itself. The semi-colon is currently in decline, and some linguists advocate abandoning the apostrophe. We no longer use as much punctuation in address blocks in letters. The balance will continue to shift as each generation adjusts its rhetorical emphasis. But there will always remain a core of grammatical rules, and these are worth learning.

KEY TIP Make sure that any rhetorical punctuation choice will not impair grammatical clarity.

Power tools

Join and separate with hyphens, dashes and slashes

The earliest punctuation marks were those showing the breaks between groups of words to aid reading aloud. As the system evolved, we developed symbols that could also show the connections between words. The most complex of these is the hyphen.

Hyphens

Despite differences of opinion between punctuation authorities, one thing attracts a great degree of consensus: if you take hyphens too seriously, you will surely go mad. This relates to their role with compound words. One of the features English inherited from its Germanic origins is the ability to create new words by linking two existing ones. Compounds generally start off as separate words, such as *pay* and *roll,* but gradually come together as a new noun:

pay roll
pay-roll
payroll

The middle stage of this process uses a hyphen. Different compounds are at different stages of this process in different parts of the world, and if you tried to work out a definitive system you could expect a visit from the nice people in white coats. There is only one real solution: use your dictionary. If it gives you more than one alternative, pick the first one. Then get on with your life.

To save you a little time looking hyphens up, however, here is a list of the most common hyphen dilemmas and their solutions:

The quick guide to hyphenation

Compounds	Example
Compounds with 'well', 'ill' and 'semi'	a semi-skilled worker
Numbers, quantities and fractions	two-thirds
Where the last vowel of the prefix and the first letter of the main word are the same	pre-eminent de-emphasise
To avoid changing a word's meaning	re-form (form again) reform (improve)
To link a multi-word phrase with 'co-', 'ex-' and 'e-'	co-worker ex-president
If the base word begins with a capital letter or number	pre-2005
Suffixes that use a hyphen with numbers such as '-odd' or '-fold'	30-odd two-fold
A verb + adverb	go-ahead
A noun + verb	tailor-made
Not an adverb + verb	bypass
Not an adverb + noun	downwind
Not an adjective followed by a noun, unless forming a compound adjective	red tape red-letter day

Dashes

There is also confusion in the workplace about the difference between a hyphen and a dash. To further confuse things, there are actually two types of dashes to choose from—the en dash and the em dash—which are named that way because they are roughly as wide as the letters 'n' and 'm'.

hyphen	-
en dash	–
em dash	—

It is worth learning the difference between the three marks, because they have different functions and can help you join and separate with precision.

Most word compounding is carried out by the hyphen. The extra function of the en dash (–) is to show spans of figures, time and distance, and places. The longer mark helps to convey a range between points and numbers rather than the tighter compound of two words.

pages 2–3
2003–04
a Sydney–Perth flight

A useful hint is to test whether you could insert the word 'to' between two words or numbers. If so, use an en dash.

The em dash (—) is much more about emphasis, generally involving whole phrases and clauses rather than pairs of words. It separates but at the same time draws attention to whatever is on the other side. Here's a sample that would have benefited from a stronger mark than a comma:

> Our lead article looks at the new transition to retirement legislation, a fantastic initiative to help give you more flexibility about how and when you retire.

See how much more impact the dash has:

> Our lead article looks at the new transition to retirement legislation—a fantastic initiative to help give you more flexibility about how and when you retire.

Em dashes can also signal an abrupt change of tack or opinion:

> There were no discernible procedures—but that isn't the issue.

The second broad use of the em dash is when you want a more heightened form of parenthesis that separates but at the same time draws attention to the text it encloses:

> The government may change at the next election—many commentators think it will—but the law will remain.

As a powerful punctuation mark, reserve this for the occasions that call for extra weight.

Slashes

The slash today is associated with the very latest in computer technology. Most of us first encountered it as the 'forward slash' in an Internet address:

<http://www.plainenglishfoundation.com/index.html>

In fact, the forward slash is one of the oldest forms of punctuation, and keeps returning despite regular attempts to knock it off. Originally known as the virgule, its first function was similar to that of the comma, which eventually replaced it. But it refused to say die, and at times reinvented itself as the bar, diagonal, oblique and solidus. The internet seems as though it will preserve the mark for at least a while yet. Its other main use is to indicate alternatives such as 'yes/no', 'male/female' and 'and/or'.

Use colons for introduction and apposition

Like the semi-colon, the colon has become much less common than it was even 50 years ago. It used to have a rhetorical function as a heavy stop somewhere in weight between a semi-colon and a full stop, but this has more or less died out. Today, the colon is more of an introducer for a quotation or a list:

> We distribute this publication to: secondary schools, universities and state government departments.

In short lists like this, you can use some discretion and leave the colon out. Definitely keep it, however, when introducing a larger block quote or a bulleted list.

The more important task of the colon is to divide a sentence so that what follows amplifies, explains, questions, summarises or contrasts with what precedes it:

> There is one word for the agency's procedures: inadequate.
> The question is: what criteria shall we use?

Here, the colon is a less dramatic form of apposition than the em dash.

Use brackets for less important parenthetical elements

Our next set of marks gives you advanced options for parenthetical elements—for when you want to separate less important information from the main flow of the sentence.

There are four types of brackets you can use:

1. Round brackets ( )
2. Square brackets [ ]
3. Angle brackets < >
4. Brace brackets { }

Use round brackets to add secondary or specific detail without killing the flow of the sentence:

> The Country Fire Authority (CFA) was called to the area again.
>
> There are proposed increases in investment ($8.3 billion), jobs (30,812 full-time) and exports ($5.8 billion).

When you find yourself wanting to add brackets in a sentence, ask yourself whether the delete key might not work better. If your sentence is a long one, breaking it up might also help you integrate the material more effectively.

Use square brackets for editorial interventions, particularly within a quote:

> The manager promised to double-check them [the percentages] before close of business.

You can also use them to point out errors, but be careful as this can look a little sarcastic:

> The report argues: 'they have not omited [*sic*] any information'.

Angle brackets until recently have been reserved for fairly scholarly tasks, such as in mathematical proofs or to show where text was missing in a transcription of an ancient manuscript. But the web has given them, like the virgule, a new lease on life as a way of quoting electronic addresses without merging them with the sentence punctuation:

> <www.plainenglishfoundation.com.au>
> Contact me at <mail@plainenglishfoundation.com.au>.

Braces are the fourth kind of bracket still in use, albeit in specific disciplines such as mathematics and grammar. But as digital media continues to expand, braces may well be the next punctuation mark to re-enter the mainstream. Like the virgule or forward slash, an emerging requirement may soon be calling on them for a new job. Until then, they will be rare in most workplaces.

Terminate with full stops or question marks and avoid exclamation marks

Full stops are the most obvious of the terminators, and the one mark everyone can use with confidence. Use them:

- at the end of a sentence that isn't a question or exclamation
- after the final point in a bulleted list
- when numbering subsections and paragraphs
- to separate elements in web and email addresses
- as the decimal point in numbers and currency
- when expressing the time.

The most contentious point about full stops in the workplace is whether to insert one space or two before the capital letter that starts the next sentence. The old standard used to be two spaces because the typewriter carriage did not always move accurately and it was safer to leave an extra space. Word-processing software and printing technology now makes this redundant. Adding a second space will simply waste it.

Use a question mark after questions that are in question form. These include headings and titles that form a question.

> Can you send the shipment to the warehouse?
> What is best for the market?

You do not need to use a question mark after indirect questions or polite requests.

> Our officer asked the company if it could send the bill to our office.
> Would you please send us your bill by Monday.

Exclamation marks provide emotional emphasis, but they are rather dangerous in workplace writing. Some use them as an easy way to signal what their words have failed to convey. Here's an extract from an optometrist's newsletter:

> **Soon I'll be saying Happy 2006!!!** I cannot believe how quickly this year has passed. I know I say this every year ... time just escapes me ... I guess I really am getting older!!!! (just like fine wine, I'd like to believe I'm improving!!!!!)

Prefer single to double quotation marks

Our final area of punctuation is one of divided practice. The main issues with quotations are:

- Do you use single or double quotation marks?
- How do you show quotes within quotes?
- Where do you place the surrounding punctuation when quoting speech or dialogue?

Media and most publishers go for double quotation marks, while corporate and government style tends towards the single. Single quotation marks look cleaner and are easier to key in, but doubles have a tenacious hold because of their presence in publishing. Whichever system you adopt, if you need to show a quote within a quote, use the opposite mark for the inside quote:

> The convener reported, 'The committee said that it "did not receive the new guidelines" on time.'

Use quote marks when you are incorporating an incomplete piece of text within your own sentence:

> The committee said that it 'believed it had met the criteria'.

If you have a passage longer than three lines to quote, generally drop to the next line, indent it and quote it in normal text. You do not then need to place quote marks around it, nor to place it in italics.

If punctuation authorities will continue to disagree about commas and apostrophes, there seems little hope of ever unifying their practices for punctuating quoted speech. The main differences are over whether to place sentence punctuation within the quotation marks or outside them. A typical Australian practice is to place the full stop outside the quotation marks if there is a 'carrier expression' such as 'the CEO said':

> 'We are looking forward to improved sales figures,' the CEO said, 'but that will depend on what happens to interest rates'.

On the other hand, if the quote is a complete sentence and there is no carrier expression, tuck the full stop inside the quotation mark:

> 'We are looking forward to improved sales figures, but that will depend on what happens to interest rates.'

Whichever style or combination you decide to apply, do it consciously and consistently.

15 Style

At a glance

The toolbox

- Apply four principles to guide style choices 281
- Refer to a national dictionary for your spelling 283
- Minimise shortened forms 284
- Minimise capital letters 285
- Use inclusive language 286
- Number for clarity and efficiency 286
- Choose a system for citations 287
- Know your document formats 289

The living language

- Understand the changing meaning of style 289
- Be aware of the major style guides 290
- Keep up to date with changes in style 291

Power tools

- Choose the right style for your context 292
- Use style sheets for individual documents 293
- Develop an in-house manual 296

The toolbox

William Sabin, editor of the *Gregg Reference Manual*, tells a great story about the frustrations of style. A zookeeper in America wanted to expand his mongoose stocks. When ordering animals from a breeder, he was having a great deal of trouble describing them. He wanted two animals, and his first draft wrote asking for two mongooses. This sounded awkward, so he thought perhaps he should ask for two mongeese. But mongeese didn't sound quite right either. So finally, he wrote asking the supplier to send him a mongoose. Then, in the next paragraph, he asked the supplier to send a second mongoose.

The story may be apocryphal, but it illustrates the lengths we sometimes go to when trying to get around uncertainties of style. These commonly involve conventions such as how to format a date, spell a word or punctuate a bulleted list. Most of these choices are of a lower order than those you need to make for content, structure and expression, but they still have an impact on your message.

Issues of style can also consume an enormous amount of time in the workplace. Everyone has a pet hate or style preference, whether in commas or capitalisation, percentages or personal pronouns. The problem is that often you can make a rational case for several options. As a result, style choices vary between Australia and Britain, and both vary significantly from American practice.

Apply four principles to guide style choices

This chapter cannot cover the intricacies that style manuals take hundreds of pages to deal with, so we will start by looking at four guiding principles. When you need to make a style decision, these will help you to reach a more informed conclusion:

1. Clarity
2. Legibility
3. Efficiency
4. Consistency

The first principle is perhaps the most important: does one option make the text clearer than another, or does it increase the likelihood of a misreading? A classic example is the formatting for a date. The American approach is to write:

October 23, 2006

Americans have long debates about whether to omit the comma here. Some keep it because otherwise the two sets of numbers tend to run together. Others leave it out because it can read like a thousand division. The Australian approach removes the ambiguity altogether:

23 October 2006

Legibility has more to do with the physical appearance of the text. The trend towards minimal punctuation, for example, is motivated by the idea that cleaner text gives readers less to decode. The same applies to minimising capitalisation and italics because these are harder for the eye to decipher. Compare the legibility of these two options:

> The SEPTEMBER 2002 PLAN states that '*The development of plantations is an integral part of the state government's overall environmental strategy.*'

> The September 2002 Plan states that the 'development of plantations is an integral part of the state government's overall environmental strategy.'

Efficiency comes into play when one style choice takes longer to produce. Sometimes even a few extra keystrokes add up when you are making millions of them. Which of these two would you prefer to key in:

$126.50
One hundred and twenty-six dollars and fifty cents

Consistency is probably the most important principle of style. At a minimum, always be consistent within a document. People will distrust a text if it punctuates bulleted lists in three different ways. Also try to conform with the accepted style choices of your organisation and your community. Don't, for example, use American conventions for the serial comma in Australia:

The T-shirts are available in red, green, and blue.

An Australian audience will read this as a grammatical error, and correct it to:

The T-shirts are available in red, green and blue.

There are five major areas of style you will need to apply these principles to:

The style checklist

1. Language
2. Numbering
3. Punctuation
4. Sourcing
5. Formatting

Refer to a national dictionary for your spelling

Your first language choice is which reference you should use for spelling. Because of continual shifts in pronunciation, English has a complex spelling system. While for many the *Oxford English Dictionary* remains the standard, in America *Merriam-Webster's Dictionary* is preferred. In Australia, the *Macquarie Dictionary* is attuned to Australian idiom and usage.

So your dictionary will principally be a geographical choice. If your readers are in Australia, use the latest edition of the *Macquarie Dictionary*. If you are writing documents for other countries as well, you will need to be aware of the major differences. Beware of the dictionaries built into word-processing software, as they mostly use American spelling.

Some major spelling variations

Variation	Australia	United Kingdom	America
ize / ise	organise	organise / organize	organize
or / our	colour	colour	color
m / mme	program	programme / program	program
g / gue	catalogue	catalogue	catalog
re / er	centre	centre	center

You may also need to look at words specific to your profession, and decide how to spell compounds such as 'pay roll', 'pay-roll' or 'payroll'.

Minimise shortened forms

There are five main ways to shorten a word or a phrase:

The shortened forms checklist

1. Abbreviations
2. Contractions
3. Acronyms
4. Initialisms
5. Symbols

	Examples	Meaning	Conventions
Abbreviation	Aust. cont.	Australia continued	Use the first but not last letter of a word, ending with a full stop.
Contraction	Dr Pty Ltd	Doctor Proprietary Limited	Use the first and last letters of a word, and do not use a full stop.
Acronym	Qantas DoCS	Queensland and Northern Territory Air Service Department of Community Services	Use the first letters of a phrase, which are then pronounced as a word. These start out in capitals, but can become their own word.
Initialism	NSW CD	New South Wales compact disc	These are like acronyms but they stay in capitals and each letter is pronounced.
Symbol	km ©	kilometre copyright	Use the established conventions set by international bodies.

Abbreviated forms like these are a short cut for the workplace writer. If your readers are familiar with a particular form, it may save them time as well. If you are less certain that your reader will know an abbreviation, spell it out the first time you use it and place the abbreviation in brackets. But don't take this as licence to render every name into an acronym or initialism, as it will slow down reading:

> PDC's representative, LL, recently approached DOH with a proposal for DOH to purchase PDC and thereby merge the interests of the tenant and landlord. LL claims this will have benefits for DOH.

A more balanced usage is a mix of acronyms, full spelling and short titles rather than acronyms or initialisms alone:

> Lend Lease recently proposed that the department purchase the Property Development Corporation (PDC) to merge the interests of the tenant and the landlord. It claims this will benefit the department.

Minimise capital letters

Workplace writers habitually overuse capital letters, mainly because they make some words seem more important. Chapter 9 has discussed how capitals have changed over the centuries and how they are continuing to evolve. The current Australian standards are as follows.

The capitalisation checklist

Use capitals:

- at the start of each sentence
- for proper nouns such as names of people, countries and languages
- for geographical names
- for the names of months, historical periods or official holidays
- for the full title of an organisation
- for the initial letter in a heading
- for a specific reference, as in 'Phase 2'
- for elements of a report, such as Findings, Notes, Chapter, Figure, Table and Part
- for each important letter in a publication title.

Do not use capitals:

- for short titles such as 'the company'
- when a name is used as an adjective, such as 'federal politics' and 'university policy'
- for a general report reference, as in 'the lower chart on page 16'
- for abbreviations, as in 'vol.' and 'no.'
- for emphasis, as it looks like SHOUTING.

Use inclusive language

Another source of uncertainty is how to use inclusive rather than gender-specific references. Too often in the past, writers used 'he' when referring to both genders. The disclaimer that 'the masculine pronoun implies both the masculine and feminine' is no longer acceptable. To write inclusively, try these approaches in order of priority:

An applicant must submit his form on time.

	Alternative	Example
1	Use the plural	Applicants must submit their forms on time.
2	Use the gender-free pronoun 'you'	You must submit the application form on time.
3	Leave the pronoun out	Every applicant must submit forms on time.
4	Repeat the noun	Applicants must submit the application forms on time.
5	Use the gender-free pronoun 'they'	They must submit the application forms on time.
6	Use the alternative pronouns 'his' or 'her' or 'his/her'	Every applicant must submit his or her forms on time.

Also be careful with value-laden terms that define people based on ethnicity, sexual orientation or ability. Refer to people using more neutral descriptions, such as geography rather than ethnicity ('African–American'), and by using prepositions rather than adjectives ('people with a disability' rather than 'disabled people').

Number for clarity and efficiency

The main confusion that arises with numbers is when to spell them out in words and when to use numerals. The governing convention is partly determined by clarity and partly by efficiency. The case for using numerals as an efficiency measure is clear-cut. But problems can emerge when the numbers are small, when they start a sentence or when two numbers collide:

We need to order another 2 30 mm boards to finish the job. 1 board was damaged in the last order, so please make sure the 2 are well padded.

Here, clarity is better served by turning some of these into words:

> We need to order another two 30 mm boards to finish the job. One board was damaged in the last order, so please make sure the two are well padded.

Spell out numbers in words:

- for numbers one to nine in the text
- if a number starts a sentence
- to indicate millions, billions and trillions.

Use numerals:

- for 10 to 999,999
- in tables
- with units of measurement, such as 30 mm or 5°C
- for numbers with decimals, such as 6.25
- for the time, such as 6.30 am
- for angles, such as 90°
- for percentages in tables, graphs, charts and diagrams
- in mathematical or scientific equations.

The key point of contention is at what digit to convert from spelling to numerals. Single-digit numbers can get lost within text, so these are best spelt out from one to nine. Double digits will be more prominent, so use numerals at 10 or higher.

Choose a system for citations

Many workplace documents will need to incorporate material from somewhere else. This may mean paraphrasing someone else's idea, adding a quotation, or simply referring to an intellectual debt. Effective sourcing can boost your credibility by showing the depth of your research. There are significant legal implications as well, as the expression of ideas constitutes intellectual property, and unacknowledged use of someone else's property is a form of theft.

On the other hand, overly scrupulous sourcing of every point can become distracting for a reader, constantly interrupting the flow of a document. The right balance will vary with the context. In an academic setting, full and careful citation will be far more important than when a small business writes a letter to a customer. The conventions you choose may differ, but you must always acknowledge where you are using someone else's words.

There are two main approaches to citation and referencing: the author–date system and the documentary note system. The first was developed for use in the sciences, although it is increasingly popular in the humanities as well. It places the author's name and the date of the source's publication in brackets next to the text that draws from it:

> Recent studies have confirmed the original results (Radcliffe 2003, p. 28; Whatmore and Coombs 2000).

If readers want to pursue the reference, they can turn to an alphabetical list of the works cited at the end of the document. There are many minor variations to this system, but they all have the key feature of citing the author and date in the text immediately next to where it is used.

The documentary note system does not interrupt the text with the reference in brackets, but places a superscript number in the text, linked to a citation at the bottom of the page (footnote) or at the end of the text (endnote).

> Recent studies have confirmed the original results.[1]

One of the advantages of the documentary note system is that you can add commentary that amplifies the point you are making in the main text. However, readers are getting increasingly intolerant of this convention because it slows them down as they jump up and down the page or turn to the end of the text. It is best to limit your references solely to citing your source material. If a point of discussion is important enough, incorporate it into the main body of the text or press the delete key.

The two systems also differ in how they present the full reference for a work in a bibliography:

Author–date

James, N. 2007, *Writing at Work*, Allen & Unwin, Sydney.

Documentary note

N. James, *Writing at Work*, Sydney, Allen & Unwin, 2007.

Whichever you choose, use it consistently. More importantly, decide in advance what conventions you will follow, and make sure everyone working on a project knows them. Copy editing several pages of inconsistent referencing at the late stage of a report can be soul-destroying.

Know your document formats

In most workplaces, the format you use is pre-set in document templates, often in electronic form. However, word-processing software can play havoc with the set dimensions, particularly when you cut and paste text from elsewhere. Always find out what your formatting parameters are so you can re-set your documents. The basic elements to check are:

1. Body text—font, size, line spacing, paragraph spacing, alignment.
2. Headings—font, size, line spacing, alignment.
3. Page size and margins.
4. Tables and graphs—conventions for numbering them and placing captions.

Where you don't have any established conventions, Chapter 7 on design can help you choose your typography and page design.

The living language

Understand the changing meaning of style

Part of the problem with style is that the meaning of the word has constantly shifted. It initially referred to a set of characteristics that defined a particular thing. Its first recorded use emerged in the 14th century, when Chaucer wrote a story 'in frankis stile', meaning in a manner characteristic of French writers. But style then took on the sense of some kind of judgement or sanction about those characteristics.

By the 18th century, style often referred to the admirable qualities of a piece of writing. 'Proper words in the proper places, make the true definition of style,' said Jonathan Swift in 1720. English translators used the word when rendering classical texts on rhetoric into English. While Greek rhetoricians wrote 'lexis' and Roman orators 'elocutio', both words in English became 'style'. In this rhetorical sense, style could be any aspect of expression: word usage, grammar, sentence structures or figures of speech.

With the rise of industrialisation, however, style started to narrow in meaning. In Scottish law it referred to an authorised form for drawing up a deed. In 1871, the *American Encyclopaedia of Printing* used it to refer to the rules and methods of typography that a particular printing house followed. This led to the development of style manuals, which set out the best way to produce specific texts such as books, newspapers and magazines.

Early printers had apprenticeship systems that passed on knowledge about typesetting and production. At the turn of the 19th century, expanding markets for books placed considerable pressure on these systems and their output. As the *Oxford Style Manual* describes it, 'suddenly, the length of time formerly taken to learn the skills associated with producing books appeared antiquated when measured against the new realities of mechanisation and high volume'.

Be aware of the major style guides

In 1893, the printer to Oxford University, Horace Hart, compiled a sheet of rules on typography and usage for his rapidly expanding staff. When he found copies being sold to the general public, he decided to issue *Hart's Rules* as a book. It has never been out of print. The text covered the different parts of a book, how to prepare a manuscript, how to handle proofs, and how to treat capitalisation, abbreviations, punctuation, spelling of foreign words, numbers, and lists and tables. Oxford followed up this success with its *Author's and Printer's Dictionary*, a dictionary of usage, listing 'common editorial conundrums' in alphabetical order.

The Oxford volumes were immensely influential throughout the English-speaking world. As compulsory education and increasing literacy boosted the demand for books of all kinds, there was a felt need for standards. Books that varied their spelling, sourcing, numbers or referencing looked sloppy and careless, and this took time to fix.

Not to be outdone, the Americans decided to develop their own reference more suited to local circumstances. An academic publisher took the lead when the University of Chicago Press adapted a single sheet of typographical basics to create the first *Chicago Manual of Style* in 1906. Like its Oxford predecessor, its focus was on how to prepare and publish a physical book, but it also covered punctuation, language, spelling, numbers, quotations and referencing. Now in its 15th edition, it has radically altered many of its rulings down the decades.

If increased book production drove the initial wave of publishing on style, the expansion of different professions also played a part. The first business-writing guide emerged in 1916 in George Burton Hotchkiss and Celia Ann Drew's *Business English*. *The Gregg Reference Manual* was written by the man who devised a popular form of shorthand, and it remains in print decades later.

The rise of tertiary education spawned shorter guides for students, of which William Strunk Jr's *The Elements of Style* is the best known. But specific academic disciplines were also finding that the Oxford and Chicago manuals were not comprehensive enough for their needs. They started to develop style sheets, like that of the American Psychological Association, as separate publications. The *APA Style Manual* was first issued in 1952. Only the year before, the Modern Language Association developed its own style sheet, which took a little longer to reach book form, finally being published in 1985.

The next major developments also came in the middle of the century, with the entry of government into the style game. Smaller countries such as Australia and New Zealand did not have a local reference and were feeling increasingly distant from the British outlook. The first *New Zealand Style Book* was published in 1958 to overcome what was seen as the chaotic use of styles across the public sector. As postwar government expanded, there was more need for an authoritative reference for internal and external publications. The Australian *Style Manual* followed suit in 1966. Both became key references, not only for government but for their expanding local publishing industries as well.

The last major influence on style comes from newspapers and magazines. Like their book publishing counterparts, newspapers evolved in-house style manuals to ensure that their publications followed consistent conventions. This is even more crucial when copy must be prepared for publication in less than a day, rather than the months that book publishers have to finish their work.

In the US, the most popular and available media style manuals are the *New York Times* and the Associated Press style books. In the UK, there are the *Times Style Guide*, the *Economist Style Guide* and the *Guardian Style Manual*. For Australian media, News Limited publishes its style guide for the general public.

Keep up to date with changes in style

We have now had just on a century of published style manuals in the narrower sense of the word. If one trend has emerged, it is that the styles they dictate will never be entirely fixed. The first edition of *The Chicago Manual of Style* could speak for all when it declared in its first edition:

> Rules and regulations such as these, in the nature of the case, cannot be endowed with the fixity of rock-ribbed law. They are meant for the average case, and must be applied with a certain degree of elasticity.

That elasticity has been driven first and foremost by technology. Time and again changes in production have led to changes in style. We used to underline text for emphasis because it was the best that typewriters could do, but now word processors have more legible options such as bolding. We used to punctuate sentence lists with semi-colons, but most of these have given way to bulleted lists. As the technology changes, so too will our style manuals.

Just as significantly, style choices will vary with the context of communication. What may work for a newspaper may not be appropriate for a small business, let alone for a government department or an academic journal. Style is diversifying. While some basic standards will always run through different style manuals, you also have the freedom to adapt your style to your own context.

Power tools

Choose the right style for your context

When choosing your style parameters, the first step is to decide which of the major style guides you will follow. Adopting a single reference gives you an instant set of standards. You may depart from them in some areas, but working from one text will be less frustrating than having to juggle differences of opinion on any style question.

The trick, of course, is determining which reference to adopt. Start by checking whether your organisation already has an in-house style manual, and what published source it is based on. Above all, you should write to be consistent with your organisation's voice.

If you don't have an internal guide, your next reference point will be geographical. Choose a general guide that is in use in your country, whether that is *The Gregg Reference Manual* in the US, the *Oxford Style Manual* in the United Kingdom, or the *Style Manual* in Australia. Depart from these only where there is an alternative specific to your profession, such as in publishing, engineering, academia or psychology. Then follow the principles of your chosen guide. Its authors will have thought a lot about the choices they recommend, and that saves you having to do so.

KEY TIP Try to set your style options before you draft.

Use style sheets for individual documents

When you are writing a longer document or report, it is also worth preparing an individual style sheet. This is particularly important when you are writing complex reports that include tables, graphs, case studies, references, footnotes and appendixes. Here, the potential for inconsistency is high, particularly when you import material electronically. A style sheet also helps when you are writing a document as part of a team. If all the contributors go in different style directions, it will be a nightmarish job to edit the text into a consistent whole.

When you are the sole writer of a document, a style sheet will encourage you to set your style parameters while you draft. This is especially useful if your writing is interrupted by other priorities, or where you cannot give your report exclusive attention. By defining your styles, you will draft with more consistency, and reduce the burden of proofreading in the final stages.

Start your style sheet with the five basic categories: formatting, language, numbers, punctuation and sourcing. Include the styles that are specific to the document, such as its fonts, margins and headings. You can then add the style issues not covered in your general reference, or those that you commonly confuse. Following is an example of a style sheet for an individual report.

You don't need to identify everything for your style sheet at the outset. Jot down the major formatting parameters and decide which sourcing method you will use. The style choices for language, numbers and punctuation will emerge as you are writing. Whenever one comes up, make a choice and note it on your style sheet. This will keep your text more consistent as you draft. You will also build up a complete style standard to edit against when reviewing the text. While this will take some extra time as you are writing, it will save you three times that at the back end.

Sample style sheet

1. Formatting

Normal text	Palatino 12 point Line spacing 'at least 14 points'
Heading 1	Chapter titles
Font:	18 point Arial bold
Capitals:	Initial caps only
Spacing:	At least 14 points, 18 points after
Numbering:	'Chapter 1 …'
Alignment:	Left, ragged right
Heading 2	
Font:	14 point Arial bold
Capitals:	Initial caps only
Spacing:	At least 14 points, 12 points before and after
Numbering:	1.1, 1.2, 1.3, etc.
Alignment:	Left, ragged right
Heading 3	
Font:	12 point Arial bold
Capitals:	Initial caps only
Spacing:	At least 14 points, 12 points before, 6 points after
Numbering:	None
Alignment:	Left, ragged right
Figures	Place caption underneath each figure Number consecutively throughout the text For caption, use 'Figure 1:' then title
Tables	Place caption underneath each table Number consecutively throughout the text For caption, use 'Table 1:' then title Font Arial 10 point bold, at least 14 points

Formatting (cont.)

Bulleted lists	Use a square bullet, indented 10 mm Hanging indent 0.5 mm

2. Language

Shortened forms	Per cent not percent or % in text % in tables 10 km/h
Spelling	One space after full stop payroll not pay roll the company (lower case) judgement not judgment (unless legal) focused not focussed 'ise' not 'ize'

3. Numbers	Spell out numbers one to nine Numerals for numbers 10 and over '11 May 2006' for dates 3000 30,000 100,000 one million
4. Punctuation	No semi-colons in a bulleted list Use em dash with no spaces either side
5. Sourcing	Use documentary note system Endnotes not footnotes, numbered from 1 within each chapter Save citations for sources only Indent block quotes (10 mm) not in italics with a line space above and below

Develop an in-house manual

Developing a style sheet is also a good way to start an in-house style manual if you don't have one. Emphasise the content that is not covered by one of the general style manuals, or that needs adapting for your own circumstances. If you are a two-person small business, even a quick two-page reference will increase the consistency of your documents.

In larger organisations, you may want to develop an in-house manual in more detail. Many people find the comprehensive style guides rather forbidding, and appreciate a shorter, more tailored text. This might run to 50, 60 or 70 pages, but avoid making it over 100 pages. Let one of the dedicated publications be your backstop, supplemented with your in-house guide listing the style choices that are more specific to you.

16 Editing

At a glance

The toolbox

- Always edit your text 298
- Edit objectively and systematically 298
- Apply the editing checklist 300

The living language

- Understand the editing spectrum 302
- Learn some lessons from the history of editing 303

Power tools

- Scope your editing tasks 306
- Don't change it unless you need to 308
- Choose the right form of feedback 308
- Learn a mark-up system 309
- Use the editing checklist in performance review 312
- As an editor, rewrite only as a last resort 312

The toolbox

Always edit your text

Editing is all about quality control. After sweating blood to get your draft down and agonising over the expression, the last thing you want is to go over the whole thing again. Yet go over it you must.

In 2005, the Royal Mail in Britain surveyed the public about the writing they receive from businesses. It found that 'bad design, poor grammar and atrocious spelling could be costing UK businesses a staggering £41 billion in lost sales'. Seventy-four per cent of consumers said they wouldn't trust businesses that used poor spelling and grammar, while 30 per cent said they would not buy a product from a company with error-prone writing.

In the businesses surveyed, 56 per cent of employees said they used only the computer spell-checker when reviewing their documents, and seldom asked colleagues to double-check for errors. Up to a quarter lacked the confidence to correct their managers' grammar, even when they did spot an error.

These costs are preventable. There are two ways you will use editing tools at work:

1 When self-reviewing text you have drafted yourself.
2 When reviewing text written by others.

Editing starts with the understanding that editing is a separate process from drafting. When generating text, you focus on the content and the sheer physical task of sweating the words onto the page. The editor's eye then steps in to mediate between the writer and the reader, sitting somewhere between the two. This must be the case whether you are editing your own work or the work of others.

Edit objectively and systematically

Effective editing applies two basic principles: objectivity and system. Most workplace writers edit in an unstructured way, simply rereading the text and looking for problems that might leap out. The trouble is, you are often too close to the material, so you lack objectivity. You know what you are trying to say, and as you read it is likely that the text will say exactly that. Far from leaping out at you, the errors seem to go to ground.

There are several ways you can bring objectivity to your text. The first tip is simple: leave as much time as you can between drafting and editing. Leave the draft for a week, and you will come back with a fresh eye. Some writers put their draft into a drawer for a period of 'freezing'. Return to it after a cooling-off period, and you are more likely to make revisions than when the memory of your drafting effort is still fresh. The problem, of course, is not having the luxury of time. Then your cooling-off period might be overnight or half a day. Even a 15-minute break will give you some distance.

The second way to gain objectivity is to show your text to somebody else. If they were not involved in the research or the drafting, they should quickly spot major problems. Here you will need to work with our second principle: some kind of system. Don't just hand over the text and ask them to review it, for it will inevitably come back with some minor suggestions about commas and apostrophes. Brief your reviewers about what you need them to assess by breaking down the editing task into four stages:

The four elements of editing

1 Content
2 Structure
3 Expression
4 Style

When self-editing, ideally work your way through the text four times, looking at each stage separately. First assess the core messages in the text, the arguments you are mounting, the evidence you are using to support them and the accuracy of your information. Keep your head in the big picture and don't be distracted by the minutiae of punctuation and expression.

Second, review the way you have arranged the material. What structural models are you using, how well is your design working, what is the balance between descriptive and analytical content, and how well does the text flow from paragraph to paragraph? Is the text focused or does it have too much detail?

Then—and only then—start to assess the expression. What tone does the text establish, and is it appropriate for its audience? How effective is the word choice, and can you simplify your expression? What is the average sentence length, and can you vary the sentence mechanics? How are you using verbs, and what is the balance between active and passive voice?

Finally, turn to the lowest level of review: issues of style. Check the punctuation, make sure the formatting complies with your organisation's conventions, review the numbers and capitalisation, scan for spelling errors and double-check your sourcing.

KEY TIP Allocate as much time to editing as you do to drafting.

Without a formal system of this kind to direct your energies, your brain when you review your text will work like water flowing down a slope: it will take the path of least resistance. That usually means neglecting the higher-level issues of content and structure because these call for greater intellectual effort. The easiest course is to read the text, mark up expression, and look for errors of style in a haphazard way. This is an inefficient use of time and not particularly effective. You will condemn yourself to draft after draft after draft without guaranteeing a good result.

With a systematic approach, you can also direct the flow of editing resources—both yours and those of any reviewer you might have. If you are not sure about the strength of your argument, ask your reviewer to assess it. If you lack confidence with your grammar, direct the reviewer to check for errors. If you have a good eye for typos, save that job for yourself and let your reviewer know not to bother with it. They will appreciate a specific brief because it will save them time as well. You will both benefit from the more effective feedback that will result.

Apply the editing checklist

Here is a complete editing system identifying 20 elements to assess.

The editing checklist

Editing stage	Check	Assess
Content	1. Clarity	Message and purpose clear to readers
	2. Accuracy	Facts and figures correct
	3. Objectivity	Opinions supported by facts
	4. Logic	Argument or instruction sequence effective
	5. Completeness	Depth and breadth sufficient
Structure	6. Focus	Right level of detail for reader
	7. Structure	Good structure design, balance and navigation
	8. Coherence	Unified purpose and smooth transitions
	9. Design	Visual elements reinforce content
Expression	10. Tone	Right level of formality for reader
	11. Word choice	Minimise complexity, jargon and abstraction
	12. Mechanics	Good average length, structure and variation
	13. Verbs	Mostly active verbs
	14. Efficiency	Tight expression
	15. Grammar	Correct pronoun references, modifiers, verb agreement, verb tenses and word order
Style	16. Formatting	Consistent layout or correct use of a template
	17. Language	Correct spelling, capitals and shortened forms
	18. Numbering	Correct dates, time, money and numerals
	19. Punctuation	Grammatically correct and consistent
	20. Sourcing	Consistent and complete references

Work your way through the checklist in descending order of focus, starting with content and structure and gradually narrowing your gaze to expression and style. Your review of the big picture may lead you to delete whole slabs of text, so get those out of the way and don't waste time honing their expression. And be warned: it is very tempting to start with the small stuff. It is far easier to mark up the punctuation or correct the spelling than think about the structural design or the strength of argument. Force yourself to start from on high.

Of course, real-world deadlines will not always allow you to apply the system in its full glory. When your time is limited, make at least two passes through the text: first for content and structure and second for expression and style. These areas seem to tap into different parts of the brain, so by working through them one at a time you will get the best return on your invested time. If you try to do both together, one of them will capture your attention, and it will usually be the small stuff.

The living language

Understand the editing spectrum

The editing checklist highlights the complexity involved in editing even short documents. When you work through a longer publication such as a report, this complexity accelerates exponentially. Publishers of books and newspapers break up the editing roles among separate people. Some editors work at the higher, conceptual end of content and structure, while others focus on the minutiae of expression, style and production. Professional editors tend to divide into two camps: substantive editors and copy editors.

Here is how we might place the two camps on a spectrum next to the editing checklist:

Editing spectrum	Editing stages	Elements to check
▼ Substantive editor	Content	1. Clarity 2. Accuracy 3. Objectivity 4. Logic 5. Completeness
	Structure	6. Focus 7. Structure 8. Coherence 9. Design
	Expression	10. Tone 11. Word choice 12. Mechanics 13. Verbs 14. Efficiency 15. Grammar
▲ Copy editor	Style	16. Formatting 17. Language 18. Numbering 19. Punctuation 20. Sourcing

At either end of the spectrum, each type of editor has some specific responsibilities. Expression is the middle ground that they share. Copy editors have an important role in checking expression for sense and clarity, but they do not generally rewrite large slabs of text. They traditionally mark up the physical copy with suggestions, which then go back to the author. Substantive editors, on the other hand, take a much more interventionist role in rewriting the text. The balance of these roles varies considerably from publisher to publisher, but specialisation always exists to some degree.

Workplaces can also introduce specialisation when setting up their quality control systems for writing. A small legal office, for example, might train one member of staff to focus specifically on copy editing while asking other colleagues to review a document for content and structure. A team in a corporation might separate these roles when preparing an annual report. In a government agency, reports and briefing notes often go through a chain of middle and upper managers on their way to a Director General or a Minister. You could assign different people in that chain to focus on different areas.

Learn some lessons from the history of editing

If there is one thing we can learn from the history of editing, it is that there is no single editing system that will work in every context. More than most professional skills, editing is closely allied to the technology and the medium you are using, and these are constantly changing. You will always need to adapt your editing systems.

The first editors were simple copyists, verbatim transcribers of texts. In ancient Egypt, copyists did a roaring trade writing out papyrus scrolls of the Book of the Dead, which were buried with prominent people to help them navigate the afterlife. They didn't change the text during the copying. The Romans took this business opportunity further by using literate slaves—often 30 at a time—to copy down a work as it was read aloud. They operated like a human printing press.

Then the trend-setting Christians embraced the new technologies of codices to replace scrolls and vellum to replace papyrus. Monasteries set up scriptoriums to produce religious works and sometimes to preserve pagan classical works as well. Cassiodorus in 540 wrote a text explaining how to run these scriptoriums, and this brought more of what we would today call copy editing. Scribes spent their days copying the texts, but would pass them on to others to check, add titles and notes. Finally, the codex would move into production by being illustrated and bound as a book.

When universities were established from the 12th century on, they applied these processes to academic works by establishing publishing houses called stationers. Although the books were handwritten and their market was small, publishing of a sort was born. As the books became more complex, copyists kept evolving their role until they became known as 'correctors' of text.

Christian scholars continued to improve the practices of correction, wanting to reproduce religious texts that were uniform and free from error. In 1417, the monk Oswald wrote a Latin treatise called the *Opus Pacis* to 'discuss the theoretical ground for correcting and emending a text'. Thirteen copies of this astonishing work survive, and much of it would still apply to today's writing.

Then one shift in technology took the editing trade far beyond the copyist and corrector: the printing press. Before Gutenberg invented movable type and printed the first books in the 1440s, the handwritten books circulating around Europe would have numbered in the thousands. By 1500, the number of printed books available was more like nine million. It was really only with this surge in production that editing processes as we might recognise them emerged.

The first century of printing was a free-for-all, as printers grabbed hold of any manuscript that might be popular and produced as many copies as they could sell. Aldus Manutius in Venice revolutionised book production by producing editions of 1000 copies instead of 250. That's small when compared with today's print runs, but a 33-fold increase on the output of the Roman slave copyists. Competition was intense and there was little control. A rival printer could get an edition of your book and produce it himself. Printers complained that they had to rush books through the press 'more quickly than asparagus could be cooked'. The quality of production was initially poor, but as the market matured it demanded a more skilled worker.

The copyists and correctors were in greater demand than ever, and as the technology evolved so did their role. By the 15th century, they were starting to apply standardised spelling to chaotic national languages and produce text as uniform and free from error as possible. When the printer ran a small operation, he did the selecting, setting, correcting and printing himself. He might use the services of an external corrector, or he might employ an in-house corrector. As the business grew, these roles would separate and be done by different staff.

By the 18th century, the role of the publisher, in the sense of selecting texts to produce, financing the operation and reaping the profits, was separating from that of the printer, who remained responsible for the physical production. The word 'editor' was first applied to this publisher, as it still is today with commissioning editors. It was only in the 20th century that the correctors of the printing press started to transfer to the publishing houses themselves. Sometimes overlapping with the editor who selects works, but increasingly taking over and professionalising the role of the corrector, the copy editor was born.

A similar evolution occurred in the development of newspapers and magazines, which had to wait for the printing press to take off and for literacy to be widespread enough to create a market. Early presses were often one-man bands, with the publisher doing the writing, editing, printing and distribution. As circulation increased, these roles separated and specialised. As in the book world, a separate position of copy editor (US term) or sub-editor (UK term) emerged.

This history partly explains why the skills of correction are so lacking in the workplace. The role of the editor has never stood still for long enough to establish a coherent and stable method. Only where complexity of publication demands specialist editors, such as in book or newspaper publishing, has the role become established. Because workplace documents were mostly internal and not subjected to the scrutiny of publication, organisations did not see the value of an editorial role except in specific cases. As a result, workplaces have failed to apply comparable systems. It is little wonder their documents are so error-prone.

When upgrading this part of your professional practice, you can draw a number of lessons from the history of editing:

- Separate the review process from the writing process.
- Use a systematic approach.
- Tailor that approach to your own context.
- Update your processes as technology evolves.

Power tools

Scope your editing tasks

Adapting an editing system for your individual needs is easier said than done. Seven factors will influence how you work as an editor:

1. The readers of the document
2. The type of document
3. The size of the document
4. The quality of the text
5. The time frame
6. The writer
7. The budget

Thinking about these factors will help you answer the key questions every editor faces:

- How much do I intervene?
- What is the best method of intervention?

Many internal workplace documents are relatively short—between one and three pages—and should need a low to medium level of editing. This means up to two passes through the text by a reviewer who is not also the writer. In many organisations, however, these documents are redrafted up to a dozen times by as many as half a dozen people. Published reports, on the other hand, usually need more thorough editing, with specialisation by a number of people in the different stages of review. Yet these reports are sometimes dumped onto the desk of a sole individual, and receive far less quality control than their public exposure warrants. Use the following matrix to help you decide how to allocate your editing resources.

Levels of intervention

	Low intervention	Medium intervention	High intervention
	Single reading Verbal feedback Minimal mark-up of text Quick turnaround	More than one reading Text passes between writer and editor once Text possibly reviewed by others Text marked up to indicate general changes without rewriting Systematic review of different elements, such as content, structure, expression and style Medium response time	Several readings to evaluate text thoroughly Text passes between writer and editor more than once Changes so substantive that some of the text is rewritten Professional production Multiple passes between several people, each looking at specific areas such as content, structure, expression and style Systematic checking of style conventions against a professional reference Lengthy time frame from research and drafting to editing and publishing
1	Personal readers or close colleagues	Internal but senior readership	Diverse readership, or small but informed readership
2	Professional or personal documents	Internal and external professional documents	Published professional documents
3	Short documents	Medium documents	Long documents
4	Good-quality draft	Moderate-quality draft	Poor-quality draft
5	Short deadline	Medium time frame	Long time frame
6	Highly skilled writers	Moderately skilled or sensitive writers	Inexperienced, sensitive or poorly skilled writers
7	No budget except limited staff time	Adequate staff time and perhaps some budget for external support	Extensive staff time and dedicated budget for external support, production and distribution

Don't change it unless you need to

As you are assessing these factors, remember the editor's golden rule: don't change it unless you have to. Early in our career, we usually sort out a writing style that works, combining organisational standards with our own skills and experience. When you start to move into middle management and review the text of others, your first impulse will be to adjust everyone else's writing to your way. The most common mistake you can make is to rewrite the text according to your own ear. That is not editing. It is co-authoring. You will drown in a sea of words.

Heavy-handed intervention is costly, ineffective and will not motivate your staff. The quality of successive drafts declines because staff feel 'you're only going to change it anyway'. Your co-authoring workload will increase exponentially, preventing you from getting on with the higher-level work you are being paid for. By scoping your editing and grounding it in a formal system, you can distinguish more objectively between changes of substance and your own personal preferences.

If you use an objective system, you will also find you can explain not just *what* needs changing, but *why*. There is nothing worse than rewriting someone's text and explaining that it 'just sounds better this way'. This is particularly so if the edit does indeed sound better. Unless staff understand why, you will have to rewrite their text every time. If you can explain your changes objectively, staff will accept them, learn from them and be able to apply them in the future. The quality of successive drafts will improve, motivation will increase and your quality control tasks will ease.

Choose the right form of feedback

Scoping your work and diagnosing the text will lead you to choose the most effective level of feedback, in increasing order of intervention:

1. Verbal feedback
2. Mark-up of the text
3. Editing report or assessment
4. Rewriting of text

Effective managers mainly use a mixture of verbal feedback and text mark-up, with occasional formal assessment as part of their performance review. Only rarely should you need to rewrite large slabs of text.

The happy managers are those who only need to give some verbal guidance to staff they are reviewing. It helps if you have prepared thoroughly. Read through the text before sitting down with the writer, and diagnose both its achievements and its shortcomings. The nearest your pen should come to the document is to write some separate notes.

While diagnosing, it is usually best to work your way through in descending order from the big picture to the details, but this is not always the best order in which to give feedback. Staff can take editorial criticism very personally. So look for the things that a document does well as much as the things that need to improve. Start with some positives, then work your way through in descending order of priority. Think about what will have the greatest impact on the document and deal with that early. If you give structured feedback, your writer will then revise in a structured way as well.

Learn a mark-up system

The next level of intervention combines verbal feedback with physical mark-up of the text, which will guide writers when they are sitting back at their desk. The chief temptation to resist is rewriting. Instead, try to read and diagnose, then mark up your diagnosis with some editorial symbols. Place these in the margins, with minimal lines and circles in the text itself.

Minimising the mark-up will be cleaner and less demoralising for a sensitive author, as well as saving your time. You can put the structure marks in the left margin and the expression marks on the right.

The following symbols correspond with the tools covered throughout this book:

Structure mark-up

Text mark	Margin note	Meaning
None	✗	Cut this paragraph
None	✔	Good point, keep this paragraph
None	↓	Reduce this paragraph
None	↑	Expand this paragraph
None	→	Move below
None	←	Bring forward
None	N	Narrative
None	P	Proof
None	K	Key material
None	↯	Check flow between paragraphs
None	*design*	Consider using layout rather than text

Expression mark-up

Text mark	Margin note	Meaning
the approximate time of commencement	KISS	Simplify
In light of the above, particularly in relation to these issues, it is recommended that...	cl.	Reduce clutter
is provided	pass.	Make passive voice active
provision	h.v.	Make hidden verb active
However; the Office will call it's...	punct.	Check punctuation
In light of the above, particularly in relation to these issues, it is recommended that...	mech.	Improve sentence mechanics

In addition to marking up the margins, you may want to add a general comment at the start or end of a document about the structure and expression. This might be something like: 'The document uses an effective telescoping structure, but there seems to be more detail than the readers need. Write a core message test and see if you can trim. The expression is generally clear, but reduce the passive voice and watch for some long sentences, as well as incorrect punctuation.' The mark-up will then guide your author to specific areas in the text.

Here is an example of some text marked up as a workplace manager might use it:

Audit Observation

It was noted by audit that the following clearing accounts had not been reconciled and cleared on a regular basis and that at as of 16 March 2007 they exhibited outstanding balances.

These accounts included number 167843, the Head Office Sales Clearing Account, with a balance of $16,623 credit; number 443564, the Direct Debit Clearing Account with a balance of $3,768.30 debit; the Receivable Clearing Account, with a balance of $35,687.22 credit, and the Consulting Fee Clearing Account, with a balance of $6,728.54 debit.

Audit reviewed account information during the recent audit engagement for the corporation. Discussions with staff revealed what appears to be a limited understanding of the operation of these accounts, and the associated transactions. It is audits understanding that Finance is in the process of investigating the balances of these accounts, and will clear them as it is considered appropriate.

The Reconciliations – Head Office Accounts Procedure requires reconciliation of the Head Office Sales Clearing Account on a monthly basis however there are no documented procedures in relation to reconciliation and clearing of the other clearing accounts.

Implications

Transactions are not appropriately reflected in the general ledger.

General ledger discrepancies are not identified and addressed in a timely manner.

Recommendation

It is recommended by audit that the corporation proceed with documentation of the purpose of each clearing account and that the required reconciliation and clearing procedure be identified.

It is further recommended by audit that each account be cleared and reconciled on a monthly basis.

Use the editing checklist in performance review

For more extensive documents, or for formal assessment of staff performance, you can write a separate report of your diagnosis using the editing checklist. This becomes more important if you need to coach a particular individual who is struggling with skills or with attitude. It also gives you an objective record of your efforts to help.

You can also use this full system as part of an annual performance review. Let staff know that you will select some documents in a given month, and formally assess them against the criteria in the checklist. When you have done so, sit down and go through the documents with them. It will give you a structure to talk through their strengths and weaknesses and develop an agreed plan of action to upgrade their skills. Staff will appreciate structured feedback.

As an editor, rewrite only as a last resort

The last resort is to apply the most comprehensive kind of substantive editing, with heavy intervention and rewriting of the text. This is a valid option, but in the workplace it is a short-term one to be applied only when circumstances demand it. The main case where you will need to rewrite is if time is short and you have to get the text out the door. For the most part, if the text is so bad, return it to the author to rewrite taking account of your feedback.

If you find yourself having to take this step regularly, it is a sign that you need to make some more fundamental changes to the editorial workflow. Review the way you are diagnosing text, giving feedback and coaching staff. You now have a full range of tools and methods to draw from to design an effective system.

17 Proofing

At a glance

The toolbox

- Pay your proofing premium 314
- Know the difference between proofing and editing 315
- Proof the big picture for sequence, layout and typography 316
- Proof the little picture for sense, spelling, grammar and style 318
- Always do one final proof 320

The living language

- Learn from an endangered profession 321
- Use the top 10 proofreaders' tips 323

Power tools

- Learn some proofreading marks 324
- Mark up text efficiently 327
- Work with some electronic aids 328

The toolbox

Pay your proofing premium

If editing is your main form of quality control, think of proofing as a kind of insurance. If your editing was effective, proofing should not pick up all that much. But little things can and will go wrong: gremlins in the typesetting, typos the spell-checker won't recognise or figures in tables that don't add up. Just as you need a separate editing stage after drafting, you will always need to take one final look at the text.

Proofing seems like an expensive premium to pay given the comparatively small things it picks up. Although there is as much method to learn in proofing as there is in editing, proofing will rarely transform a document in the way that editing does. Final proofing corrections usually have little material impact on meaning, but they can have a magnified impact on your credibility. A new industry magazine a few years ago led with a story about strategic planning. On its front cover, in bright red, 64-point type, its credibility crashed with the headline 'STRAGETIC PLANNING—WHY IT MATTERS'.

When readers notice a typo or a misspelling in the text, it can distract them so much that they are no longer persuaded by the content. It doesn't matter how much effort the authors invested or how strong their case—one error can make all the difference. At other times, the cost is even more obvious. There is a thriving sub-business on the online auction site eBay specifically attuned to the misspelling of items such as 'camras', 'labtop' computers, 'telefones', 'dimonds' and 'antiks'. Savvy entrepreneurs comb the site for these errors, pick up the items cheaply, then re-sell them with the correct spelling at a considerable mark-up. You must pay your premium.

Yet despite these costs, professionals often devote little time to proofing their documents, believing that their drafting and editing will have found any errors. The problem is, during these earlier stages you are more often reading for meaning, skimming through text with only enough concentration to get the sense of a passage. As a result, you see what you expect to be there. The proofreader must escape this mindset and look at the text from a fresh angle. This ensures that what you see is actually on the page.

Know the difference between proofing and editing

The first difference between proofing and editing is that you do not start to proof until you have a final document. This means the text is edited and complete, and set in its final form. For internal documents produced on a word processor, the layout may not have changed much along the road. For published reports, it may be typeset separately using a desktop publishing program. If this is the case, do not even think about proofing until you have a final print-out. If you start the proofing any earlier, you will only double or triple your work.

The second difference is that you proof with two sets of the text in front of you: the latest print-out as your proof copy, and the previous edited version of the document. This way you can cross-check against the original, clarify the initial intentions and assess where errors have crept in. This is easier on paper than on the screen, particularly if the document will be read off the page in its final form. If you are proofing an electronic document such as a website, you should certainly check it on screen as well, but most proofreaders find that a paper print-out detects more than on-screen proofing alone.

But the third difference between editing and proofing is the vital one. You are not reading a proof to make *any* major changes to the text. Substantial improvements in structure or expression are for the editing stage. You are checking for minor errors of sense, layout, language and typography. If your document is being printed professionally, major corrections of final proofs can be very expensive.

For this reason, it is also best if someone other than the writer, and preferably other than the editor as well, do the proofing. They will bring a fresh eye and spot things that those previously involved may not see. A new reader is also less likely to rewrite whole slabs of text.

Like effective editing, proofing works best when done systematically, in at least two phases:

1 The 'big picture'—sequence, layout, headings and typography.
2 The 'little picture'—sense, spelling, typos, punctuation, grammar and style.

Some proofreaders break these stages down further, working through the text a number of times. This will depend on the time you have available, the length of the work and the level of perfection you need. You can also reverse the order if this works better for you: start with the little picture, then scan the pages for the overall layout.

Proof the big picture for sequence, layout and typography

Looking at the big picture means taking a satellite view as you turn through the text, casting your eye over the sequence of sections and headings, the way they are laid out and the typography on each page. Proofreaders talk about 'sweeping the page', moving through the proof without being distracted by the minutiae of sense, spelling, punctuation or grammar. Following are the 10 elements to look for as you beam down from above.

The proofing checklist

Running text elements

1. Are all parts of the document complete and in the right order?
2. Are the headings, tables and graphs consistent and numbered in the right sequence?
3. Are the page numbers consecutive and the headers and footers correct and consistent?
4. Are the drops and margins around each page and around headings correct?
5. Do the headings match up with the table of contents if there is one?

Page elements

6. Is all the body text aligned correctly and consistently, and are there any rivers and lakes?
7. Are the word and line breaks effective, or can you adjust the typesetting?
8. Are the fonts correct in type and size throughout?
9. Is the use of italics, bolding and underlining correct?
10. Are the tables and graphs formatted correctly, and do all numbers add up?

Running text elements

Break your big picture sweep into two stages: the running elements and the page elements. It is best to check running text by turning through the entire text, as you will be comparing what is on page two with the same element on page seven. To begin, scan through the whole document and check that every section is there and in the right sequence. This sounds obvious, but even a simple letter might have left out a file or reference number.

Next, look at any headings, particularly if they are numbered. Make sure the numbering systems are consistent, and don't shift, for example, from 'Chapter 1' to 'Chapter Five'. There may have been some restructuring during the editing, so check that the sequence doesn't jump from Chapter 4 to Chapter 6, making the final number of chapters wrong as well. If tables, graphs or diagrams are numbered, make sure the numbering is sequential, either within each chapter or over the whole document. Assess the placement of captions, labels and legends, and make sure they use consistent styles.

Next, look at the page numbers and the headers and footers, and make sure they are correct and consistent. Footers can suddenly vary in size or placement, or the number itself might appear in a different font. The drops, or space between footers and headers and the page text also need checking, as well as the spaces before and after headings.

Finally, turn to the contents page and make a further pass through the entire document, cross-checking that all the headings, page numbers and references to figures correlate with the contents. When editors are improving the wording of headings, for example, they do not always move back to the contents to update the new title. During typesetting, the placement of a particular figure or table may have shifted over to the next page.

Page elements

The first five elements are like checking the formwork of the document. The next pass through the document's big picture is slower and its focus narrower. Here you are not scanning for running elements, but assessing the typography on each page. The elements you are viewing here are best checked by viewing one page at a time, and sweeping down the page rather than reading word for word.

Start by looking at the alignment of text. Is it ranged left or fully justified, and are any paragraphs out of alignment? If fully justified, are there bad gaps between words and letters, creating the effect of rivers and lakes down the page? If so, look at changing some of the word breaks or line breaks to even out the text spacing. At the same time, look for short lines (a couple of isolated words on the last line of a paragraph) and widows (an isolated line at the end of a paragraph that breaks over onto the next page). See if you can adjust the wording or the spacing to even these up.

Next, look at the font used on the page. Cross-check against any style sheet or design specifications you have. Is the right font being used, particularly if there are different fonts for headings and body text? If the fonts themselves are right, are they of a uniform size? It is very easy for a word or even a line to be set one point too large or small. Look at the spacing between lines, as any variation will give the text an uneven look. Look for bold, italic or underlined text, and check that it is in line with the document's standards for emphasis.

Finally, look again at the tables, graphs, diagrams, illustrations and other visual material. Check that the columns of numbers line up, or that the shapes in a flow chart are correct. If these visual elements are being imported from external files, they may be out of proportion to the surrounding text. Do a spot check on any figure totals—particularly any not automatically calculated by your software—to test that they add up. You don't want your reader pointing out that a table total is an impossible 107 per cent.

Proof the little picture for sense, spelling, grammar and style

Once you have finished your satellite view, it's time to work through the text again, this time coming down from orbit and getting right in next to each word and character. This level of proofreading demands very slow, careful reading. You are looking for the following 10 elements:

The proofing checklist

1. Does the text make sense and is its meaning clear?
2. Are there any grammatical problems?
3. Are words spelled correctly and consistently?
4. Are there any typos?
5. Are there any incorrect word doubles such as there/their or it's/its?
6. Are any words accidentally repeated?

7 Is the punctuation correct and complete?
8 Is the formatting of numbers consistent and correct?
9 Are the cross-references in the text complete and do they point to the right page?
10 Is the sourcing and referencing complete and correct?

Reading for sense is perhaps the most difficult element to incorporate into your proofing, because you can fall into the trap of re-editing. The proofreader's task is not to re-word text that doesn't seem clear, but to query any sentence that doesn't make sense and let the editor or writer decide whether to change it. Of course, if you are the writer and the proofreader, you will be having that conversation with yourself. But maintain your discipline and change only what is essential. You can endlessly improve expression. Proofread to correct rank errors.

A common error of sense is where a sentence has more than one meaning. If the writer and editor are close to the material, the fresh eye of the proofreader can be the one that saves the day. The writer of this sentence in an insurance claim could have used a proofreader:

> I pulled away from the side of the road, glanced at my mother-in-law, and headed over the embankment.

In another case, a small business probably wasted its money with this advertisement:

> No matter what your coat is made of, this miracle spray will make it really repellent.

Closely related to sense is a final check of the grammar. The copy editor should have done this carefully, but it is always worth a look. Even if you don't consciously assess the grammar of every sentence, do it regularly enough to pick up any problems. The sort of grammar problem a proofreader will find is not the glaring error that will jar to your ear. It may be lack of agreement between subjects and verbs, or the wrong pronoun being used for a noun, or an ambiguous modifier generating a second meaning:

> For those of you who have children and don't know it, we have a nursery downstairs.
>
> Please take time to look over the brochure that is enclosed with your family.

Then there is the stage that most people associate with proofing: picking up spelling errors and typos. Even a professional typist will make errors when transcribing text, particularly if working with poor handwriting. More commonly, authors will key in text directly themselves. As a result, the number of typos in workplace documents has probably increased.

Online spell-checkers can help you to correct the obvious errors, but they won't pick up wrong words that happen to be spelled correctly. The spell-checker passed all of these as correct:

Get rid of aunts: Zap does the job in 24 hours

Modular sofas. Only $299. For rest or fore play.

When proofing, the most valuable reference you can have is a style manual or style sheet. This will give you the standards to follow for spelling, punctuation, numbers and referencing. If the writer or editor has not established a style sheet, you may need to make one up as you go, marking variations in the text and deciding, usually by what occurs most often, which version to use.

Start by looking at the spelling. Does the writer (or the writer's automatic spell-checker) use British or American spelling for -our/-or and -ise/-ize words? What standards are they using to punctuate a bulleted list? Look for variations in 'per cent', 'percent' and '%', and in date formats, such as 1 July 2006 and 6th of August 2007. Here your task is to bring consistency. Readers may not be able to diagnose where there is variation, but they will get a sense that things are messy. The effect can be just as pronounced as that of a spelling error.

The final little-picture check is of the references. Often, the text will refer to other parts of the document, such as 'see page 122'. Make sure that the contents referred to are actually on the page indicated, and that the number is filled in. Too many publications reach the printer with 'see page xx' still there. Also cross-check every footnote, endnote and asterisk to confirm that they are correct.

Always do one final proof

Just when you thought it was safe to send off your document, one task remains: a final proof. If you have made any changes, no matter how small, take the time to print out new pages after the corrections have been entered. This final round of corrections is even more focused. You are not revisiting the entire proofing checklist but comparing the new version against the marked-up corrections on the previous set of proofs. Place a tick next to each one when you have confirmed it. Chances are, if there were a number of changes, there will be one or two corrections that went awry. Even when you are most pressed for time, it is always best to do this final check. As the production manager in an advertising agency once observed, 'we never have time for a final proof, but we always find the time to re-print'.

The living language

Learn from an endangered profession

Although proofreading requires different skills and experience to editing, specialist proofreaders are becoming something of an endangered species. There has always been overlap between the things a proofreader checks and the things a copy editor works on. Now they are tending to merge.

In the world of newspaper publishing, the distinction between the two is certainly dissolving, and the proofreader is disappearing altogether. According to Rooney and Witte, 'In journalism, the job title of proofreader is almost obsolete. Most newspapers have turned the job over to the copy desk.' Proofreading as a specialty is holding on in book publishing, but its practitioners tend to be poorly paid freelancers. There are virtually no dedicated proofreaders in the workplace.

The decline of the proofreader is perhaps not surprising, since the craft itself is one of the most recent additions to the world of writing. While the concepts of style and editing have been with us for many centuries, proofing is but a few centuries old. Its birth somewhere in the 17th century came as a result of the printing press.

When type metal was arranged in galley trays ready for printing, it was first necessary to make a trial run on the press to test how it would fare. The document generated was called the 'galley proof' or 'proof sheet' because it was used to 'prove' that the typesetting would work. The printer or editor would check the proof and make any adjustments to the type before proceeding with the print run.

It took two more centuries of industrialisation before the task of checking proofs was influential enough to become a verb: proofing. As the output of printeries rose exponentially in response to compulsory education and spreading literacy, it was necessary to systematise this final quality control. Printers established 'reading' departments, which were usually in a back room next to the print shop and staffed by women.

A typical operation was that of Halstead Press, the largest book printer in Australia in the middle years of the 20th century. Its reading department would work in pairs: a copy holder and a proofreader. One would read aloud from the original manuscript, while the other would check that the original wording was reflected perfectly in the proof. It was a very literal reading: 'open bracket word word, close bracket, full stop space new sentence capital letter ...'

Reading departments and proofreaders were initially attached to printeries for very practical reasons. A typical book used some tons of type metal, so it couldn't be moved around easily. That means the typesetting had to be done in the print shop, and it made sense for the reader checking the proofs to be close by. Then, in the middle of last century, offset lithography changed printing forever. Instead of casting metal letters and setting them up in trays to be pressed against paper, printers could use photography to create plates.

With lithographic printing, and within a few decades digital printing, there was no longer any practical reason for the typesetting or the proofreading to be done in the print shop. Your typeset text could be put in an envelope or on a disk. Publishers started to transfer these roles into their own offices where they had greater control. At first they established their own reading departments, but increasingly many of the tasks of the proofreader merged with those of the copy editor.

Give it another 50 years, and it is unlikely that there will be many dedicated proofreader positions. This does not mean that the work proofreaders have been doing will disappear. It simply means that it will increasingly be done by a non-specialist.

In the workplace, there has been comparable generalisation of writing, editing, typesetting and proofreading tasks. Only 20 years ago, many organisations still maintained a typing pool, a group of (mostly) women who would type letters and reports and proofread them. Authors in professional positions would hand-write text and place it in an out tray, from where it would head off to the pool. It might be days before it returned typed to the in tray.

The desktop computer has changed everything, and once again technology has restructured the responsibilities in writing and production. Increasingly, authors typeset as they write on a computer, which will send exactly what they have on screen to a printer sitting just feet away. A writer may then have to be his or her own editor, checking the content, structure and expression, and understanding and adhering to style. Finally, there may be a colleague to proof the text, but more likely the writer will take on this task as well.

In essence, the technological changes of the last 50 years have merged three or four different roles, once fulfilled by different people often in completely different locations. Now, one multiskilled professional is writer, editor, typesetter, designer, proofreader and e-publisher. As well as the professional skills of your particular area, you will need to develop the skills to do most if not all of these things.

Use the top 10 proofreaders' tips

Are there any tips we can learn from specialist proofreaders before they disappear? The methods in this chapter are synthesised from textbooks and manuals on proofreading. These also give us general tips that could only come from decades of collective experience:

Top 10 proofreaders' tips

1. Read against the original copy.
2. Read aloud.
3. Force yourself to read word by word using a card, pen or ruler.
4. Read text backwards.
5. Be aware of your blind spots.
6. Re-check the early pages of a text.
7. Never trust a machine.
8. Assess the flow-on impact of any changes.
9. Read in short bursts rather than marathon sessions.
10. Check everything.

KEY TIP | Always try to proof with a style sheet or style manual.

Power tools

Learn some proofreading marks

Probably the most useful tool proofreaders have developed is the proofreading mark. Anyone encountering these for the first time would be forgiven for thinking they had entered an arcane world of hieroglyphs, understood by the exalted few. Why would it be worthwhile for a professional to learn an entirely new language?

If your writing tasks are fairly simple, and you are your own editor and proofreader, you probably do not need a standard set of proofreading symbols. Use whatever private language makes sense to you. Where you are writing more complex documents, in particular where you are writing in a team environment, an agreed form of mark-up becomes more important. If you do desktop publishing and work with external designers and printers as well, then learning the marks becomes crucial.

Proofreaders' marks have two priorities:

1 To indicate a correction with maximum accuracy.
2 To convey a correction using minimum space on the page.

The marks were originally developed because space was limited in the final proofs of books or newspapers, which were set fairly tightly on the page. There simply wasn't room to write out in full something like 'delete this word, change the first letter of the second one to capitals and transpose it with the word that follows'. Instead, proofreaders minimised the mark-up in the text and placed symbols in the margins.

Here are the most common proofreading marks, grouped into four areas:

Text mark	Margin note	Meaning
Inserting and deleting text		
Text should been clear		Delete
Text should ~~have~~ be clear		Delete
Text should clear	be	Insert missing material
Text should beclear	#	Insert space
Text shoould be clear		Delete and close up
Text should be cle ar		Close up
Text should be ~~clear~~	stet	Reinstate text
Formatting text		
text should be readable	cap	Change to capital letters
TEXt SHOuld be readable	lc	Change to lower case
Text should be readable	ital	Change to italics
Text should be readable	bold	Change to bold
Text *should* be readable	rom	Change to normal roman type

Text mark	Margin note	Meaning
Moving text		
Text be should efficient	(trs)	Transpose
… by the Office. Text should be efficient …	(np)	Begin a new paragraph
… by the Office. Text should be efficient …	(run on)	No new paragraph
Text should be efficient	(take over)	Move to next line, next page or specified page
Text should be efficient	(take back)	Move to previous line, page or specified page
Text should be efficient		Move to the left
Text should be efficient		Move to the right
Punctuating text		
by the Office which should	, /	Insert comma
Please note the following	(:) /	Insert colon
… by the Office should text be usable …	; /	Insert semi-colon
… by the Office Should text be usable …	(.) /	Insert full stop

Text mark	Margin note	Meaning
Is this text usable	? /	Insert question mark
This text is not usable	! /	Insert exclamation mark
… the text which is not usable should be clearer …	(/) /	Insert round brackets
This is a crystal clear text	/-/	Insert a hyphen
We'll edit the text over April June	/en/	Insert an en dash
This text is persuasive a rare thing indeed	/em/	Insert an em dash
The Offices position	' /	Insert apostrophe
The Office's position	' / ' /	Insert quote marks
… as several studies show.	3 /	Insert superscript/footnote

Mark up text efficiently

To mark up proofs effectively, work mainly in the margins and not between the lines. Minimise the marks you place in the text itself, concentrating on deletion and insertion lines. This helps immensely with keying in, because the corrector's eye can scan down the margin rather than moving around the page, when it is more likely to miss corrections. Use a pencil to mark corrections, because inevitably you will change your mind about some of them, and crossing out pen marks is messy.

To decrease the ambiguity in your marks, enclose any comments or instructions in a circle. This will make it clear that these words are not to be keyed in as new text (it happens). Where you are adding words to be inserted in the text, place them between forward slashes to make it clear where the new text starts and ends. If you have a number of corrections to make to a line, sequence them in the margin from left to right to minimise the chances of misreading.

Above all, be patient and mark up the text as precisely as possible. Time you might save with rushed and unclear mark-up will be more than lost with errors and further proofing.

Work with some electronic aids

At the same time as professionals are finding they have to do more of their own proofreading, they are also having to change where they do it. While proofing on paper is still the most accurate way to pick up final errors, increasingly you will be proofing on screen as well.

As this shift occurs, proofreaders' tools are turning up as electronic aids, and in some cases these are best used on screen. The first are the spell-checker and grammar-checker built into your word-processing software. As the Royal Mail study showed, this is often the only kind of proofing that many documents undergo. These are useful but limited tools. Spell-checkers will not pick up correct but wrong words:

Eye halve a spelling checker
It came with my pea sea.
It plainly marques four my revue
Miss steaks eye kin knot sea.

The grammar-checker is even less reliable. The rules embedded into its program are rather simplistic, so while it will be right half of the time, the other half of its suggestions will be questionable or downright silly. By all means use it to pick up problems, but don't ever rely on it. Its 'readability' calculations are notoriously inaccurate. It is reasonably accurate about sentence length unless you have a lot of bulleted lists. Its passive voice recognition is incomplete, and the Flesch–Kincaid readability score often only calculates as far as grade 12.

More recently, sophisticated style-checking programs have been developed which are separate from the built-in grammar-checker, and some of these can also calculate readability. These are much more effective and accurate, but you will still need to judge what they suggest. Never trust a machine.

Of more use for final corrections are the 'find' and 'replace' functions in the word processor. When you find a variant spelling such as 'recognise' versus 'recognize', you can do a global search and replace rather than key each correction in by hand. Check each replacement, however, particularly in shorter words, or you might insert the word where you don't intend to. For example, a global change on the word 'author' to 'writer' can also change the word 'authority' to 'writerity'.

Finally, experiment with the 'track changes' function, particularly if you are working with others electronically. If you are proofing a text for someone in another city, you can track your changes and send the text by email, embedding extra notes where you need to. They can work through the changes and accept or reject them, while preserving the layout of the text. The old proofreaders would hate it, but this kind of tool shows just how far the craft of proofing has shifted from the back rooms of the printeries to the workstations of the workplace.

Further reading

Writing at Work draws on a broad sweep of disciplines—from grammar, readability and rhetoric to plain English, usability and information design. What follows is a list of current sources for those who want to take a topic further. The books are representative of their genres, with a focus on those that are readily available.

Business communications

Business writing

Most business writing books are slim guides pitched at busy workplace managers.

Bailey, Edward P., *Writing and Speaking at Work: A practical guide for business communication,* 3rd edn, New Jersey, Pearson Prentice Hall, 2005.

Blake, Gary and Bly, Robert W., *The Elements of Business Writing,* New York, Longman, 1991.

Danziger, Elizabeth, *Get to the Point,* New York, Three Rivers Press, 2001.

Minto, Barbara, *The Pyramid Principle: Logic in writing and thinking,* 3rd edn, London, Financial Times Prentice Hall, 2002.

Munter, Mary, *Guide to Managerial Communication: Effective business writing and speaking,* 7th edn, New Jersey, Pearson Prentice Hall, 2006.

Poor, Edith, *The Executive Writer: A guide to managing words, ideas and people,* New York, Grove Weidenfield, 1992.

Smith, Edward L. and Bernhardt, Stephen A., *Writing at Work: Professional writing skills for people on the job,* New York, McGraw Hill, 1997.

Communications

Then there are the communications textbooks, used mainly in university undergraduate courses.

Hartley, Peter and Bruckman, Clive G., *Business Communication,* London, Routledge, 2002.

Kolin, Philip C., *Successful Writing at Work,* concise edition, Boston, Houghton Mifflin Company, 2006.

Oliu, Walter E., Brusaw, Charles T. and Alred, Gerald J., *Writing that Works: Communicating effectively on the job*, 9th edn, Boston, Bedford St Martin's, 2007.
Petelin, Roslyn and Durham, Marsha, *The Professional Writing Guide: Writing well and knowing why*, Sydney, Business and Professional Publishing, 1992.
Windschuttle, Keith and Windschuttle, Elizabeth, *Writing, Researching, Communication: Communication skills for the information age*, Sydney, McGraw Hill, 1989.

Design

Typography

Typography focuses on the most effective presentation of words on a page or screen.

Bringhurst, Robert, *The Elements of Typographic Style*, version 3.1, Washington, Hartley and Marks, 2005.
Lupton, Ellen, *Thinking with Type: A critical guide for designers, writers, editors and students*, New York, Princeton Architectural Press, 2004.
Wheildon, Colin, *Communicating or Just Making Pretty Shapes*, revised edition, North Sydney, Newspaper Advertising Bureau of Australia, 1986.
Wheildon, Colin, *Type and Layout: How typography and design can get your message across—or get in the way*, Berkeley, Strathmore Press, 1995.

Information design

Because information design is relatively new, the definitive book is yet to be written, but there are plenty of useful texts.

Mijksenaar, Paul, *Visual Function: An introduction to information design*, New York, Princeton Architectural Press, 1997.
Schriver, Karen A., *Dynamics in Document Design: Creating text for readers*, New York, John Wiley & Sons, 1996.
Sevilla, Christine, *Information Design Desk Reference*, Menlo Park, California, Crisp Learning, 2002.
Williams, Robin, *The Non-Designer's Design Book: Design and typographic principles for the visual novice*, 2nd edn, Berkeley, Peachpit Press, 2004.
Williams, Robin and Tollett, John, *Robin Williams Design Workshop*, Berkeley, Peachpit Press, 2001.

Information graphics

When you need a more sophisticated reference on graphics, mostly there is Edward Tufte.

Harris, Robert L., *Information Graphics: A comprehensive illustrated reference*, New York, Oxford University Press, 1999.
Tufte, Edward, *Envisioning Information*, Cheshire, Connecticut, Graphics Press, 1990.

Tufte, Edward, *Visual Explanations: Images and quantities, evidence and narrative*, Cheshire Connecticut, Graphics Press, 1997.

Tufte, Edward, *The Visual Display of Quantitative Information*, 2nd edn, Cheshire, Connecticut, Graphics Press, 2001.

Editing and proofreading

Book and newspaper copy editing

Many of the texts on editing are specific to book publishing or newspaper editing.

Butcher, Judith, *Copy-editing: The Cambridge handbook for editors, authors and publishers*, 3rd edn, Cambridge, Cambridge University Press, 1992.

Flann, Elizabeth and Hill, Beryl, *The Australian Editing Handbook*, 2nd edn, Milton, John Wiley & Sons, 2004.

Plotnik, Arthur, *The Elements of Editing: A modern guide for editors and journalists*, New York, Macmillan, 1982.

Rooney, Dr Edmund J. and Witte, Oliver R., *Copy Editing for Professionals*, New York, Stipes Publishing, 2000.

Editing in a professional context

These are more directly relevant to editing in the workplace.

Billingham, Jo, *Editing and Revising Text*, Oxford, Oxford University Press, 2002.

Einsohn, Amy, *The Copyeditor's Handbook: A guide for book publishing and corporate communications*, 2nd edn, Berkeley, University of California Press, 2006.

Kehrwald Cook, Claire, *Line by Line: How to edit your own writing*, Modern Language Association, Boston, Houghton Mifflin, 1985.

Ross-Larson, Bruce, *Edit Yourself: A manual for everyone who works with words*, New York, Norton, 1996.

Samson, Donald C. Jr, *Editing Technical Writing*, New York, Oxford University Press, 1993.

Tarutz, Judith A., *Technical Editing: The practical guide for editors and writers*, New York, Basic Books, 1992.

E-writing

New technology calls for new techniques, although the basic principles of writing don't change.

Angell, David and Heslop, Brent, *The Elements of E-mail Style: Communicate effectively via electronic mail*, Boston, Addison-Wesley, 1994.

Booher, Dianne, *E-Writing: 21st-century tools for effective communication*, New York, Pocket Books, 2001.

Cavanagh, Christina, *Managing Your E-Mail: Thinking outside the inbox*, New Jersey, John Wiley & Sons, 2003.
Dorner, Jane, *Writing for the Internet*, Oxford, Oxford University Press, 2002.
Smith, Lisa A., *Business E-Mail: How to make it professional and effective*, San Anselmo, Writing and Editing at Work, 2002.

Grammar

Dictionaries

When you are already familiar with grammar, these make accessible references.

Aitchison, James, *Cassell's Dictionary of English Grammar*, London, Cassell & Co., 2001.
Chalker, Sylvia and Weiner, Edmund, *The Oxford Dictionary of English Grammar*, Oxford, Oxford University Press, 1998.
Stern, George, *The Grammar Dictionary*, Canberra, RIC Publications, 2002.

General guides

To brush up on your grammar, look at one of the practical guides for adults.

King, Graham, *Good Grammar*, London, Collins, 2005.
Seeley, John, *Everyday Grammar*, Oxford, Oxford University Press, 2004.

Academic grammars

For those wanting to pursue grammar further, here are the more comprehensive texts.

Greenbaum, Sidney, *Oxford English Grammar*, Oxford, Oxford University Press, 1996.
Huddleston, Rodney and Pullum, Geoffrey K., *The Cambridge Grammar of the English Language*, Cambridge, Cambridge University Press, 2002.
Leech, Geoffrey, Deuchar, Margaret and Hoogenraad, Robert, *English Grammar for Today: A new introduction*, 2nd edn, Hampshire, Palgrave Macmillan, 2006.
Leech, Geoffrey and Svartik, Jan, *A Communicative Grammar of English*, 3rd edn, London, Longman, 2002.
Quirk, Randolph, Greenbaum, Sidney, Leech, Geoffrey and Svartik, Jan, *A Comprehensive Grammar of the English Language*, Harlow, Longman, 1985.

English as a second language

Then there are the texts designed for those whose first language is not English.

Swan, Michael, *Practical English Usage*, 2nd edn, Oxford, Oxford University Press, 2001.

Thomson, A.J. and Martinet, A.V., *A Practical English Grammar*, 4th edn, Oxford, Oxford University Press, 2001.

Linguistics

Here are some books for the curious who want to delve into linguistics.

Allerton, D.J., *Essentials of Grammatical Theory: A consensus view of syntax and morphology*, London, Routledge and Kegan Paul, 1979.

Butt, David, Fahey, Rhondda, Feez, Susan, Spinks, Sue and Yallop, Colin, *Using Functional Grammar: An explorer's guide*, Sydney, National Centre of English Language Teaching and Research, Macquarie University, 2001.

Crystal, David, *Linguistics*, 2nd edn, London, Penguin Books, 1985.

Freedle, Roy O. (ed.), *Discourse Production and Comprehension, Volume 1*, New Jersey, Ablex Publishing Corporation, 1977.

Halliday, M.A.K., *An Introduction to Functional Grammar*, 2nd edn, London, Edward Arnold, 1994.

Historical grammars

If you are interested in the history of grammar, look out for the following books.

Cobbett, William, *A Grammar of the English Language*, Oxford, Oxford University Press, 2002.

Fries, Charles Carpenter, *American English Grammar*, New York, Appleton Century Crofts, 1940.

Lowth, Robert, *A Short Introduction to English Grammar*, Scholar Press, 1967.

Mulroy, David, *The War Against Grammar*, Portsmouth, Boynton Cook Publishers, 2003.

History of English

Histories of English

In the last half a century, books on the history of English have reached a popular audience, partly through related television series.

Baugh, Albert and Cable, Thomas, *A History of the English Language*, 5th edn, London, Routledge, 2002.

Bragg, Melvyn, *The Adventure of English, 500AD to 2000: The biography of a language*, London, Hodder and Stoughton, 2003.

Bryson, Bill, *Mother Tongue: The English language*, London, Penguin Books, 1991.

Burchfield, Robert, *The English Language*, Oxford, Oxford University Press, 1985.

Howard, Philip, *The State of the Language: English observed*, London, Hamish Hamilton, 1984.
Lederer, Richard, *Anguished English: An anthology of accidental assaults upon our language*, Dell Publishing, 1987.
McCrum, Robert, MacNeil, Robert, and Cran, William, *The Story of English*, 3rd edn, London, Faber and Faber, 2002.
Winchester, Simon, *The Surgeon of Crowthorne: A tale of murder, madness and the love of words*, London, Viking, 1998.
Winchester, Simon, *The Meaning of Everything: The story of the Oxford English Dictionary*, Oxford, Oxford University Press, 2003.
Wren, C.L., *The English Language*, London, Methuen, 1962.

Reference works

Some important general reference works on English emerged in the 1990s.

Crystal, David, *The Cambridge Encyclopedia of the English Language*, 2nd edn, Cambridge, Cambridge University Press, 2003.
MacArthur, Tom, *The Oxford Companion to the English Language*, Oxford, Oxford University Press, 1992.

Jargon

Without doubt, the most influential discussion of the abuse of jargon and cliché is a single essay: George Orwell's 'Politics and the English Language', published in 1946. Many of the subsequent books have taken a lexical approach.

Hudson, Kenneth, *The Dictionary of Diseased English*, London, Harper and Row, 1977.
Hudson, Kenneth, *The Dictionary of Even More Diseased English*, London, Macmillan, 1983.
Partridge, Eric, *A Dictionary of Clichés*, 5th edn, London, Routledge and Kegan Paul, 2000.
Watson, Don, *Watson's Dictionary of Weasel Words*, Sydney, Knopf, 2004.
Webb, Nick, *The Dictionary of Bullshit*, London, Robson Books, 2005.

General works

You can find some more general discussion of language abuse in these.

Lutz, William D., *Doublespeak*, New York, HarperCollins, 1990.
Poole, Steven, *Unspeak*, London, Little Brown, 2006.
Watson, Don, *Death Sentence: The decay of public language*, Sydney, Knopf, 2003.

Wheen, Francis, *How Mumbo Jumbo Conquered the World: A short history of modern delusions*, London, Harper Perennial, 2004.

Plain English

The pioneers

Foundational books on plain English include:

Cutts, Martin, *The Oxford Guide to Plain English*, Oxford, Oxford University Press, 2004.
Eagleson, Robert, *Writing in Plain English*, Canberra, AGPS, 1990.
Gowers, Ernest, *The Complete Plain Words*, London, Her Majesty's Stationery Office, 1954.

Plain language and the law

The law is the profession best served with writing guides.

Asprey, Michele M., *Plain Language for Lawyers*, 3rd edn, Sydney, The Federation Press, 2003.
Butt, Peter and Castle, Richard, *Modern Legal Drafting: A guide to using clearer language*, 2nd edn, Cambridge, Cambridge University Press, 2006.
Garner, Bryan A., *Legal Writing in Plain English*, Chicago, University of Chicago Press, 2001.
Gibbons, John, *Forensic Linguistics: An introduction to language in the justice system*, Melbourne, Blackwell Publishing, 2003.
Kimble, Joseph, 'Writing for Dollars, Writing to Please', *The Scribes Journal of Legal Writing*, vol. 6, 1996–97.
Law Reform Commission of Victoria, *Plain English and the Law*, Report Number 9, Melbourne, Law Reform Commission of Victoria, 1984.
Mowat, Christine, *A Plain Language Handbook for Legal Writers*, Scarborough, Carswell Legal Publications, 1998.

Punctuation

Punctuation guides

While books on writing tend to carry a chapter on punctuation, few writers have made the transition to a dedicated volume.

Cappon, Rene J., *The Associated Press Guide to Punctuation*, New York, Basic Books, 2003.
Carey, G.V., *Mind the Stop: A brief guide to punctuation with a note on proof correction*, Cambridge, Cambridge University Press, 1939.
Gordon, Karen Elizabeth, *The New Well-tempered Sentence: A punctuation handbook for the innocent, the eager, and the doomed*, Boston, Houghton Mifflin, 2003.

Partridge, Eric, *You Have a Point There: A guide to punctuation and its allies*, London, Hamish Hamilton, 1953.
Todd, Loreto, *Cassell's Guide to Punctuation*, London, Cassell and Co, 2001.
Trask, R.L., *The Penguin Guide to Punctuation*, London, Penguin Books, 1997.
Truss, Lynne, *Eats, Shoots and Leaves: The zero tolerance guide to punctuation*, London, Profile Books, 2003.

Readability

Chall, Jeanne S., *Readability: An appraisal of research and application*, Ohio, Ohio State University Press, 1958.
Du Bay, William, *Smart Language: Readers, readability, and the grading of text*, South Carolina, Book Surge Publishing, 2007.
Flesch, Rudolph, *The Art of Readable Writing*, New York, Harper, 1949.
Fry, Edward, 'Fry's readability graph: Clarifications, validity and extension to level 17', *Journal of Reading*, vol. 21, no. 3: pp. 242–52.
Gunning, Robert, *The Technique of Clear Writing*, New York, McGraw Hill, 1952.
Klare, George and Buck, Byron, *Know Your Reader: The scientific approach to readability*, New York, Hermitage, 1954.
Redish, Janice and Selzer, Jack, 'The place of readability formulas in technical communication', *Technical Communication*, vol. 32, no. 4: pp. 46–52.

Rhetoric

Primary texts

Aristotle, *The Art of Rhetoric*, translated with an introduction and notes by H.C. Lawson Tancred, London, Penguin Books, 1991.
[Cicero], *Rhetorica Ad Herennium*, translated by Harry Caplan, Loeb Classical Library, Cambridge, Harvard University Press, 1999.
Cicero, *On the Orator, Books I–II*, translated by E.W. Sutton and H. Rackham, Loeb Classical Library, Cambridge, Harvard University Press, 2001.
Cicero, *On the Orator, Book III, Divisions of Oratory*, translated by H. Rackham, Loeb Classical Library, Cambridge, Harvard University Press, 2004.
Cicero, *On Invention, Best Kind of Orator*, and *Topics*, translated by H.M. Hubbell, Loeb Classical Library, Cambridge, Harvard University Press, 2000.
Quintilian, *The Orator's Education, Books 1–12 (4 vols)*, edited and translated by Donald A. Russell, Loeb Classical Library, Cambridge, Harvard University Press, 2001.

History of rhetoric

Although you could read the primary sources by Aristotle, Cicero and Quintilian, probably a more accessible introduction to the area is through a more general work.

Blair, Hugh, *Lectures on Rhetoric*, New York, William E. Dean, 1840.

Corbett, Edward P.J. and Connors, Robert J., *Classical Rhetoric for the Modern Student*, 4th edn, New York, Oxford University Press, 1999.
Herrick, James A., *The History of Theory of Rhetoric: An introduction*, 3rd edn, Boston, Allyn & Bacon, 2005.
Kennedy, George A., *A New History of Classical Rhetoric*, Princeton, Princeton University Press, 1994.

The new rhetoric

More specialist readers may want to delve into these:

Perelman, Chaim and Olbrechts-Tyteca, L., *The New Rhetoric: A treatise on argumentation*, translated by John Wilkinson and Purcell Weaver, Notre Dame, University of Notre Dame Press, 2003.
Perelman, Chaim, *The Realm of Rhetoric*, translated by William Kluback, Notre Dame, University of Notre Dame Press, 2003.

Argument and invention

If you want to explore the methods of research and argument more closely, try these texts.

Booth, Wayne C., Colomb, Gregory G. and Williams, Joseph, *The Craft of Research*, 2nd edn, Chicago, University of Chicago Press, 2003.
Weston, Anthony, *A Rulebook for Arguments*, 3rd edn, Indianapolis, Hackett Publishing Company, 2000.
Williams, Joseph M. and Colomb, Gregory G., *The Craft of Argument*, 2nd edn, New York, Longman, 2003.

Public speaking

Useful but very different treatments of making an effective speech are:

O'Loghlin, James, *Umm ... A Complete Guide to Public Speaking*, Sydney, Allen & Unwin, 2006.
Porter, Chester, *The Gentle Art of Persuasion: How to argue effectively*, Sydney, Random House, 2005.

Style

The originals

By far the most influential style manuals are the oldest.

The Chicago Manual of Style, 15th edn, Chicago, University of Chicago Press, 2003.
Ritter, R.M., *The Oxford Style Manual*, Oxford, Oxford University Press, 2003.

Business and academic style manuals

Style is growing and specialising in different areas.

American Institute of Physics, *AIP Style Manual*, 4th edn, Stanford, American Institute of Physics, 1990.

American Psychological Association, *Publication Manual of the American Psychological Association*, Washington, American Psychological Association, 2001.

Atlas, Michel C., *Author's Handbook of Styles for Life Science Journals*, Florida, CRC Press, 1996.

Beer, David F. and McMurrey, David, *A Guide to Writing as an Engineer*, New Jersey, John Wiley & Sons, 2005.

Dodd, Janet S., *The ACS Style Guide: A manual for authors and editors*, Washington, American Chemistry Society, 1997.

Gibaldi, Joseph, *MLA Style Manual and Guide to Scholarly Publishing*, 2nd edn, New York, Modern Language Association of America, 1998.

Sabin, William A., *The Gregg Reference Manual*, 10th edn, Boston, McGraw Hill, 2004.

Scientific Style and Format: The CBE manual for authors, editors and publishers, 6th edn, Cambridge, Cambridge University Press, 1994.

National style manuals

Snooks & Co., *Style Manual: For authors, editors and printers*, 6th edn, Canberra, John Wiley & Sons, 2002.

Wallace, Derek and Hughes, Janet, *Style Book: A guide for New Zealand writers and editors*, Wellington, GP Publications, 1995.

Media style guides

Many newspapers found the Oxford and Chicago manuals too book-centric, so they developed their own.

Goldstein, Norm (ed.), *The Associated Press Stylebook*, New York, Basic Books, 2004.

Lockwood, Kim, *Style: A guide for journalists*, Melbourne, Nationwide News Limited, 2003.

Siegal, Allan M. and Connolly, William G., *The New York Times Manual of Style and Usage*, New York, Times Books, 1999.

The Economist Style Guide, London, The Economist, in Association with Profile Books, 2005.

Washington Post Deskbook on Style, Ohio, McGraw Hill, 1978.

Technical writing

With a significant presence in university curriculums, there are several excellent textbooks on technical writing.

Anderson, Paul V., *Technical Writing: A reader-centered approach*, 2nd edn, San Diego, Harcourt Brace Jovanovich, 1991.

Pickett, Nell Ann, Laster, Ann A. and Staples, Katherine E., *Technical English: Writing, reading and speaking*, 8th edn, New York, Longman, 2001.

Pringle, Alan S. and O'Keefe, Sarah S., *Technical Writing 101: A real-world guide to planning and writing technical documentation*, 2nd edn, NC, Scriptorium Press, 2003.

Usability

The first generation of texts about usability are all written by foundational practitioners.

Dumas, Joseph S. and Redish, Janice C., *A Practical Guide to Usability Testing*, revised edition, Exeter, Intellect Books, 1999.

Hackos, JoAnn T. and Redish, Janice C., *User and Task Analysis for Interface Design*, New York, John Wiley & Sons, 1998.

Rubin, Jeffrey, *Handbook of Usability Testing: How to plan, design, and conduct effective tests*, New York, John Wiley & Sons, 1994.

Usage

Usage guides commonly compile an alphabetical list of rulings on acceptable practice in spelling, pronunciation, points of grammar and punctuation.

The originals

Fowler, H.W., *A Dictionary of Modern English Usage*, 2nd edn revised by Sir Ernest Gowers, Oxford, Oxford University Press, 1996.

Fowler, H.W. and Fowler, F.G., *The King's English*, 2nd edn, Oxford University Press, 1919.

Partridge, Eric, *Usage and Abusage*, new edition, London, Hamish Hamilton, 1971.

More recent usage dictionaries

Bernard, J.R.L. (ed.), *Macquarie Writer's Friend*, Sydney, The Macquarie Library, 1999.

Bernstein, Theodore M.; *The Careful Writer: A modern guide to English usage*, New York, The Free Press, 1965.

Bernstein, Theodore M., *Miss Thistlebottom's Hobgoblins: The careful writer's guide to the taboos, bugbears and outmoded rules of English usage*, Centro Books, 2000.

Hughes, Barrie (ed.), *Penguin Working Words*, Melbourne, Penguin Books, 1993.

Murray-Smith, Stephen, *Right Words: A guide to English usage in Australia*, Melbourne, Viking, 1987.

Peters, Pam, *The Cambridge Guide to English Usage*, Melbourne, Cambridge University Press, 2004.

Walsh, Bill, *Lapsing into a Comma: A curmudgeon's guide to the many things that can go wrong in print—and how to avoid them*, New York, McGraw Hill, 2000.

Writing guides

Some classics

For general guidance on writing, it is hard to go past a handful of tried and true works that have proved popular for decades. These references are to the currently available edition.

Flesch, Rudolf and Lass, A.H., *The Classic Guide to Better Writing: Step-by-step techniques and exercises to write simply, clearly, and correctly*, 50th anniversary edition, New York, HarperCollins, 1996.

Strunk, William and White, E.B., *The Elements of Style*, 4th edn, New York, Longman, 2000.

Williams, Joseph M., *Style: Ten lessons in clarity and grace*, 8th edn, New York, Pearson Longman, 2005.

Zinsser, William, *On Writing Well: The classic guide to writing non-fiction*, 25th anniversary edition, New York, Collins, 2001.

Nuts and bolts books

There is a lively sub-genre of writing books that look at specific areas of writing.

Fiske, Robert Hartwell, *The Dictionary of Concise Writing: 10,000 alternatives to wordy phrases*, Oak Park, Marion Street Press, 2002.

Longknife, Ann and Sullivan, K.D., *The Art of Styling Sentences*, 4th edn, New York, Barron's, 2002.

Pellegrino, Victor C., *A Writer's Guide to Using 8 Methods of Transition*, revised edition, Wailuku, Maui Arthoughts Company, 2004.

Pellegrino, Victor C., *A Writer's Guide to Transitional Words and Expressions*, revised edition, Wailuku, Maui Arthoughts Company, 2004.

Pellegrino, Victor C., *A Writer's Guide to Powerful Paragraphs*, Wailuku, Maui Arthoughts Company, 2003.

Ross-Larson, Bruce, *Powerful Paragraphs*, New York, W.W. Norton & Co., 1999.

Ross-Larson, Bruce, *Stunning Sentences*, New York, W.W. Norton & Co., 1999.

Seeley, John, *Writing Reports*, Oxford, Oxford University Press, 2002.

Other general writing books

This leaves a useful collection of more general guides.

Blamires, Harry, *The Penguin Guide to Plain English*, London, Penguin Books, 2000.

Blamires, Harry, *Compose Yourself and Write Good English*, London, Penguin Books, 2003.

Kane, Thomas S., *The New Oxford Guide to Writing*, New York, Oxford University Press, 1988.

Manser, Martin and Curtis, Stephen, *The Penguin Writer's Manual*, London, Penguin Books, 2002.

Vallins, G.H., *Good English: How to Write it*, London, Pan Books, 1951.

Vallins, G.H., *Better English*, London, Pan Books, 1953.

Vallins, G.H., *The Best English*, London, Pan Books, 1960.

Wilbers, Stephen, *Keys to Great Writing*, Cincinnati, Writer's Digest Books, 2000.

Chapter notes

To make this book as readable as possible, I have minimised the interruption of footnotes throughout the text. For those wanting more detail, these notes offer specific references and acknowledge intellectual debts. They run continuously, grouped into the three chapter sections, with notes separated by the ■ symbol.

Where a note refers to a source not included in the Further Reading section, I cite it fully below. Where a work is already fully cited in the Further Reading section, I give a short author and year reference, along with the section containing the full reference. For example, 'Herrick (2005, Rhetoric)' means you can find the full citation in the Rhetoric section of Further Reading.

One of the challenges of writing this book was finding a broad range of real workplace samples to illustrate each tool. Organisations do not generally make internal documents publicly available, and clients I work with naturally enjoy full confidentiality. Fortunately, many people have offered me samples, so every example in the text is based on a real-life scenario. The origins of some have been disguised, however, at the request of their authors. The Internet has been a second major source, as workplaces are increasingly using it to post all kinds of documents. Every sample sourced from there is acknowledged below. Where a viewing date for an electronic address is not included, it was last checked in March or April 2007.

Chapter 1: Readers

Toolbox

Details on the Teesdale District Council report come from 'Report "incomprehensible to any normal person"', *Teesdale Mercury*, 23 November 2006, viewed on 28 November 2006 at <www.teesdalemercury.co.uk/teesdale-news/story.1182.html>.

The living language

For more background on the history of rhetoric, see Corbett and Connors (1999, Rhetoric), Herrick (2005, Rhetoric), Kennedy (1994, Rhetoric), Lawson-Tancred's introduction to Aristotle's *The Art of Rhetoric* (1991, Rhetoric), and the primary works of Cicero and Quintilian. ■ On the relationship between rhetoric and technical writing, see Hackos and Redish (1998, Usability). ■ Grice's account of the cooperative principle can be found in his *Logic and Conversation* (1967), although I encountered it in Herbert H. Clark and Susan E. Haviland, 'Comprehension and the Given-New Contract', in Freedle (1977, Grammar).

Power tools

While the scale of document testing is my own, it draws on the emergent literature on usability, particularly Dumas and Redish (1999, Usability), Hackos and Redish (1998, Usability) and Rubin (1994, Usability). There is also a useful chapter on testing in Asprey (2003, Plain English). ■ The Communications Research Institute of Australia has further articles on testing at <www.communication.org.au/html/papers_to_read.php>. A current guru of web usability is Jacob Nielsen, whose work you can explore through the Nielsen Norman Group website <www.nngroup.com>. The Society of Technical Communicators also has some useful checklists and tools for testing at <www.stcsig.org/usability/resources/toolkit/toolkit.html>.

Chapter 2: Content

Toolbox

The content checklist for workplace writing is greatly influenced by Booth, Colomb and Williams, *The Craft of Research* (2003, Rhetoric). While this book is directed mainly at academic writing, its underlying method is equally appropriate to workplace documents.

The living language

Corbett and Connors (1999, Rhetoric) and Herrick (2005, Rhetoric) both discuss the practical applications of rhetorical tools in the process of invention. ■ The checklist for evaluating conclusions draws heavily from Booth, Colomb and Williams (2003, Rhetoric).

Power tools

For a useful overview of content development techniques, you can try James Mankeltow's electronic book *Mind Tools: Essential skills for an excellent career*, 4th edn, Swindon, Mind Tools Ltd, 2005, which is available at <www.mindtools.com>. This covers all the techniques mentioned here and many more. ■ Some of these are also discussed in Petelin and Durham (2001, Business Communications). ■ For more on mind mapping, see Tony Buzan, *The Mind Map Book*, New York, Penguin Books, 1991. ■ For the six thinking hats technique, see Edward de Bono, *Six Thinking Hats*, Back Bay Books,

1999. ■ For background on fishbone diagrams, see Kaoru Ishikawa, *What is Total Quality Control? The Japanese way*, New York, Prentice Hall, 1985.

Chapter 3: Structure

Toolbox

The idea of setting out basic structural models was influenced by a chapter in John Seely's *Writing Reports* (2002, pp. 45–55, Writing Guides), from which I have taken two terms: 'narrative' and 'exposition'. Martin Cutts' (2004, pp. 132–42, Plain English) chapter on 'reader-centred structures' traverses similar terrain. However, most models are based on my own work with over 30,000 pages of workplace documents over the last decade.

Power tools

Structural mapping has evolved over five years of working with a number of agencies that publish longer reports. I am grateful for their feedback on this system. I first presented it publicly as part of the workshop 'Will it work? Measuring effective writing' at the 2006 WriteMark Plain English Conference in Wellington, New Zealand, in October 2006.

Chapter 4: Focus

Toolbox

I've been using the core message test tool in writing courses since 2000. I am pleased that some organisations have found it useful enough to structure into their templates.

The living language

While the magpie anecdote is drawn from my own experience of a particularly vicious beast, the connection to thinking versus communication structures was suggested by a teaching script of Pamela Freeman. ■ The available works of Cicero and Quintilian are all listed under Rhetoric in Further Reading.

Power tools

The 'Work Choices' memo was published by the Pharmacy Guild of Australia at <www.psa.org.au/ecms.cfm?id=186>, viewed in August 2006. ■ For further discussion about structuring bad news, see Anderson (1991, pp. 154–9, Technical Writing), Munter (2006, pp. 18–22, Business Communications) or Wilbers (2000, pp. 173–80, Writing Guides). ■ The bank letter is one I received as a customer of the Commonwealth Bank of Australia.

Chapter 5: Persuasion

Toolbox

For Aristotle's account of the parts of an argument, see section 10 of H.C. Lawson-Tancred's translation of *The Art of Rhetoric* (1991, Rhetoric). I had developed the value analysis tool as part of our writing workshops, only to discover that Aristotle had beat me to the concept by some 2000 years.

The living language

On the three modes of persuasion and the different kinds of logic, see Aristotle (1991, Rhetoric) and Corbett and Connors (1999, Rhetoric). Anthony Weston's *A Rulebook for Arguments* (2000, Rhetoric) is a useful pocket guide to the different forms of argument. ■ I first encountered the anecdote about swans and inductive logic in Windschuttle and Windschuttle (1988, Business Communications). ■ While the selection of 12 rhetorical arguments for workplace writing is mine, it draws on the primary works of Aristotle, Cicero and Quintilian. As always, however, Corbett and Connors (1999, Rhetoric) is a seminal secondary reference.

Power tools

A major influence in this classification of proofs was Chaim Perelman and Lucy Olbrechts-Tyteca's work (2003, 1982, Rhetoric). I first presented my own map of the most common workplace proofs used in government writing in 'No, Minister: Intention and reality in the rhetoric of government', a paper presented to the What Is the New Rhetoric? conference at the University of Sydney in September 2005. ■ The examples of consequence arguments come, in turn, from 'Climate Change and Water in Australia', published by Climate Action Network Australia, <www.cana.net.au/water/farmers/index.html>; Tobias Gurock, 'Keeping a product idea secret', 18 August 2005, <http://software.gurock.com/postings/date/2005/08/>; and Andrew Skegg, 'Slippery When Wet?' in the *Risk Engineering and Safety Solutions* newsletter, SEMF, <www.semf.com.au/risk/?m=200610>. ■ The first instance of an example argument could come from almost any government department. The comparison example was written by Graeme Hunt, President of Western Australian Iron Ore and Bodarie Iron, *BHP Billiton Iron Chronicle*, <http://ironore.bhpbilliton.com/docs/FEBChroniclepart1.pdf>, January 2007. The first analogy example comes from Toby and Gayle Allan's 'Internet Technology Primer', a paper presented to the CMGA conference in 1999, <www.apms.com.au/papers/allan99b.pdf>. The second analogy sample is excerpted from a marketing letter signed by Andrew Cox, Technology Consultant, iocom. ■ The sample of authority comes from a University of Sydney paper on its University Learning Management System (WebCT) Upgrade Project, <www.usyd.edu.au/learning/governance/elearning_docs/webct_upgrade_communication_aug2006.pdf>. The precedent sample comes from a post by 21_blue to the WebmasterWorld forum on Google AdSense, viewed January 2007, <www.webmasterworld.com/forum89/11943.htm>. The argument of principle example is taken from Lisa Hill's article 'Compulsory Voting' at <http://arts.anu.edu.au/democratic audit/papers/20030604_hiil_comp.pdf>. ■ The definition argument about junk food was written by the Confectionery Manufacturers of Australasia as part of a Q&A document on nutrition, <www.candy.net.au/consumer-information.asp?pgID=179#Q03>. The final examples of responsibility arguments regularly come out of government agencies.

Chapter 6: Coherence

Toolbox

The Greenspan quotation comes from David and Hilary Crystal's *Words on Words: Quotations about language and literature*, London, Penguin Books, 2000, p. 152. ■ *Cosmos* is an excellent magazine chock full of good writing on science. The subscriber letter was signed by publisher Dr Alan Finkel in January 2006.

The living language

For more on the history of the paragraph, see Corbett and Connors (1999, pp. 511–38, Rhetoric). ■ Also useful is Wilbers' (2000, pp. 195–215, Writing Guides) chapter on coherence. ■ Of the many works that discuss paragraphing, Pellegrino (2003, 2004 and 2004, Writing Guides) and Ross-Larson (1999, Writing Guides) offer dedicated and extensive accounts, while Anderson (1991, Technical Writing) is the best of the technical writing texts on the subject.

Power tools

One of the major contributions of linguistics to the theory of coherence is the 'old before new' principle, which I first encountered in Herbert H. Clark and Susan E. Haviland, 'Comprehension and the given-new contract' in Freedle (1977, Grammar). The topic is also covered well in Halliday (1994, Grammar) and Butt *et al.* (2001, Grammar). ■ The extract from Martin Luther King's 'I have a dream' speech is reproduced from Brian MacArthur (ed.), *The Penguin Book of Historic Speeches*, London, Penguin Books, 1996, pp. 487–8. ■ The most extensive collection of transitional words and phrases is in the books of Pellegrino (2004 and 2004, Writing Guides), although Angell and Heslop (1994, pp. 62–4, E-writing) have a more accessible list. ■ The final quotation was originally published in the *Sydney Morning Herald*, although it is reproduced here from Petelin and Durham (2001, p. 20, Business Communication).

Chapter 7: Design

Toolbox

The principles of type in this section are well established in the printing and publishing industries, and are reflected in most major style guides. Useful references on the topic are Sevilla (2002, Design) and Bringhurst (2005, Design). ■ The estimate of 60,000 fonts comes from Bringhurst (2005, Design). ■ The 'two and a half alphabets' rule on line length comes from Anthony Barker, former editor of book publisher Angus & Robertson, AR 12–13, Angus & Robertson Oral History Collection, Mitchell Library, Sydney. ■ For information on the impact of contrast or other type features for readers with visual impairment, see the Fact Sheets published by Vision Australia at <www.visionaustralia.org.au/info.aspx?page=795>.

The living language

For background on the history of information design, see Janice Redish, 'What is information design?', *Technical Communication*, second quarter, 2000, pp. 163–6. ■ Information designers are also by nature web savvy, and have posted extensive resources about their profession. Key references include the information design timeline published by the Society of Technical Communicators, <http://stc-on.org/id/category/history-of-idia/>, as well as its definition page, <http://stc-on.org/id/category/definition/>. See also David Sless, 'Transitions in information design', published by the Communications Research Institute of Australia, <www.communication.org.au/cria_publications/publication_id_46_1659832486.html>. You can find some biographies of early pioneers at <http://dao.rit.edu/dao/designers/pioneer.html>. ■ On the coining of the term information architecture, see <www.asis.org/SIG/SIGIA/definition.html>.

Power tools

The sample text used to illustrate a short table comes from a standard 'receipt notice' used by the Office of Charities in NSW in 2006. ■ When it comes to information graphics, Tufte (1990, 1997, 2001, Design) is a field unto himself, although technical writing texts such as Anderson (1991, pp. 360–85, Technical Writing) cover visual aids effectively.

Chapter 8: Tone

Toolbox

Halliday was my linguistics lecturer at the University of Sydney, and this opening quip has stayed with me for 20 years. ■ Zinsser's quote comes from his classic guide to writing non-fiction (2005, Writing Guides). ■ Elizabeth Newton's music tapping study is in her unpublished doctoral dissertation, 'Overconfidence in the Communication of Intent: Heard and unheard melodies', Stanford University, cited in Justin Kruger, Nicholas Epley, Jason Parker and Zhi-Wen Ng, 'Egocentrism over E-mail: Can we communicate as well as we think we can?', *Journal of Personality and Social Psychology*, 2005, vol. 89, no. 6, pp. 925–36. ■ The tone scale is my own invention, developed to help workplace writers hear the impact of their words and attune their ear to a less officious tone. The idea for the scale was suggested in part by *Communicating in Writing*, a training handbook developed by the Australian Public Service Board Personnel Development Branch, Canberra, Australian Government Publishing Service, 1975, p. 8. ■ The tone sample comes from a NSW local government letter, but might easily have been written by any local council. ■ The Bristol police's attempt at using text language was reported by David Smith, 'Too Trendy Text by Police Force Backfires', *Observer*, 29 January 2006, viewed at <http://observer.guardian.co.uk/print/0,,5386442-102285,00.html> on 31 January 2006.

The living language

Thomas Elyot's quote comes from Baugh and Cable's (2002, History of English) definitive account of the English language, p. 214. Thomas Wilson's rejoinder comes from the same text, p. 218. ■ The Internet security sample is part of the privacy statement of Rural Law Online, <www.rurallaw.org.au/cb_pages/privacy.php>. ■ The two quotes from mobile phone company 3 were viewed at <http:www.three.com.au/index.cfm?pid=2148&pageid=3176> and <http:www.three.com.au/index.cfm?pid=2148&pageid=2148> in August 2006. ■ The child support letter is from a standard template used by the Australian Government Child Support Agency in 2004. Only the names have been changed. ■ Virgin's quote comes from Virgin Mobile's 'Safe Chatting Tips', <www.virginmobile.com.au/companyinfo/corporateresponsibility/safechattingtips.html>. ■ Jonas Blank's infamous email has been the subject of considerable media coverage since he sent it in 2003. Ben McGrath covered it in 'Oops', *New Yorker*, 30 June 2003, <www.newyorker.com/printables/talk/030630ta_talk_mcgrath>. ■ The case of the abusive marquee supplier was reported by Jonathan Marshall, 'Cheap and Tacky Wedding Email that Went Global', *New Zealand Herald*, 19 November 2006, <www.nzherald.co.nz/section/story.cfm?c_id=1&objectid=10411458>. ■ The email study is Justin Kruger, Nicholas Epley, Jason Parker and Zhi-Wen Ng, 'Egocentrism over E-mail: Can we communicate as well as we think we can?' in the *Journal of Personality and Social Psychology*, 2005, vol. 89, no. 6, pp. 925–36.

Power tools

The seven elements are among those studied by Kruger *et al.* above. ■ The sample on certification comes from 'Post-Certification: Maintenance issues' published by AGA Certification Services on the AGA website at <www.aga.asn.au/post_certification_issues>. ■ There is a useful discussion of point of view and person in Wilbers (2000, pp. 143–63, Writing Guides). ■ The IntraConnect sample was supplied by an IT manager who wishes not to be identified. The names have been changed.

Chapter 9: Grammar

Toolbox

A single chapter on grammar cannot hope to match the definitive coverage of texts such as Huddleston and Pullum (2002, Grammar) or Greenbaum (1996, Grammar), the first of which extends towards 2000 pages. The approach here is to present enough of traditional grammar to help workplace writers understand what happens in a sentence. I have included here what I find most helpful when training professionals, and the text I turn to most often is Thomson and Martinet (2001, Grammar), although Swan (2001, Grammar), King (2005, Grammar) and Leech, Deuchar and Hoogenraad (2006, Grammar) were also influences. ■ The story of schoolyard burial of the word 'got' has been related to me by some half dozen professionals who went to school in different areas. I don't know how widespread the practice was, nor how it started. ■ The analogy of writing with practising chemistry comes from Mulroy (2003, Grammar). ■ There is a well-informed discussion of the history of capitalisation in Snooks & Co. (2002, pp. 119–20, Style).

The living language

For more on the history of grammar in English, see Mulroy (2003, Grammar), Baugh and Cable (2002, History of English), Burchfield (1985, History of English), Bryson (1991, History of English), and Bragg (2003, History of English). ■ The split infinitive anecdote on treaty negotiation comes from Crystal (2003, p. 195, History of English). For an account of the attack on grammar in the 20th century, see Mulroy (2003, Grammar) and Fries (1940, Grammar).

Power tools

The pronoun reference example comes from Lederer (1987, p. 156, History of English). ■ The sample on starting a sentence with a conjunction comes from the Railway Engineering Company case study on the Wimbledon Signalling Centre, <www.theraileng.co.uk/pdfs/wmbn_sigcent.pdf>. ■ Of the many accounts of Churchill's famous rejoinder on prepositions, Crystal (2003, p. 194, History of English) discusses the myth in a useful context. The Churchill Centre argues that the attribution to Churchill is apocryphal at <www.winstonchurchill.org/i4a/pages/index.cfm?pageid=388>.

Chapter 10: Words

Toolbox

The estimates on the size of the English vocabulary come from Bryson (1990, p. 3, History of English). ■ The wide variety of estimates for Shakespeare's vocabulary stems from what you classify as a word. Those who count every word, such as McCrum (2002, History of English) end up with 30,000, but this count includes every variant of a word in different tenses, plurals and spelling. Those counting 'lexemes', such as David Crystal, reach around 17,000 to 20,000 words. ■ The sick leave sample comes from the University of Melbourne *Personnel Policy and Procedures Manual*, <www.unimelb.edu.au/ppp/docs/9.html#9.7.3>. ■ Although many writers feel that using bigger words will impress and persuade their readers, a recent study of university essays has found that needless complexity has negative consequences. See Daniel M. Oppenheimer, 'Consequences of Erudite Vernacular Utilized Irrespective of Necessity: Problems with using long words needlessly,' *Applied Cognitive Psychology*, 20, 2006, pp. 139–56. ■ Churchill's memo is widely quoted in books and on websites. A full version of the text can be viewed at <http://www-unix.oit.umass.edu/~mee/writing_churcill_mm5.htm>. My thanks to Judy Keena for this reference.

The living language

The most authoritative source for this brief history of the language is Baugh and Cable (2002, History of English), although Burchfield (1985, History of English), Bryson (1991, History of English), and Bragg (2003, History of English) were also helpful. ■ The percentage of Latinate words in officialese comes from studies completed by communications company Optimum, which it has used to develop proprietary editing software. Contact <www.optimum-uk.com> for details. ■ The accident compensation sample comes from the Accident Compensation Regulations 2001: Version No. 010: SR No. 21/2001, published by the Victorian WorkCover Authority.

Power tools

Perhaps the leading contemporary advocate of readability measures is William DuBay, who published *The Principles of Readability* in 2004 on his website <www.impact-information.com>. Much of the history of readability is drawn from this text. DuBay has since published his work in book form as *Smart Language: Readers, readability and the grading of text*, BookSurge Publishing, 2007. ■ For more on the Fry Readability Graph, see 'Fry's Readability Graph: Clarification, validity and extension to level 17', *Journal of Reading* 21, no. 4, pp. 46–52. ■ The audit sample comes from a standard audit letter template used by one of the 'big four' accounting firms in Australia. ■ The Victorian Law Reform Commission's study was published in *Plain English and the Law*. Report no. 9, 1984, p. 70. ■ The breastfeeding policy text comes from a 'policy pending comment' posted on the Victoria University intranet, viewed in January 2006. ■ For papers critical of readability formulas, see Janice Redish and Jack Selzer, 'The Place of Readability Formulas in Technical Communication' in *Technical Communication* 32, no. 4, pp. 46–52, and Janice Redish, 'Readability Formulas Have Even More Limitations than Klare Discusses' in *ACM Journal of Computer Documentation*, August 2000, vol. 24, no. 3, pp. 132–7.

Chapter 11: Clutter

Toolbox

The school notice about hot dogs comes from the 'Newsletter of the Immaculate Heart of Mary Primary School', viewed in August 2006 at <www.ihm.adl.catholic.edu.au/notice0.html>. ■ The quote from Samuel Johnson comes from a list compiled for the Plain Language International website <http://plainlanguagenetwork.org/Resources/quotations.htm> by Annette Corrigan. ■ The more senior education example comes from Carolyn Dowling, 'Academic Discourse in the Age of the Internet', published by the Australian Catholic University, <www.ascilite.org.au/aset-archives/confs/edtech98/pubs/articles/dowling.html>. ■ The Management Essentials sample was posted by Steve Dowse at the *Sydney Morning Herald* website on 21 February 2006; he said it was 'an actual exerpt from an actual email sent by one of my colleagues'. Only the name was changed. <http://blogs.smh.com.au/newsblog/archives/frankenstein/003636.html> ■ The council road-sealing policy comes from a Ballarat Council document, viewed in August 2006 at <www.ballarat.vic.gov.au/Files/SealingUnsealedRoadsPolicy.pdf>.

The living language

The business registration and web-based education campaign samples were written by A. Tilley in a March 2004 AMPICTA 'Submission on Business Names and RTMs', written in response to the ACIP issues paper 'A Review of the Relationship Between Trademarks and Business Names, Company Names and Domain Names', released in

January 2004. The submission was signed by Bryan Dwyer, President of AMPICTA, an organisation that represents Australian intellectual property owners but does not explain its acronym on its website. You can try to guess at <www.ampicta.org.au/publications/Submission%20on%20Business%20Names.pdf>. ■ The leadership sample comes from Kenneth Bartell's PhD thesis 'Leadership in a Lutheran School: An exploration of principal and school pastor worldviews and their potential impact on the transformation of the school learning community', submitted in July 2004 at the Australian Catholic University and published at <dlibrary.acu.edu.au/digitaltheses/public/adt-acuvp43.29082005/01front.pdf>. ■ The BHP press release 'Update on BHP Billiton's Investigation into the Financing of a 1996 Grain Shipment to Iraq' was released on 31 January 2006, <www.bhpbilliton.com/bb/investorsMedia/news/2006/updateOnBhpBillitonsInvestigation IntoTheFinancingOfA1996GrainShipmentToIraq.jsp>. ■ I transcribed the Federal Attorney General's quote from a television interview broadcast on ABC television in 2005. ■ For more on the relationship between word doublets and triplets and the language of the law, see Butt and Castle (2006, pp. 19–26, Plain English). ■ The informed consent sample comes from a Melbourne University document, '4.7.3 Human Resources Ethics Committee', <www.unimelb.edu.au/unisec/Srvol1/pdf/r$-073.pdf>. ■ The TT-Line sample comes from the standard 'terms and conditions of carriage' for the Spirit of Tasmania ferry service, <www.spiritoftasmania.com.au/terms.htm>.

Power tools

The most comprehensive reference on grammatical clutter is Robert Hartwell-Fiske's *The Dictionary of Concise Writing: 10,000 alternatives to wordy phrases* (Fiske, 2002, Writing Guides). Other useful chapters on the forms of clutter can be found in Williams (2005, pp. 109–29, Writing Guides), Wilbers (2000, pp. 10–36, Writing Guides), and Zinsser (2005, pp. 13–17, Writing Guides). ■ The Board appraisal sample of long-winded verb phrases comes from Suncorp's 'Corporate Governance Statement—2006', <www.suncorp.com.au/suncorp/img/assets/3639/corporate_governance.pdf>. ■ The tautological adverb sample was written by a young graduate professional, who went too red when the effect was pointed out to be named here. ■ The opinion on the Druce moth comes from Associate Professor Paul Adam, 'Phyllodes imperialis, southern Subspecies (a Moth)—Endangered species listing', <www.nationalparks.nsw.gov.au/npws.nsf/Content/Phyllodes_imperialis_southern_subspecies_endangered>.

Chapter 12: Verbs

Toolbox

The OH&S sample comes from a policy document in a corporation, but it is typical of the 'HR speak' in large organisations. ■ The initial verb example is based on an anecdote given by an executive director of a state Office of Revenue, who quoted this as a sample of poor writing culture. ■ The business model sample with hidden verbs is a generic sample, based on board minutes in public and private sector organisations. ■ The Charrow and Charrow studies are cited in Gibbons (2003, Plain English). ■ The audit of leave processing example comes from an internal document of a NSW government agency, but it is typical of public sector finance-speak. ■ The sample on new residential premises comes from the Gilbert and Tobin online law 'tax.biz' newsletter, viewed in April 2006 at <http://itechne.com/gtnewslettertax>. ■ The Bob Mackay International Marinas sample comes from 'About Yamaha', <www.yamaha-motor.com.au/corporate/index.htm?corporate.asp>. ■ The Privacy Act sample comes from a submission of the Australian Law Reform Commission to the Senate Legal and Constitutional References Committee review of the *Privacy Act 1988* (25 February 2005), <www.alrc.goc.au/submissions/ALRCsubs/2005/2502.htm>.

The living language

The experiments on the reading time to comprehend the passive voice are discussed in Herbert H. Clark and Susan E. Haviland, 'Comprehension and the Given-new Contract' in Freedle (1977, Grammar). ■ The Judge order sample is a generic example based on Australian court documents. ■ The sample on new program funding arrangements comes from a NSW government agency. ■ The Victoria University sample comes from an email to staff responding to a spate of brain tumors in RMIT, possibly caused by electromagnetic radiation from mobile phone receptors, 23 May 2006. ■ Arthur Levitt championed the use of plain English in all corporate disclosure documents. Under his chairmanship of the US Securities and Exchange Commission, the SEC published the influential *Plain English Handbook*, available at <www.SEC.gov/pdf/handbook.pdf>. When Christopher Cox took over as Chair on 4 August 2005, his first speech reiterated that commitment. His speech is available at <www.sec.gov/news/speech/spch080405cc.htm>, posted to the PLAIN E-Mail Forum <plainlanguage@yahoogroups.com> by William Lutz on 6 August 2006. ■ The performance indicators sample comes from a state government briefing note. ■ The Heritage Council example comes from the web document 'Development Deferrals' by the Heritage Council of Western Australia, <www.heritage.wa.gov.au/b_development_referrals.html>. ■ The Flowerpoint example comes from 'Flowerpoint Delivery', viewed at <www.flowerpoint.com.au/delivery.php> in May 2006. ■ The digestibility studies sample comes from the 'Aquaculture Research Information Sheet: Nutrition Research', viewed at <www.fisheries.nsw.gov.au/aquaculture/general/information_sheet_nutrition_research> in April 2006. ■ The BBC sample comes from the BBC 'Editorial Guidelines', <www.bbc.co.uk/guidelines/editorialguidelines/edguide/crime/investigationsi.shtml>. ■ The Palmedia sample comes from 'About Insto' viewed at <www.palmedia.com.au/index.php?option=com_content&task=view&id=1&Itemid=29> in May 2006. ■ The sample on the ILO examination of Howard Government laws comes from the Australian Council of Trade Unions press release 'Federal Government to Reduce Australian Workers' Rights Will be Examined by ILO' on 10 June 2005, <www.actu.asn.au/Archive/MediaandCommunication/ACTUNews/FederalGovernmentToReduceAustralianWorkersRightsWillBeExaminedByILO.aspx>. ■ The Décor Pebble sample comes from Spec-Net, 'Product News', <www.spec-net.com.au/press/0406/decorpbl_050406.htm>. ■ The bank reconciliation sample comes from a typical audit management letter. ■ For more on linguistic flow, see Halliday (1994, Grammar), Butt *et al.* (2001, Grammar) and Billingham (2002, Editing and Proofreading). ■ The digestibility sample is cited above.

Power tools

The data-processing sample comes from a government agency document. ■ The AME sample comes from 'AME Off-shore Products', viewed at <www.amepl.com.au/offprojects.html> in April 2006. ■ The AAMI sample comes from the 'Online Insurance Quote Terms' at AAMI, viewed at <www.aami.com.au/insurance_quotes_australia/insurance_quote_terms.asp> in April 2006. ■ For more on gerunds, see Joseph Williams (2005, Writing Guides). ■ Most of the short samples used to demonstrate gerunds are generic examples based on workplace documents in the private and public sectors. ■ The audit sample on report generation comes from an audit working paper.

Chapter 13: Sentences

Toolbox

The product marketing sample comes from an internal workplace memo. ■ The 18-word sentence length claim comes from Robert Eagleson, author of the influential *Writing in Plain English* (1990, Plain English). ■ The trade globalisation sample came from the website of the SGS Group, an international trade certification company, viewed at <www.sgs.com/assessment> in August 2006. ■ For a more detailed exercise in evaluating passages' percentages of sentences above and below the average length, see Corbett and Connors (1999, pp. 369–74, Rhetoric).

The living language

For more on sentence schemes, see the primary works of Aristotle, Cicero and Quintilian (Rhetoric). Corbett and Connors (1999, pp. 377–411, Rhetoric) summarise most of the rhetorical schemes and tropes. I have selected those of most use for workplace writing, but this hardly exhausts the subject. ■ The FORGACS sample comes from the 'Welcome to Forgacs' page at <www.forgacs.com.au/>. Forgacs is a ship repair, construction and engineering company. ■ Other useful texts on sentence rhythms and structures include Williams (2005, pp. 154–73, Writing Guides) and Wilbers (2000, pp. 66–104, Writing Guides). ■ The HouseWorks sample comes from the Wesfarmers website, viewed at <www.wesfarmers.com.au/default.aspx?MenuID=14> in August 2006. ■ Most of the samples of repetition are generic workplace examples. The exception is of course President John F. Kennedy's famous 'ask not what your country can do for you' speech, reprinted in Brian MacArthur (ed.), *The Penguin Book of Historic Speeches*, London, Penguin Books, 1996. ■ The sample on the engineers career planning presentation comes from 'Engineering Queensland', the website of the Engineers Australia Queensland Division, viewed at <http://qld.engineersaustralia.org.au/jetspeed/> in May 2006. ■ The legal sample about a retrial comes from a judgment of Justice Kirby, High Court of Australia: *Antoun v The Queen* [2006] HCA 1 (8 February 2006), <www.austlii.edu.au/au/cases/cth/high_ct/2006/2.html>. ■ The ADGP sample comes from the Australian Divisions of General Practice, '2006 Federal Budget: Brief overview and analysis of measures of interest to Divisions of General Practice', 10 May 2006, <www.adgp.com.au/client_images/43340.pdf>.

Power tools

For useful coverage of sentence types and patterns, see Williams (2005, pp. 228–9, Writing Guides), Wilbers (2000, pp. 88–104, Writing Guides), Corbett and Connors (1999, pp. 361–76, Rhetoric), Petelin and Durham (1992, pp. 99–124, Business Communications) and Kane (1988, pp. 111–39, Writing Guides). ■ The mail guidelines sample comes from a policy document within a government agency. ■ The Property Development Corporation sample is a generic example based on a real estate document. ■ The market prediction sample is based on the style adopted by an investment division of a major Australian bank. The division had been ill-advised to make its marketing documents more readable by writing only simple sentences. The cumulative effect was a kind of baby talk. ■ The information disclosure sample was cited by Mark Hochhauser, 'Compliance vs. Communication: Readability of HIPAA notices', posted on the Privacy Rights Clearinghouse at <www.privacyrights.org/ar/HIPAA-Reading.htm>, but reprinted with permission from *Clarity*, no. 50, November 2003. ■ The award-winning web-development sample is based on text at the FirmSite home page, <www.firmsite.com.au>. ■ The sample on the review of the Privacy Act comes from a submission of the Australian Law Reform Commission to the Senate Legal and Constitutional References Committee Review of the *Privacy Act 1988* (25 February 2005), <www.alrc.goc.au/submissions/ALRCsubs/2005/2502.htm>. ■ The legal sample on expert witnesses comes from the law firm Freehills, 'A Lesson for Expert Witnesses', 28 April 2005, <www.freehills.com/publications/publications_4990.asp>. ■ The global leader sample is an edited version of a job advertisement for a site manager posted on <http://cracker.com.au/classified/perth/jobs/automotive/myc4313430.aspz>, viewed in August 2006.

Chapter 14: Punctuation

Toolbox

The Rogers case was reported by Grant Robertson, 'Comma Quirk Irks Rogers', *The Globe and Mail*, 6 August 2006, viewed at <www.theglobeandmail.com/servlet/story/RTGAM.20060806.wr-rogers07/EmailBNStory/Business/home>. The legal aspects of the case are discussed by Mark Painter, Judge of the Ohio First District Court of Appeals, *Lawyers Weekly USA*, 25 September 2006, <www.judgepainter.org/legalwriter48.htm>. ■ The audit comma sample comes from an audit document within one of the 'big four' accounting firms. ■ Most of the short samples demonstrating comma guidelines are generic workplace examples. ■ For a discussion on the Oxford or serial comma, see Truss (2003, pp. 83–7, Punctuation). ■ The wartime pilot training manual sample comes from Gowers (1954, p. 181, Plain English). ■ The land tax sample was in a draft letter that came within a whisker of being sent out to thousands of people. ■ The customer profile example was supplied by a professional working for a car manufacturer in Australia. ■ On the history and use of the apostrophe, see Todd (1995, pp. 32–8, Punctuation), Howard (1984, pp. 170–2, History of English), and Snooks & Co. (2002, pp. 85–8, Style).

The living language

For accessible discussions of the history of punctuation, see Howard (1984, pp. 155–72, History of English), Crystal (2003, pp. 278–83, History of English), Truss (2003, Punctuation) and Todd (1995, pp. 7–25, Punctuation). ■ Eric Partridge's quote on American punctuation comes from Partridge (1953, Punctuation). ■ The classic rejoinder on behalf of American practice comes from Louis Menand, 'Bad Comma: Lynne Truss's strange grammar', *New Yorker*, 28 June 2004, p. 102. Bryan Garner takes up the cudgels against Truss even more vehemently in 'Don't Know Much About Punctuation: Notes on a wannabe stickler', *Texas Law Review*, April, 2005, vol. 83, no. 5, pp. 1443–52. Garner's article is particularly valuable for its footnotes, which constitute a bibliography on punctuation. It also shows why the British and American outlooks are as divided as they were in Partridge's day. ■ For an example of a linguist advocating abandoning the apostrophe altogether, see Kate Burridge, *Blooming English: Observations on the roots, cultivation and hybrids of the English language*, Sydney, ABC Books, 2003, pp. 194–6, although grammarians such as Burchfield have made much the same suggestion (see Burchfield, 1985, p. 25, History of English).

Power tools

The link between madness and taking hyphens seriously comes from an Oxford University Press style guide in New York, cited by Gowers (1954, p. 188, Punctuation). ■ The short samples illustrating the power tools of punctuation are from generic workplace documents. ■ The sample on new retirement laws comes from a newsletter sent by the financial services group Genisys. ■ The exclamation mark sample came from Karen Zoellner, 'Karen Zoellner's Voice', in the newsletter *Oxford Eyes*, edition 1, vol. 13, 2005. ■ For examples of media style for quotation marks, see Lockwood (2003, Style), Goldstein (2004, Style) or Siegal and Connolly (1999, Style). For Australian government style, see Snooks & Co. (2002, Style). See also the discussions of quotation marks in the *Chicago Manual of Style* (2003, Style) and Ritter (2003, Style).

Chapter 15: Style

Toolbox

The mongoose story comes from a presentation by Bill Sabin, editor of the *Gregg Reference Manual*, at Adding Up the Benefits, the fifth PLAIN Language international conference, 5 November 2005, in Washington DC. See <www.plainlanguagenetwork.org/conferences/2005/FinalProgram.pdf>. ■ For the differences between the American and Australian date formats, compare the *Chicago Manual of Style* (2003, p. 253, Style) and Snooks & Co. (2002, p. 170, Style). ■ The plantation sample comes from a public sector audit report. ■ On the readability of capital letters, see Snooks & Co. (2002, Style). ■ The main dictionaries in Australia, the United Kingdom and America are the *Macquarie Dictionary*, 4th edition, Sydney, Macquarie Library, 2005; the *New Shorter Oxford Dictionary*, Oxford, Clarendon Press, 1993; and either *Webster's Ninth New Collegiate Dictionary*, Springfield, Merriam-Webster, 1983, or the *American Heritage Dictionary of the English Language*, New York, Random House, 1992. ■ The treatment of shortened forms draws heavily on Snooks & Co. (2002, pp. 150–61, Style). ■ The acronym sample comes from the asset management division of a government agency. ■ For more detailed discussion of capitalisation, see Snooks & Co. (2002, pp. 118–35, Style), Ritter (2003, pp. 71–111, Style) and the *Chicago Manual of Style* (2003, p. 253, Style) ■ On the use of inclusive language, see Casey Miller and Kate Swift, *The Handbook of Nonsexist Writing for Writers, Editors and Speakers*, 2nd edn, Harper & Row, 1992, and Snooks & Co. (2002, pp. 55–62, Style). ■ On the treatment of numbers, see Snooks & Co. (2002, pp. 162–77, Style), Ritter (2003, pp. 166–91, Style) and the *Chicago Manual of Style* (2003, pp. 379–98, Style). ■ For a straightforward discussion of the various citation systems, see Snooks & Co. (2002, pp. 190–1, Style).

The living language

For more on the early history of style manuals, see Ritter (2003, pp. v–x, Style), 'The History of *The Chicago Manual of Style*' viewed at <www.chicagomanualofstyle.org/home.html> in May 2006, and Sabin (2004, Style). ■ For William Strunk's *The Elements of Style*, see Strunk and White (2000, Writing Guides). ■ For typical academic, national and media style manuals, see the Style section of Further Reading. ■ The quote from *The Chicago Manual of Style*, 1st edn, is reproduced in the 15th edn (2002, p. xiii, Style).

Power tools

See the Style section of Further Reading for a full list of the available style guides. ■ For more on working with style sheets, including further examples, see Einsohn (2006, pp. 47–54, Editing and Proofreading), Butcher (2004, pp. 66–7, Editing and Proofreading), Billingham (2002, pp. 26–9, Editing and Proofreading), Snooks & Co. (2002, p. 265, Style), and Flann and Hill (2004, pp. 49–51, Editing and Proofreading).

Chapter 16: Editing

Toolbox

The 2005 Royal Mail study surveyed 1000 people, and based its £41 billion estimate on the average value of products or services not used if the UK population matched the responses of the survey group. It was reported in 'Poor Communication Costs UK Businesses Billions in Lost Sales', 10 August 2005, at <www.royalmail.com>. ■ On the role of an editor as a mediator between the author and the reader, see Plotnik (1982, Editing and Proofreading). ■ On leaving time between drafting and revising, see Anderson (1991, pp. 465–6, Technical Writing) and Wilbers (2000, pp. 223–4, Writing Guides). ■ Writer and naturalist Aldo Leopold applied the freezing of a text before editing more literally by putting his work in a dedicated drawer to 'cool off' before he revised it. Quoted in Wilbers (2000, p. 223, Writing Guides). ■ The editing system in this chapter was first developed for an 'editing for managers' masterclass I developed and ran in several government finance agencies.

The living language

The distinction between a copy editor and a substantive editor is discussed in further detail in Snooks & Co. (2002, pp. 252–60, Style). Most texts on editing focus on the role of the copy editor; examples are Butcher (1992, Editing and Proofreading), Flann and Hill (2004, Editing and Proofreading), Rooney and Witte (2000, Editing and Proofreading), and Einsohn (2006, Editing and Proofreading). ■ For an accessible overview of the entire history of copyists, publishing and editing, see the major entry on 'Publishing' in the *Encyclopaedia Britannica*, 15th edn, Chicago, 2005, vol. 26, pp. 415–49. For more detailed accounts of the evolution of copyists, correctors and copy editors in book publishing, see Adrian Johns, *The Nature of the Book: Print and knowledge in the making*, Chicago, University of Chicago Press, 1998; Mary Rouse and Richard Rouse, *Authentic Witness: Approaches to medieval texts and manuscripts*, Notre Dame, University of Notre Dame Press, 1991; Brian Richardson, *Print Culture in Renaissance Italy: The editor and the vernacular text 470–1600*, Cambridge, Cambridge University Press, 1994; Percy Simpson, *Proof Reading in the Sixteenth, Seventeenth and Eighteenth Centuries*, London, Oxford University Press, 1935; David McKitterick, *A History of Cambridge University Press, Volumes 1–3*, Cambridge, Cambridge University Press, 2004; Harry Carter, *A History of the Oxford University Press: Volume 1, to the year 1780*, Oxford, Clarendon Press, 1975; Marcus Walsh, *Shakespeare, Milton and 18th Century Literary Editing: The beginnings of interpretive scholarship*, Cambridge, Cambridge University Press, 1997; and Elizabeth Eisenstein, *The Printing Revolution in Early Modern Europe*, Cambridge, Cambridge University Press, 2005. ■ For more detail on the development of editing within newspapers and other publications, see Joad Raymond, *The Invention of the Newspaper: English newsbooks 1641–1649*, Oxford, Clarendon Press, 1996; Joad Raymond, *Pamphlets and Pamphleteering in Early Modern Britain*, Cambridge, Cambridge University Press, 2003; Jeremy Black, *The English Press 1621–1861*, Phoenix Mill, Sutton Publishing, 2001; F.J. Mansfield, *Sub-editing: A book mainly for young journalists*, London, Pitman, 1932; Lucy Brown, *Victorian News and Newspapers*, Oxford, Clarendon Press, 1985; and Dennis Griffiths, *The Encyclopaedia of the British Press 1422–1992*, London, Macmillan, 1992.

Power tools

The seven steps on defining the scope of an editing project, and the three broad levels of intervention, come from an 'editing for managers' masterclass I developed and ran in several government finance agencies. This also helped me to map some of the common traps workplace managers fall into when reviewing the work of others. ■ There is little written about how to give effective editorial feedback in the workplace, with most texts on editing relating to book or newspaper publishing. Notable exceptions are a chapter on the 'Management of Colleagues' Writing' in Cutts (2004, pp. 149–57, Plain English), and technical writing texts such as Anderson (1991, pp. 474–88, Technical Writing). ■ The tools for plain English editorial mark-up are my own, developed in marking up over 30,000 pages of copy for more than 4000 workplace professionals over six years at the Plain English Foundation. ■ The marked up text is based on a standard management letter appendix written by an auditor.

Chapter 17: Proofing

Toolbox

The sub-business based on eBay misspellings was reported by Diana Jean Schemo, 'In Online Auctions, Misspelling in Ads often Spells Cash', *New York Times*, 28 January 2004. ■ For general texts on proofreading, see Snooks & Co. (2002, pp. 261–9, Style), Flann and Hill (2004, pp. 141–92, Editing and Proofreading), and Butcher (2004, pp. 99–104, Editing and Proofreading). The proofing checklist is drawn partly from elements discussed in these texts, combined with my own experience and practice. ■ On electronic proofing and editing, see Flann and Hill (2004, pp. 286–9, Editing and Proofreading). ■ The proofreading error examples come from the hilarious collection *Anguished English* by Richard Lederer (1987, History of English). ■ For further discussion on grammatical errors such as pronoun references, dangling modifiers and verb agreement, see Kehrwald Cook (1985, Editing and Proofreading) and Ross-Larson (1996, Editing and Proofreading).

The living language

For general background on the evolution of correctors into editors and proofreaders, see the texts quoted for the living language section of Chapter 16. The changing role of the proofreader in newspapers is discussed in Rooney and Witte (2000, Editing and Proofreading). ■ The history of the word 'proofing' comes from the full *Oxford English Dictionary*, 2nd edition, Oxford, Clarendon Press, 1989. ■ Background on the history of editing and proofing in Australia, particularly at Angus & Robertson and Halstead Press, comes from my doctoral thesis 'Spheres of Influence: Angus & Robertson and Australian literature 1939–1960', University of Sydney, 2000. In particular, I conducted over 120 hours of oral history interviews with former editors, proofreaders and production managers, tapes that now form the Angus & Robertson Oral History Collection, Mitchell Library, Sydney. Particularly useful on this topic were interviews with Ian Macarthur (AR 14–19), Tony Barker (AR 12–13) and Enid Moon (AR 100–101). See also Enid Moon, *Memoirs of a Galley Slave: A proof-reader looks back*, Book Collectors' Society of Australia, 1991. ■ The background on typing pools in the workplace comes from my own career experience, as well as discussions with older staff among the 4000 who have attended Plain English Foundation writing workshops. ■ The top 10 tips are culled from my own experience, as well as from the sources listed for this chapter.

Power tools

On the use of proofreading symbols in Australia, see Snooks & Co. (2002, pp. 521–7, Style) or Flann and Hill (2004, pp. 147–54, Editing and Proofreading). For the equivalents in the United Kingdom and North America, see Butcher (2004, pp. 421–4, Editing and Proofreading), Ritter (2003, Editing and Proofreading, pp. 54–60) and *The Chicago Manual of Style* (2003, pp. 91–104, Editing and Proofreading). ■ For the Royal Mail study, see the reference at the start of the notes for Chapter 16. ■ The 'spelling checker poem' has been kicking around the Internet in various inaccurate forms. I am grateful to William Lutz for supplying the original text, which he sources to X.J. Kennedy and Dana Gioia, whose *Literature: An introduction to fiction, poetry, drama and writing* is now in its 10th edition (Longman, 2006). ■ For more about electronic editing and proofreading, see Flann and Hill (2004, pp. 240–91, Editing and Proofreading).

Acknowledgements

There is only one name on the cover of this book, but many people made it possible.

Foremost is Peta Spear, co-founder of the Plain English Foundation, who understood its full potential even before I did. Her unwavering support for this book meant having to take over much of my workload—as well as keep up her own—for the better part of a year. As if those demands were not enough, she also increased our turnover. More importantly, Peta is my partner in life as well as in business. Her faith in the book kept me going during the many days when the project threatened to overwhelm.

The Foundation's staff also deserve credit for this achievement. Ginger Briggs, our first employee, shared so much of the back-breaking work in the early days. Ginger also contributed background research for several chapters, and her e-savvy helped to find many of the real-world samples that bring life and relevance to the text.

Other Foundation staff contributed by carrying our growing workload while I was away writing. Our trainers Ron Denholm, David Hollier and Dana Skopal continue to turn plain language theory into workplace reality. Our operations manager, Glenn James, keeps the whole show running smoothly. Catherine Casey, Daniela Shield and Brenda Mattick chipped in with vital document design, and Robert Shield held our IT systems together. Thanks also to Pamela Freeman, Nicola Robinson, Gordon Eliot, Bronwyn Sweeney and Pauline Waugh who joined us for parts of the journey.

This book is also better for the feedback of plain language practitioners at home and overseas. In particular, I would like to thank Christine Mowat and Peter Butt for their encouragement and support. For setting an unstinting good example, thanks also to Joe Kimble, Martin Cutts, William Lutz, Ginny Redish, Annetta Cheek, Robert Eagleson, William DuBay, Michele Asprey, Lynda Harris, Jacquie Harrison, David Elliot,

Christopher Balmford, Melodie Mercer, Sarah Carr, Nigel Grant, Gary Larson and Nathan McDonald.

Of course, even the best content cannot reach an audience without a publisher, and Allen & Unwin is maintaining the best traditions of Sir Stanley. Thanks firstly to Patrick Gallagher, who heard me speak at the Sydney Writers' Festival and suggested there 'must be a book in this'. Elizabeth Weiss and Angela Handley have been the best editorial team I could have hoped for—supportive, painstaking and thoroughly professional. I am also indebted to Liz Keenan for a thorough copy edit, and to Simon Paterson for the design of a most complicated book. My agent, Lyn Tranter, helped out every time I needed her.

For my family, I hope this book explains why you didn't hear from me for two years. My thanks for your patience go to Tom, Sharon and Kate.

I end this book where I began—by acknowledging the 4000 workplace writers who took up the challenge of testing these tools. In particular, I want to acknowledge Jo Grisard and Rose Williams, who were the first to give it a go. While I could easily thank another thousand personally, my top 10 would be Barry Underwood, Bob Sendt, Linda Baranov, Gül Izmir, Michael Egan, Bob Debus, Sarda Nana, Jo Fish, Perce Butterworth and Michael Milligan. This book is another legacy of your efforts.

Index

abbreviations, 284
ability, in language, 286
abstract nouns, 173, 178, 226
academic culture, 233, 287
accountability, 232
accuracy, 301
acronyms, 284–5
active voice, 25, 164–7, 225–7, 229, 231–2, 237–40
address blocks, in letters, 272
adjective phrases, 252
adjectives
  clutter caused by, 215, 217–18
  combined with verbs, 228
  for detail and colour, 176–7
  as key words, 208
  as open-class words, 171, 178, 225
  parallel forms of, 246
adverb phrases, 252, 254, 263
adverbs
  in clauses, 254
  clutter caused by, 215, 219–20
  for detail and colour, 176–7
  as key words, 208
  as open-class words, 171, 178, 225
  as transitional words, 131
advertising, 248–9
Age, 200
Age of Reason, 21
Agricola, 21
Alcuin, 270
Alfred, King, 195
alignment, of text, 138, 294, 316, 317
alliteration, 247
American Encyclopaedia of Printing, 289
American Psychological Association, 163, 291
anadiplosis, 248
analogies, in reasoning, 108–9, 111–12
analytical documents, 51, 56, 131, 148
analytical headings, 66, 67
anaphora, 248
angle brackets, 276
Angles, 195
Anglo-Saxon words, 198, 214
antimetabole, 249
antithesis, 247
APA Style Manual, 291
apostrophes, 267–9, 271, 272
appeals to ignorance, 115
appeals to pity, 115
appeals to the masses, 115
apposition, 245, 249–50
argument (rhetoric), 21, 98, 109–10, 115
  see also persuasion
Aristophanes, 270
Aristotle, 6, 20, 98, 105, 106, 124
ars dictamanus, 20
Ars Rhetorica (Aristotle), 20
The Art of Readable Writing (Flesch), 202
articles, 184
Associated Press, 202, 291
assonance, 247
asterisks, 320
audit reports, 89
Australian, 200
Australian Bureau of Statistics, 228
author–date system, 288

authority, 108–9, 112–13, 197–8
Author's and Printer's Dictionary, 290
auxiliary verbs, 175, 178, 219, 224, 237

Bacon, Francis, 21
bad news, delivery of, 95–6
Bain, Alexander, 124
bars, 275
Basic English, 189
Battle of Agincourt, 196
Battle of Britain speech (Churchill), 194
Battle of Hastings, 196
begging the question, 115
biblical tone, 155
bibliographies, 288
Blank, Jonas, 163
body text, 289, 316
bold type, 139–40, 316, 318
book printing, 140–1
books, 303–4
Booth, Wayne C., 42
brace brackets, 276–7
brackets, 250, 270, 276–7
brainstorming, 43, 44–5, 59
budgets, 306
bulleted lists, 145, 146–7, 266–7, 275, 292, 294, 320
Business English (Hotchkiss and Drew), 290
business-writing guides, 290–1

capitalisation, 139–40, 172–3, 282, 285, 294, 300
captions, 317
carbon copies, 141
cases (grammar), 183, 271
Cassiodorus, 303
cause and effect, in reasoning, 108–9, 110
Celts, 195
centre justification, 138
ceremonial speeches, 38
ceremonial tone, 155
character, and credibility, 105
Charrow, Robert, 227
Charrow, Veda, 227
charts, in documents, 148, 149
chatty tone, 155, 157
Chaucer, Geoffrey, 289
chiasmus, 249
Chicago Manual of Style, 290, 291–2
Churchill, Winston, 186, 194
Cicero, 6, 20, 38, 39, 90–1, 109, 142
citations, 287–8, 293, 295
claims, reasons for, 40–1
clarity, 3, 281–2, 286–7, 301
clauses, 252–4, 255–6
climaxes, in sentences, 248
closed-class words, 171, 182, 208
clutter in language
  avoiding deceptive clutter, 212–13
  clarifying thinking before drafting, 210–12
  grammar of, 215–20
  historical clutter, 213–15
  identifying key words, 207–10
  measuring efficiency in writing, 209–10
  recognising patterns of, 221
  reducing, 164–6
  resisting the desire to impress, 212
  types of, 206–7
  see also editing
co-authoring, 308
codices, 303
cognitive psychology, 27
coherence, 117–27, 131–2, 301
collective responsibility, 233
Colomb, Gregory C., 42
colons, 249, 270, 275
columns, in page layout, 144
comma splices, 266
commas, 250, 262–6, 270, 274, 275, 282–3
commissioning editors, 305
common nouns, 172–3
communication, process of, 15–16
comparisons, in reasoning, 108–9
complements, 253, 254
completeness, in editing, 301
complex sentences, 254, 256–7, 263, 267

compound-complex sentences, 254, 257–8
compound nouns, 272–3
compound sentences, 254, 256
computers, 141, 323, 328–9
  see also spreadsheets; word processors
concessions, in arguments, 40, 41–2
conclusion checking, 25, 26, 37, 40–2
conclusions, in arguments, 98
concrete nouns, 173, 178, 246
confirmation, 91
conjunctions
  as closed-class words, 171
  clutter caused by, 215, 217
  starting sentences with, 242
  as transitional words, 131
  uses of, 185–6
  using commas before, 263, 264, 265–6
consequences, in reasoning, 108–9, 110, 113
consistency, in style, 281, 282–3, 320
content
  checklist for, 31–2
  clarifying the purpose, 34
  defining and clarifying the topic, 32–3
  developing of, 31, 43–9
  drawing conclusions, 36–7
  editing of, 299, 301
  research, 35–6
  setting targets for results, 37–8
  testing conclusions for future actions, 40–2
  types of, 38
  using the stasis system, 39–40
contractions, 164–6, 268, 284
contrast, in page design, 139
cooperative principle, 22
coordinating conjunctions, 185
copy editors, 288, 302–3, 305, 322
copy holders, 322
copyists, 303
core meanings, 171
core message test, 25, 80–8, 90–2, 96, 118, 299
corporate sector, 159, 233
'correctors', of text, 304
The Craft of Research (Booth et al.), 42
credibility, 105
cross-references, 68, 320

Danes, 195, 196, 213
dashes, 249–51, 271, 273–4
dates, formats for, 282, 320
de Bono, Edward, 45
deception, in writing, 212–13
declarative sentences, 252
deductive reasoning, 106, 108–9
definite articles, 184
definitions, in reasoning, 39, 108–9, 113–14
delayed sentences, 257
deliberative context, of writing, 38, 40–2
delivery, to an audience, 142–3
demonstrative determiners, 184
demonstratives, 133
Denney, Joseph, 126
dependent clauses, 256–7
descriptive documents, 51, 148
descriptive grammarians, 180
descriptive headings, 66–7
design
  alignment of text, 138, 294
  checklist for, 25
  choosing a font, 135–7, 139, 294
  in editing, 301
  evolution of information design, 141–2
  impact of the computer, 141
  maximising contrast, 139
  page layout, 143–8
  as part of delivery to an audience, 142–3
  using bold type for emphasis, 139–40
  using graphics, 144–5, 148–9
  using tables, 147–9
  using white space, 145
desktop publishing, 141, 323
detail, unnecessary, 206
determiners, 171, 184
diagonals, 275
diagrams, in documents, 148, 149, 318

dictionaries, 283
Digital Equipment Corporation, 27–8
diplomacy, 235
direct objects, 253
Document Design Project, 141
document formats, 289
document outcomes, 23
document testing, 23–6
documentary note system, 288, 295
Donatus, 181
Doomsday Book, 196
dots, as punctuation, 270
double quotation marks, 278
drafting, 7, 62, 210–12, 299, 300
drawings, in documents, 148, 149
Drew, Celia Ann, 290
drops, 316, 317

eBay, 314
Economist Style Guide, 291
editing
  checklist for, 300–1, 302, 312
  complexity of, 302
  determinants of, 306
  distinguished from co-authoring, 308
  distinguished from proofing, 315
  electronic aids to, 328–9
  examining structure, 299
  feedback in, 308–9
  how much to intervene, 306–9
  importance of, 298
  learning from the history of, 303–5
  mark-up systems for, 309–10
  objectivity in, 298–9
  performance reviews of, 312
  types of, 302–3
  when to rewrite, 312
  see also clutter in language; proofing
editors, 288, 302–3, 305, 312, 322
efficiency, in writing, 4, 206–10, 281–2, 286–7, 301
electronic addresses, 275, 276
The Elements of Style (Strunk), 291
ellipsis, 132–3
Elyot, Sir Thomas, 158–9
em dashes, 273–4, 295
email addresses, 140
emails, 162–4
emotion, appeals to, 105
en dashes, 273–4
endnotes, 288, 295, 320
'Englisc', 195–6
English Composition and Rhetoric (Bain), 124
English language, 184, 189, 195, 196–7
entertainment, writing as, 34
epanalepsis, 248
epistrophe, 248
Erasmus, 181
essay writing, 54–5
ethnicity, in language, 286
ethos, 105
evidence, soundness of, 40, 41, 42
examples, in reasoning, 108–9, 111–12
exclamation marks, 271, 277–8
exclamatory sentences, 252
exordium, 91
expert evaluation, of documents, 23, 26
exposition structural model, 51, 54–6, 62–3, 64
expression, 7, 206–10, 299–301, 309
  see also clutter in language; grammar; sentences; style; tone; verbs; words

fact, issues of, 39
fallacies, 115
false arguments, 115
false dilemmas, 115
feedback, in editing, 308–9
field testing, of documents, 23, 28–9
figures, 294
'find and replace' function, word processing, 329
first person, 125, 166–7
fishbone diagrams, 43, 47–9
Fiske, Robert Hartwell, 215
Flesch, Rudolph, 202
Flesch-Kincaid readability formula, 203, 328
Flesch readability formula, 202–4
flow, in documents, 117, 127–33, 235

focus, in editing, 301
focus, on facts and ideas, 80, 81, 90, 91–5
focus groups, to test documents, 23, 26–7
fonts, 135–7, 139, 294, 316, 318
footers, 316, 317
footnotes, 288, 295, 320
force-field analysis, 43, 47
formal tone, 125, 155–60
formatting, of documents, 289, 293, 294–5, 300, 301
forward slashes, 270, 272, 275
fragments, 254–5
free-writing, 43–4
French language, 196–8, 213–14
Fries, Charles Christopher, 182
frozen verbs, 226
Fry, Edward, 199
Fry readability graph, 199–201
full justification, 138
full stops, 270, 277, 278–9, 284
future continuous tense, 174
future perfect continuous tense, 175
future perfect tense, 174, 175
future tense, 174–5, 176, 227

galley proofs, 321
gender-specific references, 286
generalisations, 107, 115
Genung, John, 124
Geographical Names Board, 269
German language, 213
gerunds, 237–8
government style manuals, 291
government writing, 233
Gowers, Ernest, 142, 194
grammar
  achieving grammatical flow, 132–3
  of cluttered language, 215–20
  distinguished from usage, 179–80
  editing of, 301
  electronic grammar-checkers, 328
  the grammar generation gap, 170, 182
  major word classes, 171–2
  overcoming phobias about, 170–1
  parallel forms, 246
  prescriptive grammar, 180–1, 185, 186–7
  proofing of, 319–20
  resisting attempts to fix the tongue, 180–1
  role of punctuation in, 271–2
  uses of, 5
  using modern grammar, 182
  using open-classed words, 178–9
  see also adjectives; adverbs; conjunctions; determiners; nouns; prepositions; pronouns; verbs
grammar-checkers, 328
graphics, in documents, 144–5, 148–9
graphs, in documents, 148, 149, 289, 316, 318
Greenspan, Alan, 117
Gregg Reference Manual (Sabin), 281, 290–1, 292
Grice, H.P., 22
Guardian Style Manual, 291
Guidelines for Document Designers, 141
Gutenberg, Johannes, 304

Halliday, M.A.K., 154
Halstead Press, 322
Harold, King, 196
Hart, Horace, 290
Hart's Rules, 290
headers, 316, 317
headings, 66–7, 122, 145–6, 289, 294, 316, 317
Henry IV, 196–7
Henry V, 196–7
Henry VIII, 181
hidden verbs, 225–9, 238–9
HIH Insurance, 201
Hotchkiss, George Burton, 290
human factors engineering, 27
humanising words, 164–6, 233
humour, in emails, 163–4
hyperlinks, 140
hyphens, 270, 272–4
hypotheses, 89

'I have a dream' speech (King), 128–30
'if . . . then' statements, 262
illustrations, 318
imperative sentences, 252
in-house style manuals, 296
inclusive language, 286
indefinite articles, 184
indefinite determiners, 184
indenting, 140
independent clauses, 255–6, 265–6
indirect objects, 253
indirect questions, 277
inductive reasoning, 106, 107
industrial design, 27
industrialisation, 289
inferences, 107
infinitives, 181, 236–7
informal tone, 125, 155, 157, 162,
164–6
information, writing as, 34
information architects, 141
information design, 5, 6, 141–2
Information Design Journal, 141
initialisms, 284, 285
'inkhorn' terms, 159
instruction structural model, 51, 56
intellectual property, 287
internet addresses, 275, 276
interrogative sentences, 252
intervention, in editing, 306–9
intransitive verbs, 228
introductions, 98
Ishikawa, Kaoru, 47
issue–discussion–action model, 51, 52
italics, 140, 282, 316, 318

Jerome, 270
John, King, 196
Johnson, Samuel, 206
judicial context, of writing, 38–40
jury instructions, 227
Jutes, 195

key words, 25, 207–10
King, Martin Luther, 128–30
King James Bible, 185, 189

labels, 317
language, 283–6, 293, 295, 301
see also English language; French
language; German language;
Latin; plain English
Latin, 181, 196, 270, 271
Law Reform Commission (Victoria),
203
layout, of pages, 143–8, 316–17
leading, 137
left justification, 138
legalese, 155, 161–2, 214, 251
legends, 317
legibility, 281, 282
Lily, William, 181
line breaks, 316, 318
line length, 137
line spacing, 137
linguistics, 127, 182
lithographic printing, 322
logic, 21, 105–6, 301
logos, 105
long words, simplifying, 190–4
Lowth, Robert, 181

Macquarie Dictionary, 283
magazines, 291, 305
mail-merge software, 141
Manutius, Aldus, 270, 304
maps, in documents, 148, 149
margins, 145, 289, 316
marking up, of text, 309–10, 324–8
media style manuals, 291
Merriam-Webster's Dictionary, 283
metaphors, 111–12
mind-mapping, 43, 44, 46
misspellings, 314
modal auxiliary verbs, 175, 178, 219,
224, 237
Modern Language Association, 291
mosaic structural model, 51, 57–8
music-tapping, 154

narration, 91, 98, 99
narrative structural model, 51–3, 61, 63–4, 90–1, 102
National Commission on Writing (US), 1
National Council of Teachers of English (US), 182
National Institute of Education (US), 141
NATO, 141
New York Times style book, 291
New Yorker, 271
New Zealand Style Book, 291
News Limited, 291
newspaper writing, 52, 200, 291, 305
Newton, Elizabeth, 154
19th century tone, in text, 155
nominalisation, 226
Normans, 196, 197, 213
noun phrases, 252–3
nouns
  abstract and concrete nouns, 173, 246
  clutter caused by, 215, 217–18, 221
  combined with verbs, 226, 228
  compound nouns, 272–3
  function of adjectives in relation to, 176
  as key words, 178, 208
  as open-class words, 171, 225
  parallel forms of, 246
  possessive nouns, 268–9
  proper and common nouns, 172–3
  relation to verbs, 174
noun–verb shifts, 179–80
numbering, in documents, 67–8, 145–6, 294, 300, 301, 317
numbers, in documents, 286–7, 293, 295

objectivity, in editing, 298–9, 301
objects (grammar), 230, 234–5, 253–4
obliques, 275
official tone, 155, 157
officialese, 155, 156, 177, 191–2, 194, 197
offset lithography, 322
Ogden, C.K., 189
'old before new' principle, 127–31, 235
Old English, 183, 271
omissions, using commas to indicate, 267, 268
open-classed words, 171–2, 178–9, 208, 225
Opus Pacis (Oswald), 304
oratory, 142
Oswald (monk), 304
ownership, using apostrophes to indicate, 268–9
Oxford English Dictionary, 189, 283
Oxford Style Manual, 292
Oxford University Press, 290

page grids, 143–5
page layout, 143–8, 316–17
page numbers, 316, 317
page size, 289
papyrus scrolls, 303
Paragraph Writing (Scott and Denney), 126
paragraphs
  checklist of structures, 126
  coherence in, 117–18
  history of, 124
  layout of, 147
  making paragraphs flow, 117, 127
  'old before new' principle, 127–31
  paragraph theory, 124
  paraphrasing of, 118–23, 124
  structuring paragraphs in groups, 131
  tone and voice in, 125
  using standard paragraph structures, 126
  vocabulary in, 125
parallelism, 245, 246–7, 256, 257
paraphrasing, 118–23, 124
parenthesis, 245, 250–1, 256, 263, 274
partition, 91
Partridge, Eric, 271
passive voice, 125, 164–7, 175, 225, 229–36, 238–40, 328
past continuous tense, 174
past perfect continuous tense, 174, 175

past perfect tense, 174, 175, 176, 227
past tense, 174, 176, 230
pathos, 105
pause test, for commas, 262–3
peer review, of documents, 23, 24
performance reviews, 312
periods, 270
peroration, 91
personal pronouns, 133, 164–7
persuasion
  as a criterion of effectiveness, 4
  as a document's purpose, 34
  key parts of an argument, 98
  means of, 105–6
  using deductive reasoning, 106
  using inductive reasoning, 106, 107
  using rhetorical reasoning, 107–15
  using value analysis, 98–104
persuasive definitions, 114
Phillip, King, 196
photos, in documents, 148, 149
phrases, 252–3, 255, 257
Picts, 195
placenames, 269
plain English, 5, 6, 142, 201, 203, 214, 232
Plain Words (Gowers), 142, 194
planning, 7
Plato, 20
playing the man, 115
point size, 136–7
poisoning the well, 115
possessive adjectives, 184
possessive nouns, 268–9
possessive pronouns, 268
possibility, in reasoning, 108–9, 110–11
power, in language, 160–2, 194
Practical Elements of Rhetoric (Genung), 124
precedent, in reasoning, 108–9, 112–13
precision, 3, 173–4, 214, 223–5
premise, of arguments, 106
prepositional phrases, 215–16, 221, 252
prepositions, 171, 186–7, 242
prescriptive grammar, 180–1, 185, 186–7
present continuous tense, 174, 176
present perfect continuous tense, 174, 175
present perfect tense, 174, 175, 176
present tense, 174, 176
primary sources, 35
principles, in reasoning, 108–9, 113
printing, advent of, 270, 271, 304–5
printing press, 304, 305, 321–2
Priscian, 181
probability, levels of, 106
procedure manuals, 148
process, in reasoning, 108–9, 114
process, issues of, 39
professionalism, in tone, 158
pronouns
  to adjust tone, 164–7
  as closed-class words, 171
  to increase grammatical flow, 133
  as key words, 208
  overlap with determiners, 184
  personal pronouns, 133, 164–7
  possessive pronouns, 268
  use of to tighten expression, 183
  using gender-free language, 286
proof, in arguments, 98–9
proof analysis, 25, 26, 108–10
proof evaluation, 40–2
proof sheets, 321
proofing
  checklists for, 25, 316, 318–19
  decline of the proofreader, 321–2
  distinguished from editing, 315
  doing a final check, 320–1
  electronic aids to, 328–9
  for grammar, 319–20
  history of, 321–2
  how to mark up text, 327–8
  learning proofreading marks, 324–7
  page elements, 316, 317–18
  the proofreader's task, 319
  running text elements, 316–17
  stages of, 315–16
  'sweeping the page', 316
  tips for, 323
  why it matters, 314

in the writing process, 7
proofreading marks, 324–7
proofs of authority, 108–9, 112–13
proofs of consequence, 108–9, 110, 113
proofs of definition, 108–9, 113–14
proofs of example, 108–9, 111–12
proper nouns, 172–3
psycholinguistics, 182
public sector reports, 89
publishing, 304–5, 323
punctuation
in appositions, 249–50
editing of, 300, 301
evolution of, 270–1
gradual reduction of, 271, 282
rhetorical versus grammatical functions of, 271–2
style guidelines, 293, 295
see also specific elements of punctuation, e.g. commas; semi-colons

quality, issues of, 39
question and answer structural model, 51, 57, 131
question headings, 66, 67
question marks, 277
questions, verbs for, 175
Quintilian, 38, 91, 142
quotation marks, 270, 271, 278–9
quotations, 140, 275, 278, 295

RALLY software, 27–8
Ramus, Peter, 21
readability, 4, 25, 26, 197–204, 328
readers
checklist for adapting content to, 16–17, 25, 26
communicating with, 15–16
consideration of in editing, 306
in document tests, 26–8
feedback about documents from, 23, 24
maintaining the primacy of, 21–3
relationship between writers and, 22
role of the audience, 19–21
reason, appeals to, 105–7
reasons, for conclusions, 40, 41, 42
red herrings, 115
reference, 132–3
referencing, 287–8, 293, 295, 300, 301
refutation, 91
repetition, in writing, 214, 245, 247–9
research, 7, 35–6, 36–7
responsibility, in reasoning, 108–9
review against standards, 23, 25–6
reviewing text *see* editing
rewriting, 2
rhetoric
classical rhetoric, 5–6, 19–21
components of, 20
content in classical rhetoric, 38–40
oratory as part of, 142
Ramus's reduction of, 21
rhetorical reasoning, 107–15
rhetorical role of punctuation, 271–2
rhetorical touches in sentences, 245–51
style in, 289
testing conclusions for future actions, 40–2
Richard II, 196–7
right justification, 138
Rogers Communications Inc., 262
Romans, 195
Rooney, Edmund, 321
round brackets, 276
Royal Mail, 298, 328
running text, proofing of, 316–17

Sabin, William, 281
sales letters, 249
sans serif fonts, 135–6
sawtooth report (example), 70–5
Saxons, 195, 196
scientific method, 52, 89
Scots, 195
Scott, Fred Newton, 126
Scottish law, 289
scriptoriums, 303
second person, 125, 166–7
secondary sources, 35–6

Securities and Exchange Commission (US), 232
self-editing, 299
self-review, of documents, 23, 24
semi-colons, 266–7, 270, 272, 292, 295
sentences
  length of, 204, 244–5, 328
  one idea per sentence, 242–3
  parts of, 252–4
  spaces between, 277
  using apposition in, 245, 249–50
  using complex sentences, 254, 256–7, 263, 267
  using compound-complex sentences, 254, 257–8
  using compound sentences, 254, 256
  using fragments for emphasis, 254–5
  using parallelism in, 245, 246–7, 256, 257
  using parenthesis in, 245, 250–1, 256, 264–5, 274
  using repetition in, 245, 247–9
  using simple sentences, 254, 255–6
  varying sentence types, 252, 258
sequence structures, in paragraphs, 126
serial commas, 263, 264, 282–3
serif fonts, 135–6
sexual orientation, in language, 286
Shakespeare, William, 189, 198
A Short Introduction to Grammar (Lowth), 181
short lines, 318
sic, 276
Signet Office, 196
simple future tense, 174, 176
simple past tense, 174, 176
simple present tense, 174, 176
simple sentences, 254, 255–6
simpler words, choice of, 164–6
simplification, of writing, 15
single quotation marks, 278
six thinking hats, 43, 45, 47
slashes, 270, 272, 275
smothered verbs, 226
Society of Technical Communicators (US), 141–2
Socrates, 20
solidus, 275
sourcing, 287–8, 293, 295, 300, 301
Souther, James, 54
spaces, between sentences, 277
spacing, between lines, 294
spelling
  editing of, 300
  national variations, 283, 320
  proofing of, 314, 320
  standardisation of, 304
  in style sheets, 295
  using spell-checkers, 283, 298, 320, 328
split infinitives, 181
sports commentators, 179
spreadsheets, 148
square brackets, 276
standards, for document testing, 23, 25–6
standards, for style, 290–1
stasis system, 39–40
stationers, 304
Statute of Pleading, 196
the straw man, 115
structure, in documents
  assessing structural balance, 66
  avoiding unnecessary complexity, 66
  checklist for, 60
  delivering bad news early, 95–6
  editing of, 299, 301
  example of sawtooth report, 70–5
  mark-up of, 309
  models of, 51–64
  putting key information first, 91–5
  review of, 7
  reviewing structural design, 65
  rhetorical structuring, 90–1
  structure mapping, 25, 26, 65, 68–75
  subsections in structure, 131
  thinking versus communicating structure, 88–90
  transparency in structure, 96, 117
  unifying text around a topic, 117, 124, 125
  using headings consistently, 66–7, 122

using numbering to aid navigation, 67–8
using the core message test, 25, 80–8, 90, 91, 92, 96
see also coherence; paragraphs; persuasion
Strunk, William Jr, 291
style
changing meaning of, 289–92
checklist for, 25
for citations, 287–8
consideration of context, 292–3
developing an in-house manual, 296
editing of, 299, 300, 301
electronic style-checkers, 328
four principles of, 281–3
in language, 283–6
for numbers, 286–7
using style sheets, 293–5, 320
Style Manual, 291, 292
style manuals, 290–1, 320
sub-editors, 305
subjects (grammar), 230, 234, 235, 253–4
subordinating conjunctions, 185
subsections, in documents, 131
substantive editors, 302–3, 312
surveys, on document effectiveness, 23, 26–7
'sweeping the page', 316
Swift, Jonathan, 180, 289
Sydney Morning Herald, 200
syllogisms, 106, 107
symbols, 284

tables, in documents, 145, 147–9, 289, 294, 316, 318
tables of contents, 316, 317
tautologies, 220
technical writing, 5, 6, 27, 179
technology, 292, 303, 323
telescoping structural model, 51, 53–4, 63–4, 104
templates, 289
tenses, of verbs, 174–5
tertiary sources, 35
texting, 155, 158, 180
'that' versus 'which', 265
Third New International Dictionary (Webster's), 189
third person, 125, 166
throat-clearing openings, 210, 216
time frames, 306
Times Style Guide, 291
'to be', 175–9, 218, 230
'to do', 175
'to have', 175
tone
avoiding highly informal language, 158, 162
avoiding overdressing the text, 156–7
in editing, 301
elements which determine, 164–6
in emails, 162–4
hearing what you write, 154
humanising your prose, 166–8, 233
maintaining a professional tone, 158
overly formal tone, 158–60
in paragraphs, 125
resisting the language of power, 160–2
striking a balance of formality, 155–6
testing the tone of text, 154–5
using tone to communicate, 158–60
tone scale, 25, 155, 157, 158
topics, 32–3
'track changes' function, word processing, 329
transformational grammar, 182
transitional words and phrases, 131–2
Tufte, Edward, 141, 149
typefaces, 135–7
typewriters, 141
typing pools, 322
typography, 135–41, 289–90, 316
typos, 300, 314, 320

underlining, 140, 316, 318
United Press International, 202
universities, 304
University of Chicago Press, 290
usability, 4

usability testing, 22, 23, 27–8
usage, distinguished from grammar, 179–80
user-centred design, 22

value analysis, 98–104
vellum, 303
verb indexes, calculating, 238–40
verb phrases, 215, 218–19, 252–3
verbal nouns, 225, 236–9
verbs
  avoiding clutter, 215, 218–19, 221
  editing of, 301
  hidden verbs, 225–9
  infinitives, 181, 236–7
  as key words, 208
  as a major word class, 172
  modal auxiliary verbs, 175, 178, 219, 224, 237
  modification of with adverbs, 177
  as open-class words, 171, 178, 225
  parallel forms of, 246
  in sentences, 252–4
  split infinitives, 181
  tenses of, 174–5
  use of the verb 'to be', 175–9, 218
  uses of, 223, 230
  using verbs with precision, 173–4, 223–5, 238–40
  see also active voice; passive voice; verbal nouns
Virgin, 162
virgules, 270, 272, 275
vocabulary, 125
voice, in paragraphs, 125

warrants, for claims, 40, 42
weak verbs, 226
web pages, 57–8, 136, 139
websites, 140, 142, 249
Webster's *Third New International Dictionary*, 189
Wendell, Barrett, 124, 127
Westminster system, 233
'which' versus 'that', 265
white space, in page layout, 145
widows, 318
William, King, 196
Williams, Joseph M., 42
Wilson, Thomas, 159, 168
Witte, Oliver, 321
word breaks, 316, 317
word processors
  document formats, 289
  integration with spreadsheets, 148
  punctuation, 271
  spacing, 277
  style and style sheets, 292, 293
  using 'find and replace', 329
  using spell- and grammar-checkers, 283, 298, 320, 328
  using 'track changes', 329
words
  choice of, 164–6, 190, 301
  influence of Latinate French on, 196–7, 214
  length of, 204
  the origins of 'Englisc', 195
  readability of, 197–204
  simplifying long words, 190–4
  word stock in English, 189
writer's block, 31
writing
  as a collaborative enterprise, 142
  criteria for effective writing, 3–5
  methods for, 5–6
  purposes of, 34
  stages of, 6–7
  see also clutter; content; drafting; editing; expression; grammar; proofing; punctuation; readers; structure; style; tone
Wurman, Richard Saul, 141

Zinsser, William, 154